Total Cure

Total Cure

The Antidote to the Health Care Crisis

Harold S. Luft

Harvard University Press

Cambridge, Massachusetts

London, England

2008

Some of the ideas incorporated in the SecureChoice proposal appeared in
Harold S. Luft, "Universal Care Coverage: A Potential Hybrid Solution,"
Journal of the American Medical Association 297 (2007): 1115–1118.
Copyright © 2007, American Medical Association. All rights reserved.

A Caravan book. For more information, visit www.caravanbooks.org.

Library of Congress Cataloging-in-Publication Data

Luft, Harold S.
Total cure : the antidote to health care crisis / Harold S. Luft.
p. cm.
Includes bibliographical references and index.
ISBN 978-0-674-03210-1 (alk. paper)
1. Health care reform—United States. 2. Medical policy—United States.
3. Health planning—United States. 4. Insurance, Health—United States. I. Title.
[DNLM: 1. Health Care Reform—methods—United States.
2. Health Policy—United States. 3. Insurance, Health—United States.
WA 540 AA1 L8955t 2008]
RA395.A3L82 2008
362.1′04250973—dc22   2008016220

To Lori

. . . and to all who need a better health care system

Contents

Preface

The crisis in health care will not be solved with two aspirin and the hope we'll be OK in the morning; instead we need to restructure the system fundamentally. That is what *Total Cure* is about. Reform of the American health care system has been a recurrent issue for decades. Over those years the proportion of the gross domestic product devoted to health care has grown while the proportion of the nonelderly population with coverage has shrunk, and those trends are increasingly recognized as being unsustainable. The last major attempt to reform the system—in the beginning of the Clinton administration in the 1990s—failed to garner the necessary political consensus. A new administration taking office in 2009 with the baby boomers approaching the age of Medicare eligibility makes the time ripe for serious consideration of change.

In mid-2004, when I first considered this undertaking, these issues were obvious, as was the high likelihood that many proposals would be forthcoming from academics, policy analysts, and politicians. The question was whether I could contribute something to that discussion. For over three decades my focus had been on empirical work in understanding how the health care system functions, including topics ranging from competition to outcomes measurement, from hospitals to HMOs, from storefront clinics to high-tech equipment. Through all these investigations, this remained true: the deeper one dug into the question at hand, the less obvious were the answers. The usual analytic tools often addressed only part of the problem, and frequently there were multiple valid perspectives. Stakeholders were rarely evil but were operating within constraints and dealing with incentives they could not control. People used the same words for different concepts and misunderstood one another.

Those lessons could have been the basis of a book for my academic colleagues and future generations of researchers. The directions of the new reform proposals, however, offered another and more important opportunity. Nearly all the proposals focus on the growing problem of the uninsured; some give what I think is only superficial attention to containing health care costs. None really consider a thoroughgoing restructuring of the payment and delivery system. Simply ensuring that everyone has coverage will not change the problems we have with quality of care, insensitivity to patient preferences, overly bureaucratic systems, lack of professional autonomy, or rapid growth in costs.

Nevertheless, restructuring payment incentives, making information available in new ways, taking advantage of changes in medical specialization and inpatient care, and empowering patients can result in a system that addresses those underlying concerns while ensuring coverage for all and rates of growth in cost that are more acceptable than we now project. Thus, what had initially been a conceptual and "teaching" piece was transformed into a policy proposal. The academics could wait: the public deserved a new approach to be placed on the table for the ensuing policy debate.

As I write this in February 2008, it is still not clear who will be the candidate for either party, let alone the winner in the presidential election. This does not really matter, however; the problems we face affect us all. Moreover, the solutions I offer include features that should be attractive to both the right and the left. The public and the politicians have recognized that global warming is occurring regardless of the rhetoric used, and we need to apply a broad range of tools to deal with it. Likewise, we must recognize that improving the value our health care provides is no longer just a campaign slogan but an imperative, and we must think differently about how we move toward such improvement. I do not imagine that my proposal will be *the* answer, but I hope it begins a discussion that moves us to one.

The Robert Wood Johnson Foundation deserves much of the credit for this book. It provided direct support through an Investigator Award in Health Policy Research. More important, I have been involved in the Foundation's postdoctoral programs for over three decades and consider myself a thirty-fifth-year post-doc. Literally hundreds of fellows, with backgrounds ranging from medicine and nursing to ethics and political science, from economics and statistics to anthropology and sociology, from neonatologists and gerontologists to social workers and lawyers, have educated me while I was purportedly teaching them.

The Center for Advanced Study in the Behavioral Sciences provided the perfect setting for a sabbatical in 2006–7, when much of this book was developed. The isolation from the routine academic and administrative chores and the rigorous intellectual engagement from the staff and fellows at the Center created the optimum environment for creativity. The excellent advice I obtained there shaped much of what follows.

My colleagues at the Philip R. Lee Institute for Health Policy Studies (PHI-IHPS), the University of California at San Francisco, and the Palo Alto Medical Foundation Research Institute (PAMFRI) have been wonderful in adapting to my being distracted from day-to-day responsibilities. Special thanks are due to Eunice Chee, who, behind the scenes as always, keeps everything running smoothly.

Many people provided comments on various aspects of the proposal and draft. These include Jim Bentley, Bob Berenson, John Bertko, Erika Blacksher, Kathy Buto, Michael Chernew, Helen Darling, Steve Davidson, Zeke Emanuel, Rashi Fein, Arthur Finn, Martin Fishman, Vic Fuchs, Alan Garber, Neal Goldstein, Sterling Haidt, Lisa

Hammann, Geoff Heller, Ed Howard, Chip Kahn, Alexandra Kalev, Rick Kronick, Don Lamm, Judith Lave, Bob Leibenluft, Herb Leiderman, Victor Levadi, Mark Levine, Allen Levinson, Dick Levy, Michael Millenson, Bob Mnookin, David Mullens, Robbie Pearl, Jon Reider, Drummond Rennie, Tom Rice, Win Schachter, Leonard Schaeffer, Harvey Schloss, Samuel Sessions, Bern Shen, Steve Shortell, John Troidl, Keith Wailoo, and several anonymous reviewers. Participants in our weekly writing seminars at PRL-IHPS and PAMFRI have offered innumerable comments on many drafts. I have presented various aspects of the proposal and received helpful comments at the Blue Sky Workshop at UCLA and the FRESH-Thinking Workshop at the Center for Advanced Study in the Behavioral Sciences.

Laura J. Eaton, M.D., M.P.H., has been my collaborator in the empirical work on episodes of care that supports the plausibility of the proposal. Amy J. Markowitz, J.D., provided her expertise as an editor to help shape the manuscript into a readable form. Beth Newell came to this project a year out of college and after a week on the job had eviscerated a précis of mine. Her ability to "speak truth to power," question assumptions, offer suggestions, and track down material is truly awesome. Without her there would have been no book.

I thank Harvard University Press, and especially Michael Aronson, who believed in this book and helped it see an early publication. Amanda Heller provided expert editing with a light but instructive hand. Of course, any errors, misconceptions, and obscurity that remain are my responsibility.

I owe a special thanks to my children, Shira, Chad, and Jana, and particularly to my wife, Lori. She has been unfailingly supportive through this process, sitting through far too many repetitions of the ideas, waiting while I did just a bit more writing, and forgoing too much attention. I thank them all.

Tables and Figures

Tables

Figures

xiii

Abbreviations

ACE   avoidable compensable event
ACH   automated clearing house
CDT   care delivery team
CIM   chronic illness management
CCH   claims clearing house
DRG   diagnosis-related group
EDRG   expanded diagnosis-related group
EHR   electronic health record
FCH   Funds Clearing House
FFS   fee-for-service
FHEA   Federal Health Equity Agency
HCC   health care card
HIF   health innovation fund
HIN   health identification number
HMO   health maintenance organization
IRP   innovation reinsurance pool
ITIN   individual tax identification number
MA/I   major acute or interventional
PCP   primary care practitioner
PI   payment intermediary
UCP   universal coverage pool

Total Cure

Introduction

Health reform has reemerged on the nation's agenda. By late 2007 it had become the top domestic issue. Whether Democrat or Republican, every candidate put forward some ideas. Given electoral politics, however, it is not surprising that the proposals were often long on rhetoric and short on specifics. The experience of the Clintons in the early 1990s demonstrated the risks of being too specific before aligning the political consensus that is needed to pass legislation.

The major issues being discussed are the ever-increasing expenditures on health care, the rising cost for employers, and the falling proportion of people with insurance. In the background, and barely hinted at, is the impending burden on Medicare of the baby boomers, the first of whom will be eligible for coverage before the end of the new administration. Not surprisingly, Democrats focus on ways to reduce the proportion of those without insurance, if need be with tax increases. Republicans eschew tax increases but seem willing to discuss expanding coverage as long as it occurs primarily via the private sector.

More problematic than this ideological division, however, is the failure of both camps to look beyond coverage to more fundamental problems in our system. People *with* health insurance find the system bewilderingly complex. The Institute of Medicine, the Rand Corporation, and others have repeatedly demonstrated that quality of care

1

is far from what it should be. Patients are unnecessarily harmed by their encounters with the health care delivery system. Physicians and patients increasingly find the practice of medicine rigid and depersonalized. New technologies and drugs are announced weekly with much fanfare; many are later found to be more costly and to deliver far less than promised. "Old technologies," some as simple as routine hand-washing or careful listening to the patient's problem, are underused.

Health insurance is too often the goal of policy, yet it is merely a tool to get people the care they need, when they need it, at an affordable cost. Some innovations are thought to provide solutions. Electronic health records can certainly help, but few discuss what incentives clinicians will have to bear the costs of entering data and using the information such records can provide. Evidence-based medicine is certainly better than anecdote-based medicine, but fewer than half of well-researched quality measures are attained in practice. The techniques may be available, but much more needs to be done to translate them into practice.

Most health reform proposals fall into one of two groups. The first group attempts to increase the number of people with health insurance obtained through the patchwork of employer sponsorship, individual enrollment, and government programs. Leaving intact the existing fragmented system, such proposals need to find the money to subsidize private coverage or expand public programs, typically through some combination of tax increases and promised savings through prevention. The middle class, however, is unlikely to support increasing its taxes to pay for more coverage for the poor when the system does not work well for even those who have coverage. Prevention may improve health, but there is little solid evidence that the promised savings in reduced costs for chronic illness will appear anytime soon.

The second set of proposals envisions a single-payer, tax-financed system for everyone. Its proponents argue that while taxes will increase, overall expenditures on health care will slow because of savings that are sure to come from a unified system. The current fragmented financing system does have enormous administrative costs, but only some of these would disappear with a single-payer system. Single-payer advocates, moreover, rarely offer details about exactly how such a system would operate. In addition to the political resistance to tax increases, there are real questions about how the government would operate the system.

Neither set of proposals addresses the fundamental questions of how health care delivery should be reoriented to assure everyone high-quality care at reasonable cost. Proposals in the first group assume that the existing structure of insurance will somehow do this, despite its abject failure thus far. There is no reason to believe that increasing deductibles or building information systems will magically provide the answer. Similarly, the challenge to the single-payer advocates is to describe realistically how the administration of the new system will decide which hospitals will be closed, what procedures are unnecessary, and how fees should be set.

The approach in this book avoids the simple answers of political rhetoric. It explicitly addresses the more complex task of determining how to make the health care system work better, rather than just how to finance more of the same. Instead of focusing on getting to universal coverage while leaving the issues of long-term cost to vague promises, it focuses on how the system should be restructured to improve care for everyone. It gives providers the freedom they desire to practice and set fees but holds them more responsible for the decisions they make. Better information is needed; and with new incentives, clinicians will demand information to achieve better outcomes at lower cost. Government should make sure that the underlying data are freely available. Care will be delivered not in regimented, cookie-cutter fashion, as some allege will happen with a universal system, but in a highly individualized manner responsive to patient preferences and values. The new system will not guarantee that costs will be contained; no system can guarantee that without being willing to sacrifice quality. The new system will guarantee, however, that individual patients and the public collectively feel they get value for the money they devote to health care.

With all of the efforts of policy analysts and health economists over the decades, why should one give credence to a proposal promising far more than the best teams have offered thus far? My answer is that I began with a different question—*how to improve care* rather than *how to improve coverage*—and focused on a different approach: on realigning incentives for all the participants in health care rather than on raising enough money to continue operating the old system.

Medical expenditures include rare but very expensive events that involve uncertainty about how to care for them. People want insurance to cover the costs of care they may need; clinicians do not want to bear the financial risk of providing all the care patients may require. The reimbursement-based insurance we currently have addresses these demands, but in ways that eliminate incentives for patients and physicians to think carefully about the choices they make. The insurance carrier determines what services it will cover and what rates it will pay providers—physicians, other clinicians, and hospitals. It utilizes financial incentives such as deductibles and coinsurance to reduce patient demand, combining these blunt tools with occasional decisions about whether to pay for certain services in specific instances. Attempting to contain costs by reducing fees seems to lead physicians to increase the use of services for which they can charge extra, hence raising overall costs. In our current model a third party—neither patient nor physician—decides whether and how much to pay for a disconnected series of services.

Illnesses and injuries, however, occur in real people who have to decide whether to seek care. Clinicians make complex decisions about what is needed to treat the patient, marshalling a wide range of resources—their own and others'—to achieve the best possible outcome. Instead of a disconnected stream of services, think of those services as collected within episodes of care—just as patients and clinicians think of them. Payment should be structured to give patients and physicians the appropriate incentives and information to assess the value of various choices they need to make. People should have many choices in the care they receive and the costs they are willing to bear. People should not, however, have the option to forgo coverage. The uninsured, healthy twenty-year-old can suffer a catastrophic injury, and because we do not let people without coverage die on the streets, we end up paying for his care. Once people develop chronic conditions, they become uninsurable at reasonable cost. Those who choose to be uninsured typically regret not having insurance when they need care for major events; society must ensure that all are covered for such events. Coverage for other health needs is more discretionary; the public role in paying for those needs reflects equity and public health concerns. A just society makes certain that its least well-off members have either adequate income or assurance of basic food, housing, education, and health care needs. A society desirous of being healthy makes sure that income constraints do not deter people from preventing costly illnesses.

The plan I propose, SecureChoice, has two major components. The first is a universal coverage pool (UCP), encompassing the major risks of hospitalization and chronic illness for which everyone should have secure coverage. This pool will ensure financial access to all the services needed for such episodes of care, paying the average cost of the services needed to deliver superior outcomes. Physicians and hospitals will have both the incentives and the flexibility to deliver high-quality care efficiently. All will be in the same pool, never needing to worry about losing coverage or facing escalating premiums because they have fallen ill, their employer reduces benefits, or they change jobs. Some may be concerned that the absence of patient-based incentives will increase costs. Our current system, however, shifts costs to patients with little control over decisions in the hospital and offers no incentives for physicians to be more cost-conscious. The new episode-based payments combined with clinician-driven demands for improved quality measures will markedly increase efficiency. The UCP addresses only a quarter of the problems that bring people into contact with the medical care system, but these problems account for almost two-thirds of the cost.

The second component of the proposal emphasizes choice, flexibility, and responsibility. Plans will not constrain people in their choice of a physician to be their "medical home"—to keep track of their health records, provide much of their primary care, and offer referral information. Each physician will choose one entity—a former health insurer, credit card processor, or any other organization good at handling financial transactions—to be a payment intermediary (PI), handling all the claims for his or her patients. By processing claims, the PI automatically collects the data needed to price premiums. These premiums are essentially the ambulatory care costs incurred by that doctor's patients net of the payments received from the UCP based on their chronic illnesses. The PI can develop and offer a wide range of co-payment options from which the patient may choose. Physicians can set their own fees, practice styles, and referrals, knowing that the incremental cost implications of such choices will be borne by their patients. Some physicians will seek information on how others provide comparable-quality care at lower cost; others will demonstrate to their patients that they offer higher quality, more responsiveness, or increased satisfaction.

SecureChoice offers security for all people. All will be in one major risk pool regardless of employer and can access the UCP at the same rates even if not employed. Even if SecureChoice is not financed fully through taxes, the premium charged by the UCP will not differ on the basis of health status or use of services. Incentives to be efficient in treating major illnesses are placed on physicians and hospitals—not patients. The universal coverage pool pays enough to cover the costs of care needed by those providers who achieve superior outcomes.

SecureChoice is not about cost containment; it is about value in health care. "Cost containment" is terminology used by governments and employers wanting to keep their expenditures down, typically by squeezing provider payments and shifting costs to patients. With SecureChoice, if superior outcomes cost more than worse outcomes, the pool will pay more. Numerous studies in the United States and elsewhere reveal that medical care is far less efficient than it can be; appropriate treatments are often neglected, and unnecessary interventions are often delivered. SecureChoice includes incentives and makes available the data for clinicians to learn how to improve practice continuously so as to offer better outcomes at lower cost. In the long run, SecureChoice will lower the rate of growth in health care spending. Whether the health care share of gross domestic product rises or falls matters far less than whether we achieve the best health possible for that expenditure.

SecureChoice provides far more patient choice than even voucher-based systems, let alone plans designed by employers for their employees. People can choose their own physicians. Physicians will offer a wide range of payment options—from high deductibles to first-dollar coverage—and patients will choose the physician and payment arrangements best matching their preferences. Patient costs vary, but because of the effects of different financial incentives and the physician chosen, *not* because of the patient's chronic illnesses; the UCP offsets those costs. Members of a family can choose different doctors with differing co-payment arrangements; these choices can change over time as circumstances and preferences change.

SecureChoice allows clinicians to be the best professionals they can be. Payment structures and fees will be set not by government or health insurers but by individual physicians. If a doctor wants to provide forty-five-minute office visits, telephone consultations, or e-mail advice *and* charge for those services, that is perfectly fine. Primary care physicians will be able to refer patients to whomever they choose. Physicians will decide which payment intermediary will assist them in handling their patients' claims, choosing the one that does so with low administrative costs and hassles, and provides them and their patients with valuable information. With all this flexibility comes an appropriate degree of responsibility. Physicians who increase their fees without learning how to use other resources such as tests, scans, and new pharmaceuticals more efficiently may find that the increasing premiums passed on to their patients result in pointed discussions when patients decide whether to stay with that physician the following year.

SecureChoice will make available to clinicians, hospitals, and patients far more information than is currently the practice. Electronic health records may eventually make this easier, but at the outset the data will come from claims and other information generated in the normal care and payment processes. Instead of data being "owned" by health plans, however, SecureChoice pools all the data in a confidential manner. Converting data into useful and actionable information is not easy, but clinicians and hospitals will have strong reasons to demand such information, and independent analysts will respond. Accessible data and transparent methods will keep special interest groups from inappropriately influencing care and payment.

SecureChoice relies heavily on market incentives both to enhance flexibility *and* to reduce the power of corporate interests. Powerful interest groups often use "free market" ideology to protect the status quo while wielding power through the Congress and regulatory mechanisms. In contrast, SecureChoice includes a relatively small role for government. The UCP is managed by a semi-independent agency insulated from Congress and the executive branch. Its role is largely to pool resources, determine future premiums, and ensure that data are accessible. The payment intermediaries process claims but do not "own" patients or clinicians.

SecureChoice recognizes the importance of technological innovation in health care. Pharmaceutical companies will do what they should do best: develop new drugs. Experimental drugs will be made freely available through trials; all other drugs are implicitly included in covered benefits. Individual physicians, however, will decide which drugs to prescribe, judging when the new and more expensive ones are worth the extra cost. In making such decisions, they will ask for and receive independent assessments of what seems to work best in what circumstances. As new technologies come into use, as physicians make treatment decisions, and as the data systems follow costs and outcomes, all will learn when new technologies should be utilized.

SecureChoice is designed to be a comprehensive system, but transitions take time, and some people may never want to change. An important aspect of SecureChoice is that it moves away from making employers responsible for the funding and sponsorship of specific health plans. Depending on what policy choices are made for funding SecureChoice, employers may still be the source of much of the money that flows into the system. Some may quickly "cash out" their current contributions; others may transition slowly, using the UCP first to pay for efficient hospital care and perhaps later to handle all of the major risks for their enrollee group. At the same time, employers may focus on creating health-promoting environments and incentives for their workers and communities.

SecureChoice does rely on government in a few key areas. Safe drugs and devices will continue to be assured by the Food and Drug Administration (FDA). Fair market practices will continue to be assured by those enforcing antitrust laws. The federal, state, and local governments now pay for health insurance for the poor though Medicaid and the State Children's Health Insurance Program (SCHIP), and pay for or provide care through various safety net programs. SecureChoice envisions an income-based subsidy program that reduces the premium and out-of-pocket costs for all low-income people. This subsidy occurs behind the scenes; from the perspective of providers, everyone in SecureChoice yields the same fees. Access for the poor will improve markedly, but some safety net programs will still be needed in select geographic areas and for people for whom simply providing insurance coverage is not enough to ensure that they will get the care they need.

SecureChoice is not a formal legislative proposal but a sketch for one that might be developed in the next few years. It recognizes that fundamental changes in how we spend a sixth of our gross domestic product will be intensely political. Thus all the current players can have roles in the new system. In many instances the roles will be quite different from the present configuration, and some entities within groups may succeed even if their group loses power. For example, health insurers will no longer be center stage. Shedding their role as villains, however, insurers can use their expertise to offer physicians valuable services as payment intermediaries and as converters of data into useful information. Determining exactly how to craft a legislative proposal and build the necessary public consensus to enact something like SecureChoice is beyond the scope of this volume. The goal of this book is simply to lay the foundation for such discussions.

One challenge in moving forward is that most people think about health reform in one of two ways. Some want to adopt a system that appears to be working well in some other country—although every nation is facing its own problems. Others want to keep what we have and just make marginal improvements. SecureChoice is not a wholesale adoption of other models, nor is it minor tinkering. Instead it is a fundamental rearrangement of what exists in the United States, building on our strengths and sidestepping our weaknesses. Such a shift in thinking is not easy; if it were, we would have come to it long ago.

In Chapter 1, "Build on What You've Got, but Recognize Real-World Constraints," I explain why we cannot simply adopt the health care system of any other nation and why minor changes to our current system will not address our core problems. Chapter 2, "Overview of a Restructured Health Care System," provides a more in-depth summary of SecureChoice than in this introduction. It gives the reader a sense of the issues that will be addressed in detail in each of the successive chapters. I then give the rationale—economic, political, and value based—for the proposal. I do this because not everyone will agree with all aspects of SecureChoice, but areas of agreement should be identified whenever possible. If disagreements can be resolved by getting better data on underlying facts or behavioral factors, we should gather that information. If disagreements arise from values, we should see if compromise is possible.

Chapters 3–6 focus on the details of how SecureChoice is structured and the rationale for those design details. The discussion begins with Chapter 3, "Covering the Cost of Care: Rethinking Health Insurance," focusing on the two main aspects of the plan: (1) the universal pool to cover major acute/interventional (MA/I) care and chronic illness management (CIM) care, and (2) the patient- and provider-based premiums that will facilitate coverage and payment for minor acute and preventive care. Chapter 4, "Organizing Care and Paying Providers," focuses on the payments and incentives for clinicians and organizations delivering health care. A key aspect of SecureChoice is that it achieves many of the beneficial incentives that are possible within integrated delivery systems without requiring physicians to change markedly where and how they deliver care. Chapter 5, "Choices: Harnessing Data to Inform Decisions," describes how the new system will collect data to inform choices by clinicians and patients. Chapter 6, "Financing SecureChoice," describes financing alternatives. The simplest would be a fully tax-funded system, but because that may be politically difficult, I describe how one could build on existing financing mechanisms. A fully tax-based model implicitly guarantees equity, but one can achieve any degree of equity with a tax-funded, income-based subsidy program. Either approach would be a marked improvement over what we have now.

The last three chapters step back from the details. Chapter 7, "Malpractice, Pharmaceuticals, Medical Education, and Prevention," sketches approaches to address four key problem areas that will impinge on or can benefit by being integrated with SecureChoice. The fear of malpractice is often used today as a rationale for what is otherwise unnecessary care. SecureChoice gives physicians and hospitals much more flexibility in how they organize and deliver care and incentives to become more efficient. Unless the current fear of malpractice suits is offset, however, innovation will be slowed. Chapter 7 outlines a proposal offering better compensation for patients injured by their medical care experiences *and* reduces allegations of negligence. It simultaneously provides new roles for malpractice attorneys to reduce avoidable errors by pressing organizations to improve their systems of care. SecureChoice encourages and empowers physicians to assess critically whether expensive new drugs and devices provide enough benefits to justify the additional cost. Pharmaceutical firms and others will have to price and market their products differently, and there is a concern that this may reduce investment and research. SecureChoice can provide investment and market risk reinsurance approaches to keep innovations flowing. The medical education "pipeline" is even longer than the drug pipeline; we need to incorporate changes early to ensure the right mix of physicians. SecureChoice focuses on rebuilding the health care system, but much of what affects health lies outside of health care. Policy changes should be considered to enhance long-run behavioral and environmental factors in order to allow our population to be healthier and require less medical care.

Chapter 8, "How SecureChoice Would Work for Patients and Physicians," uses patients Harvey and Louisa and their physicians to show how SecureChoice would function. Chapter 9, "Getting There: Policy Choices, Implementation, and Transition," takes us back to the present, with a discussion of the issues that must be addressed if we are to move toward a rebuilt and better-functioning health care system for all.

The SecureChoice proposal outlines a comprehensive restructuring of American health care, a system of enormous complexity. SecureChoice is much simpler than what we have now, but nevertheless has many components and uses incentives and structures in markedly different ways. Achieving an understanding of SecureChoice is difficult if readers try to assess aspects in the context of the current system, or are unwilling to wait for information that comes later in the book. I cannot promise that every question will be answered by the time one reaches the last chapter, but many of the concerns that arise early on will be addressed. The questions and issues that remain should serve as the basis for more fruitful discussions about how to truly improve health care.

— 1 —

Build on What You've Got, but Recognize Real-World Constraints

Our health care system is like an old house that has been modified multiple times over the years but no longer meets the owners' needs, is inefficient, and appears to be falling apart. Patching holes, buying new appliances, and making minor redecorating changes is one option. Tearing down the whole structure and replacing it with a new building modeled on what appears in *Architectural Digest* is another option. These alternatives represent the primary approaches to addressing our health care system's problems. Some propose only to tweak the existing system by expanding coverage to a specific population subgroup or relying on information technology to solve shortcomings. Others feel that the solution is to scrap the current system and adopt what is in place in another country, be it Canada, France, or Germany.

Neither approach addresses problems arising from the details of how a health care system works: how care is organized and delivered, what patients want from medical care, and what clinicians need in order to practice their professions. To propose system change, however, one must recognize fundamental laws, history, and values that are not easily altered. The U.S. constitutional system differs from parliamentary systems. Americans cherish the image of the rugged individualist for whom the watchword is "That government is best which governs least." This book will not explore other nations' systems. For decades advocates have argued for the adoption of various foreign models; the political challenges surrounding change are so complex, however, that any "import" will be doomed. Just as an architect works within the physical characteristics and legal constraints of a site, health policy analysts must work within larger cultural and political constraints. Thus we begin by looking at what works well and what doesn't; at what is given and what is not.

What (If Anything) Works Well

The list of things that don't work (or appear not to be working) properly in our health care system is far longer than the list of things that function reasonably well. It is worth beginning, however, with those aspects most would want to retain.

Rapid and Wide-Reaching Technological Innovation

Americans value the pace, breadth, and dissemination of technological development and innovation in medical care. Innovation, however, may threaten the markets of existing players; this situation is not peculiar to the health care sector, as the transformation of airlines, mainframe computing, and telecommunication attests. Patients need to be assured that they are not being put at undue risk by new drugs, devices, and procedures. Under the guise of promoting safety, however, a highly centralized review and approval process may be co-opted by current market leaders to prevent the entry of competitors.

The widespread availability of technology and specialty-trained physicians means that rationing or queuing is rarely an issue in most parts of the United States—as long as one has private insurance or Medicare.[1] Put another way, patients don't perceive services as being rationed in the sense of wanting and being able to afford them but not being able to get them. The fear that one might not receive potentially life-saving care because of some bureaucratic process is a recipe for political disaster. Lobbying by patients led to mandating coverage of autologous bone marrow transplants for breast cancer in the absence of evidence of its efficacy; research eventually showed the treatment to be harmful and of no benefit.[2]

Clinical and Patient Autonomy

Clinicians generally believe that they can do whatever they feel is necessary for their patients. When managed care plans attempted in the mid-1990s to control utilization tightly, the ensuing backlash led to a reversal of such efforts. This laissez-faire approach to "practice style" means that geographic differences in patient preference and clinician practice are tolerated and go largely unchallenged, even without evidence that more care is better. All of this is consistent with the strongly held American value of individualism.

Individual values play out in complicated ways, especially when medical care intersects with religion. In some instances the government requires the availability of services some consider controversial, while in other instances it precludes their availability. Courts have ruled that employer-based plans may decide whether or not to include prescription drugs in their benefit packages, but if they choose to do so, a state may mandate that such coverage include contraceptives even if the employer objects on religious grounds.[3] Federal programs, however, have been prevented by law from paying for abortions and certain other services because those services are objectionable to certain segments of the population.[4]

Reliance on the Private Sector

Reflecting another American value, the direct role of government is currently relatively small, or at least is kept in the background. In spite of the high quality of care now delivered within the Veterans Affairs (VA) system, there is almost no interest in having the government serve as a direct provider of care. The private sector dominates, except in financing programs for the elderly and poor and some rural communities. Within both the Medicare and Medicaid programs, services are delivered primarily by independent providers, and the administration of claims is generally subcontracted to private entities. In part this is due to a historical preference for "small government."

What Doesn't Work Well

Many aspects of the health care system do not work well, ranging from the high proportion of uninsured to the high cost of care, from unsafe care to malpractice litigation, from overly restrictive pharmaceutical formularies to advertising for unnecessary treatments. Some advocates for change focus on just one or a few of these issues. A narrow focus, whether because incremental change is preferred or to protect certain interests by deflecting attention, fails to address the other issues. Incrementalism has not been effective in the past.

A comprehensive approach, while seemingly more daunting, may actually hold far more promise. From a political perspective, the threat of one type of change may be offset by the promise of another. Tying the two together offers greater potential for compromise. From a technical perspective, a change may be too costly if undertaken for a single purpose but worthwhile if multiple goals can be achieved. It is helpful to place all the problems on the table and then see whether they can be addressed together. The list of problems is unfortunately long, but reviewing it offers a glimpse of the opportunities for change. Most discussions begin with concerns about the large proportion of people without coverage and then go on to suggest ways to expand coverage. Such reforms build on a fragmented system that is both costly and inequitable. Much of the discussion, moreover, focuses on what should—or should not—be included in the benefits package. Those discussions ignore the incentive problems in the current system as well as the administrative costs of operating it. This leads to a consideration of problems in the delivery of care: variable quality, inadequate safety, and insufficient rewards for primary care, as well as the feeling common to clinicians of being deprofessionalized. Finally, most analysts see the long-term cost of the system as being driven by inexorable technological change.

The High Proportion of People without Coverage

Almost every discussion of health systems begins by citing the high proportion of Americans who lack health insurance coverage—currently about 16 percent and seemingly rising every year. Some view this with moral outrage, some with embarrassment, others simply as an unfortunate characteristic of the system, believing that most alternatives would be worse. Few argue that having so many without health insurance is desirable per se, as some believe, for instance, that the threat of unemployment creates valuable work incentives.

Even apart from the moral question of whether our society should ensure some basic level of coverage and the political question of whether leaving so many uninsured impairs our moral credibility among nations, there are other reasons for moving toward universality. Financing safety net care for people without insurance coverage through a patchwork of tax-supported public providers, shifting costs to other payers, and offering ex post facto eligibility for coverage in programs such as Medicaid is economically inefficient. These approaches also result in fragmented and poor-quality care. On those grounds alone, substantial change is warranted.

The High Cost and Inequity of Current Approaches

The majority of Americans (59.7 percent of the population) are insured through private health care coverage obtained through employers.[5] Unlike the system of employer contributions in western Europe, where the cost is often a simple percentage of wages, the U.S. system relies on the employer to negotiate the specific insurance package, enroll workers and sometimes their families, and decide how much to contribute. Most economists see the employer share of this coverage as part of the total compensation package; they believe that employers are indifferent as to whether compensation is paid as wages or as health benefits. A payment toward health insurance premiums, however, is quite different from the equivalent amount as a surcharge to wages. Health insurance coverage is "lumpy"—that is, an employee is either eligible or not—and the contribution is usually the same for each eligible worker. This contribution is a larger fraction of total compensation for low-wage or part-time workers, creating strong incentives to limit eligibility for coverage or to use "independent contractors," who are not eligible for benefits.

From the employee's perspective, the presence or absence of employer-sponsored health coverage may affect job mobility. Group policies are typically much less expensive than comparable individual coverage, and they average risk across everyone in the group, making coverage much more valuable for high-risk persons and relatively less valuable for low-risk persons. Employers recognize this, and some attempt to reduce the cost of their employee pool by attracting low- (or avoiding high-) risk workers.[6]

About 9.1 percent of the population is covered through individual policies.[7] In theory, individual policies better meet personal preferences and needs, allowing some people to choose limited coverage while others may pay more for a broader range of benefits. Insurers' flexibility in designing policies, however, is typically limited by state mandates. Marketing, underwriting, and other aspects of selling and administering individual policies add to their cost. Flexibility and choice do not come for free; these "load factors" widen the spread between the care paid for by the plan and the cost to the enrollee.

Individually purchased coverage may be eligible for some income tax deductibility; all of the employer's contribution for coverage, however, is excluded from both income and payroll taxes. Such tax incentives are more valuable for those in higher income brackets, making them an inequitable way to provide coverage. There are also equity issues for employers. Older, more experienced workforces may be more productive and warrant higher levels of compensation, but productivity does not rise as rapidly with age as do health care costs. Employers with continuing contractual responsibilities for retiree health benefits carry the contribution burden for people whom they no longer employ.[8]

Deciding What Should Be Covered

Policy analysts usually focus on specifying which broad categories of services health insurance should cover, such as inpatient care, ambulatory care, drugs, and devices. All such coverage is typically made subject to a determination of medical necessity. At an operational level, numerous decisions have to be made about whether specific services will be covered in specific instances. For example, MRI scans can be enormously valuable in many cases, but they provide no useful information—and sometimes result in harm—in others. A benefit package does not make this determination except by linking coverage to "medical necessity."

As new procedures, devices, and drugs become available with increasingly expensive price tags, these day-to-day coverage determinations are progressively more important. Advocates for guaranteed coverage of specific services include patients who think they might benefit (and who may be desperate because there is no good alternative), as well as providers and manufacturers with a financial interest at stake. (The latter often give support—sometimes covert—to providers and advocacy groups.) Payers often resist efforts to expand coverage, in part because their premiums are fixed in the short run, and in part because increases in premiums further erode the voluntary purchase of insurance. Arguments over coverage mandates fought in the legislative arena are frequently determined not by scientific evidence concerning the benefits and costs of the interventions but by the political clout of the advocates on either side.[9]

The current patchwork of state regulation of most private coverage, federal determinations for Medicare, and the exclusion of employer-administered plans from regulation creates multiple settings in which these coverage arguments are aired. A restructured system should address how such determinations are made, with the goal of increasing rational decision making and allowing the system to learn from natural "experiments" as well as randomized trials.

Ineffective or Problematic Incentives

There is substantial evidence that economic incentives influence consumer demand for health care. More questionable, however, is whether the current structure of co-payments and deductibles influences patient and clinician decision making in ways that are optimally affecting health. Deductibles clearly impact the initial decision to seek treatment, but they affect appropriate as well as inappropriate care. The general populace is not skilled at discriminating between relatively inconsequential health concerns and those needing evaluation by a clinician—an indication that medical training has value. High-deductible plans may create too much cost-based reluctance to seek care, although some preliminary results indicate otherwise.[10] The current evidence is too fragmentary, however, for an accurate assessment of this issue.[11]

A fundamental aspect of medical care, moreover, makes reliance on patient-based incentives unwise. Medical care expenditures are highly concentrated in a small proportion of the population. Typically, fewer than 20 percent of all people in a given population account for over 80 percent of expenditures (with 5 percent of the population accounting for almost half of expenditures).[12] This is the rationale for insurance to spread the risk.[13] Because financial exposure can be so great, insurance commonly sets a maximum out-of-pocket expenditure beyond which the plan pays the full cost. From the patient's perspective, once this out-of-pocket threshold is crossed, there is no economic deterrent to seeking more care.

When the need for medical care arises, the consumer becomes a patient and is usually unable to assess appropriately the precise type and amount of care needed, relying instead on clinicians to make those decisions.[14] Although ideally they reflect the patient's values, such decisions more often are based only on clinical needs as perceived by the physician. When clinicians and health care institutions receive fee-for-service payment, they have incentives to offer all services for which potential medical benefits exceed the additional cost to the patient. For most inpatient care, because the maximum out-of-pocket cost is often reached during the admission, the marginal cost to the patient of additional services may be zero. Thus, as long as a service is expected to offer some benefit, its cost is irrelevant.

To counter this incentive problem, health plans bearing some responsibility for the overall cost of care increasingly ask for information about the medical need for each service provided. This results in extensive and oftentimes problematic communications to assure "prior approval" of coverage before treatment, or retroactive refusals to pay for care already delivered. In practice, prior approval requests are rarely denied, but the process results in substantial provider frustration. Most expensive new interventions are fully (or nearly fully) covered by insurance, so there is no formal consumer-driven market test of their value. It is not surprising that biomedical product developers focus their research on areas with the greatest profit (but not necessarily clinical) potential, but this link between insurance and technology development has not been explored.

Fee-for-service payment also hampers coordination of care. Each provider (for example, physician, hospital, clinic) has economic incentives to offer his or her own "products and services." For various historical reasons, payment rates undervalue time spent with the patient relative to procedures performed. More important, if expert advice avoids the dispensing of unnecessary services, there is no way for the fee-for-service system to share those savings with the expert. Referral patterns reinforce "sequential back-scratching" and routine referral to more expensive care; such behaviors are exacerbated by subspecialization and concerns about liability. Various laws prohibit or constrain gainsharing (colloquially referred to as "anti-kickback" laws) between providers and institutions or between professionals, even if this may enhance efficiency and/or quality through better co-ordination of care.

In contrast to fee-for-service, capitation (a yearly payment to cover all services needed by a patient) offers incentives to provide no more than the necessary care, although it frequently does not work this way. The incentives work well if patients and providers are linked to-gether in a long-term relationship and if providers receive payment commensurate with the risks associated with their population of pa-tients. Clinicians then have economic incentives not to overlook a problem in the near term because it might be very costly to them in the long term. Except in highly integrated plans such as the Kaiser-Permanente system, in which the "glue" of an ongoing physician-patient relationship keeps the patient in the system, it is painless for most patients to move from one HMO to another while keeping the same clinicians.[15] This makes it easy, and far more profitable, for the plan to design ways to encourage people likely to be high cost to switch to another plan rather than to address the complicated clinical approaches needed to optimize care. These strategies need affect only a small number of very expensive patients to be highly cost-effective for the plan, and may even enhance quality for those patients if they get to see better-qualified specialists. Such schemes, however, reduce incentives for plans to seek out and effectively manage the high-cost cases, which would likely benefit the most from well-designed care.

The Cost of Operating Payment Systems

Sub-optimal incentives might be acceptable if associated with a pay-ment system that has minimal operating costs. Simple global budgets for hospitals and "no questions asked" fee-for-service reimburse-ment of clinicians may not have optimal economic incentives, but at least they are administratively inexpensive. The United States, how-ever, has the worst of both worlds. Our payment incentives encour-age ever more service delivery. To control costs, payers request progressively more detailed information about the need for each service, increasing the costs of filing claims, delaying decisions, and/or causing retroactive denials and appeals.

Payers view their administrative functions to reduce expenditures as "value added." The percentage of premiums paid to providers is referred to as the "loss ratio"; keeping this low (that is, increasing the share of both profit and administrative cost) is assessed positively by financial analysts. The feeling of providers and patients is that "the system" is designed to make the reimbursement process so cumbersome and time intensive that they sometimes simply walk away from demanding payments legitimately due them.

The multiplicity of payers and rules is part of the problem. Each payer attempts to manage its own costs. In the absence of a coordinated effort and/or dominant market player (except Medicare), providers are faced with such a cacophony of rules, requirements, and micro-incentives that most are ignored. Uniform coding of claims data to facilitate electronic submission is only now being done, decades after the credit card industry achieved this goal. The simple alternative of a single payer is politically fraught. Private payers can be expected to resist any public effort to supplant their role, but providers also seem hesitant, fearing that government-mandated rules will be driven by budget and political priorities and will be insufficiently flexible to adapt to new technologies and science.

The Highly Variable Technical Quality of Care

Health care use varies substantially across geographic areas without corresponding differences in outcomes. Some argue that outcomes are actually worse in high-use areas.[16] Although the direct connection between these observations and health care quality is not entirely clear, variations in the use of discretionary services, ranging from rates of cesarean section to days in the intensive care unit shortly before death, reflect supply variations; treatment of non-discretionary conditions, such as repair of hip fractures, however, bears little relation to supply.[17] There is not much evidence that the patterns, sometimes referred to as "practice style" variations, with higher use offer significant clinical benefit, and the current system provides little incentive for either critical assessment or change of such variations. Partly in response to such findings, in recent years evidence-based guidelines have been promulgated by panels of experts based on findings of well-designed peer-reviewed studies. Adherence by clinicians to such guidelines, however, is highly variable even when there is agreement that the guidelines are relevant.[18] Guidelines are not universally accepted as the best solution. They have been criticized for focusing too heavily on "ideal" cases rather than reflecting real-life practice.[19] There are also cases of special interest groups, such as drug companies, influencing the guideline development process.[20]

One cause of variable care is the lack of coordination across multiple providers and systems. Information on what was or was not done for a patient is often unavailable. When a patient has multiple problems, it is sometimes difficult to determine which clinician is responsible. It is hard to achieve a good balance between recognizing the unique aspects of a patient's case and developing more generic measures of quality of care that can be evaluated across many patients.

Assessing Quality of Care from a Patient Perspective

In addition to determining whether clinicians adhere to what is considered "best practice," one must also assess if it is the care the patient wants and if it is delivered in a manner the patient finds acceptable. We do not think it is enough for an airline to ensure that its planes are well maintained and do not crash; it should also get its passengers to their desired destinations in a timely and courteous fashion.

New measures focusing on patient assessments of care are gaining acceptance, such as the Consumer Assessment of Health Plans Survey (CAHPS); similar measures are available for hospital and other types of care. These weigh aspects of care that only patients can assess, such as getting needed care, receiving care quickly, completing paperwork with ease, and receiving comprehensible information, as well as doctors' communications skills and the courtesy, respect, and helpfulness shown by office staff. Still missing are tools to help patients communicate their preferences for clinical care, including trade-offs among various treatment options, and assess how well these preferences are honored.

Clinicians sometimes disagree among themselves as to what should be done in a specific case. Orthopedic surgeons are less likely to recommend conservative treatment of back problems than neurologists or physical therapists. Apart from the question of economic self-interest, clinicians naturally believe in the efficacy of approaches reflecting their own training, and know less about the skills of others. Even when the existence of alternatives is recognized, explaining options and choices to patients is complex. This is especially true in sensitive areas, such as end-of-life care, involving cultural, educational, and value-based factors that must be considered. Even the words used to describe a situation may be understood differently by various patients. Differing worldviews are part of the problem; a lack of (reimbursed) time prevents clinicians from getting beyond advice targeted to "the average" patient.

Far-from-Optimal Safety

Medical care is not always delivered in a safe manner. Although the Institute of Medicine's estimate of nearly 100,000 hospital deaths a year due to errors is debated by some, the true number is undoubtedly too high.[21] Medical care involves inherent risk, but in many instances the risk can be reduced through known, inexpensive means. Occasionally these safety problems are attributable to individuals; most, however, reflect failures of system design. Far more deadly than the incompetent surgeon is the hospital that does not enforce hand-washing by its staff. The question is: How do we improve the incentives for organizations to enhance safety?

One area in which the system has particularly flawed incentives is that of malpractice. Various studies show that the vast majority of errors do not result in malpractice claims, that most claims do not result in judgments, and that compensation levels appear random.[22] The transactional costs of litigation are substantial, involving attorneys on both sides, expert witnesses, court costs, and the time of and emotional stress on both plaintiffs and defendants.

The tort system underlying a malpractice claim is based on a specific incident involving negligence: without proof of negligence, the claim fails, irrespective of whether there was a bad outcome. "Mistakes" or "errors" are not part of the legal terminology.[23] Not surprisingly, providers have an interest in denying negligence; in addition to the financial implications, the mere accusation threatens the clinician's and/or institution's professional image. The great majority of claims are settled without any admission of guilt or public disclosure of evidence. Rather than providing incentives for organizations to identify patterns of bad outcomes leading to process redesign, however, the current system hides data and prevents learning from mistakes.[24]

Failure to Reward Primary Care Practice

Most clinicians enter their field to care for patients. For some this is accomplished through the ongoing contact of primary care, for others by delivering leading-edge specialty care. Primary care, however, is increasingly unattractive as a profession. There is pressure to raise "throughput"—that is, to see more patients in less time—partly because payment per encounter is low and the fixed costs of practice are substantial. Fee schedules do not adequately reward increased *quantity* of time spent with patients or improved *quality* of time reflected in empathy and understanding. All office visits and practitioners are generally considered by payers to be equivalent. Payers may have "preferred providers" to whom they channel patients, but selection for the panel is often based simply on the willingness to accept lower fees. Employers typically prefer broad panels of providers but offer little guidance to enrollees about how to choose a clinician. When people change employers, or employers change plans, their "covered" panels of providers may change, breaking long-standing patient-clinician relationships.

Increasing Sense among Clinicians of Deprofessionalization

Many physicians and other clinicians feel as if their "professions" are being taken away. "Professionals" are defined as people in occupations requiring extensive expertise and discretion; professionals are expected to behave according to those standards.[25] Although evidence-based practice is almost certainly preferable to practice based on anecdote or outdated training, rigid adherence to guidelines, particularly when monitored and enforced by nonclinicians, transforms their potential utility into a threat.

Whether true or not, the traditional version of professional ethics typically placed compensation in the background; currently it seems to be front and center. Physicians are encouraged to act in a business-like fashion, but when they attempt to do so by becoming owners of their practice environments, they may jeopardize their professional status, as well as occasionally running afoul of legislation intended to prevent certain types of bad economic behavior.

Perception of Technology as the Major Driver of Costs

Most U.S. health economists feel that the long-term growth in health care expenditures is driven by technology.[26] Although not all technological innovations are cost-increasing—David Cutler, J. D. Kleinke, and others argue that some innovations have produced markedly better health at lower cost—many innovations hike cost with little net effect on health.[27] A key question, however, is whether technological innovation is endogenous—that is, responsive to the incentives implicit in the health care system—or simply the result of the independent flow of new scientific exploration. Basic science is plausibly the result of researchers' independently following interesting hypotheses, but it is far less likely that the investments covering research and development (R&D) costs are independent of potential rewards. If R&D *is* responsive to payment issues, a restructured system could alter that portion of the trend in expenditures that is due to technological change.

Even if health care policy is not explicitly structured to influence the direction of R&D, R&D will be influenced by technological changes on the horizon. The specificity of drugs and devices is increasing, allowing manufacturers to identify better who will benefit from a new product. Manufacturers can then show significant benefits with fewer patients in the trial; but increased specificity limits the scope of the market, therefore raising the price needed to cover R&D costs. Higher prices will lead payers to assess more carefully whether the intervention is substantially better than the alternatives.

What Is Given and What Is Not

One way to view the different approaches to the house problem outlined at the beginning of this chapter is that the "redecorators" accept almost everything as given and think that only minor changes are possible, while the "replacers" accept almost nothing as "given." The first approach is insufficient to address the problems fully; the second is unrealistic. To get beyond these extreme approaches, it is a good idea to outline what really is unalterable.

What Needs to Be Accepted as Given

Suppose one wanted to pursue a strategy of totally revamping the U.S. health care system by "importing" what works in some other country (imagine that by some political miracle the plan was passed into law). The ongoing operation and adjustment over time of the new system would still occur in the context of the American political system. This is a system in which narrow interests have substantial veto power. The diffusion of power to congressional committees, the power of individual legislators, and the fragmented federal system make coordination and management of a single system difficult to design and operate.[28] In the United States, both constitutional interpretation and tradition reserve to the states many powers, especially in the health arena (for instance, professional licensure, the regulation of insurance), all of which challenge the creation of a national system. Although some of the separation of powers issues can be addressed, it may be difficult to do so to the extent that they affect policies outside the health arena.

Likewise, underlying public values are unlikely to change merely because a new health care system is legislated. The notion of "solidarity" (that is, citizens accepting responsibility for one another and agreeing to have everyone covered in the same plan) is common in European discussions but notably absent in the United States. Even Medicare, which comes closest to a universal plan, relies on private contractors and includes an important role for supplemental coverage paid for by individuals or employers. Since the Revolution, Americans have distrusted the ability of government to operate systems and seemingly prefer potentially complicated private sector solutions. The lack of faith in government is self-fulfilling: without respected and well-funded programs, the government has difficulty recruiting highly skilled civil servants. This results in less responsive performance and reinforces those wanting to shift programs to the private sector.

The current players in the health system will not simply disappear because a new financing plan is implemented. The ratio of procedurally oriented specialists to generalists will not change overnight, hospitals will still have too many open heart surgery and MRI units, and bondholders will still own hospital debt. Even if policymakers agree that there is an excess supply of certain health care resources, it is not clear what mechanism would be used to select which hospitals would be closed and which physicians would be excluded from the system.

Health care reform will not change the legal protections of property rights and litigation challenging government "takings." The legalities aside, appeals to a sense of "fair play" favor not harming those who legally responded to the incentives of the "old system."

Underlying economic incentives and the behaviors responding to those incentives will not change regardless of the system we implement. Most policy changes are simply intended to alter the details of the incentives to allow them to shape behavior in more desirable ways. Profit maximization will continue to be a principal driver of corporate behavior. For individuals, income maximization is tempered somewhat by both time constraints and other rewards, such as self-esteem. People and organizations generally prefer certainty to risk; many, however, are willing to accept some risk in return for increased rewards. Risk can be predicted and offset by the law of large numbers through insurance, but uncertainty is more difficult to address because the probabilities associated with various outcomes— and sometimes the outcomes themselves—are usually unknown.

What Need Not Be Taken as Given

The current players in the system will clearly be "sitting at the table" as reforms are discussed; it is unreasonable to assume that they can be eliminated from a reform plan. This does not mean, however, that all must be guaranteed the same roles they now play. Insurers, for example, serve many functions in the current system: from underwriting and risk bearing to payment and determination of medical necessity. Some of their skills may actually be underutilized currently because they cannot access the necessary data. A restructured system should consider how best to utilize the expertise and comparative advantage of all the players. We should also not assume that employers must be the primary source of specific forms of health insurance coverage, but rather consider other roles that better fit their special connections to workers.

Underlying social and political values may change at a glacial pace, if at all. New ideological labels are more likely to reflect new "framing" of positions than actual changes to the health care system's operations. That said, a restructured system should draw upon what is most beneficial from private and public sector solutions, market and collective decisions, at both local and federal levels. Changes in roles and responsibilities may be both necessary and freeing.

— 2 —

Overview of a Restructured
Health Care System

Before embarking on a detailed discussion of specific design details, this chapter offers an overview of how the U.S. health care system can be reconfigured. Like the presentation of an architect's radical new design to clients used to conventional approaches, the overview is in three parts: (1) a verbal rough sketch of the concept, followed by (2) highlights of some key features, and then (3) an explanation of the underlying values and design principles that inform the approach.

Rethinking the Coverage and Payment System

The typical questions one begins with in a health care proposal are: "Who is covered?" "What is covered?" "How is the covered part to be financed?" and "What is the function of enrollee payment?" All of these are important, but other key issues often escape scrutiny, especially those explaining how providers are paid, because the status quo is accepted as given. The incentives inherent in the current payment system, however, keep us from achieving our goals, so those issues are the focus of much of this proposal. Many proposals attempt to improve equity simply by expanding the safety net or bringing conventional coverage to those currently not able to afford it. Because our traditional reliance on multiple systems is inefficient as well as inequitable, I deal with equity in a unitary system, nonetheless relying substantially on economic incentives. This proposed system, SecureChoice, has new roles for many key players, including current health insurers.

Instead of viewing the world through the lens of conventional insurance coverage, which focuses on basic and optional *services*, maximum out-of-pocket limits, and perhaps voucher-based enrollment, SecureChoice focuses on the distinction between two broad categories of *conditions*—(1) the very expensive and uninsurable major acute and chronic illnesses, and (2) more minor acute illnesses, including some preventive care.[1] Coverage for the first category (major acute and chronic illness) is mandatory; everyone will be enrolled—directly or indirectly—in a single universal coverage pool (UCP) that will pay for all the care needed to address the first set of medical problems.[2] This category accounts for roughly 62 percent of all medical costs.[3] Even if we set aside value-based arguments for universal coverage, the only way to address the problems of risk selection effectively is to have everyone in the same pool. Coverage for all other medical care may be voluntary, in the sense that people may choose to pay for it out of pocket or buy coverage for part or all of the costs involved. Low-income people, however, will need help in meeting those costs.

The universal coverage pool concept may lead some to think that SecureChoice is a single-payer system, but in fact it is quite different. Most single-payer proposals envision a government entity tightly controlling payments and coverage decisions with little role for market forces. In contrast, SecureChoice uses government primarily to ensure equity, leaving payment decisions in other hands. Market incentives are used in many aspects of SecureChoice, and their use is highly targeted to achieve productive and informed decisions, in contrast to the problematic behavior resulting from our current use of the market.

Patient-focused financial incentives such as deductibles and coinsurance are either meaningless or harmful for the care covered by the UCP. Enormous sums are spent on hospital care, yet patients often bear no financial responsibility for decisions at the margin, and it is ethically problematic to ask them to do so in the midst of treatment.[4] Likewise, what is the rationale for deductibles that may discourage patients with chronic illness from appropriately managing their condition? Instead, incentives should be carefully designed to affect the relevant decision makers at the appropriate time. Medicare already gives hospitals a fixed payment per admission, but physicians, who make most of the decisions about what services should be delivered in the hospital, are not included in this incentive system. Under SecureChoice, the UCP will pay collaborations of physicians and hospitals a lump sum for each inpatient (or equivalent) episode of care, leaving it up to them to decide how to improve efficiency.[5] Unlike in most single-payer proposals based on tight budget controls but few incentives, payments under SecureChoice will be set at the sum required nationally for providers to deliver superior-quality care. Providers, however, may decide to charge more than that; patients can decide once a year whether they would like to purchase optional coverage for such excess charges or pay for them out of pocket.

Bundling payment for inpatient care is relatively easy. In contrast, patients receive ambulatory care from a wide range of physicians and other providers. The services needed for managing chronic illness are often delivered at the same time as those for minor acute problems, such as giving a diabetic a blood sugar check when she comes to the physician's office for a sore throat. SecureChoice therefore uses a different approach for outpatient care. People will choose a medical home, typically a primary care provider, to help coordinate their care, keep their medical records, and serve as the focal point for their coverage. Practitioners will choose a payment intermediary (PI) to handle their billing and all the claims incurred by the patients for whom they serve as the medical home. By processing these claims, the payment intermediary learns which chronic illnesses each patient has and requests monthly payments from the UCP to offset the cost of care received in the ambulatory setting for those conditions. The PI also quickly learns the practice styles of each physician and is able to calculate premiums for covering the remaining minor acute and preventive care costs.

The PI performs the bill-paying functions currently managed by most insurers. These PIs may be outgrowths of current insurers or may be other firms with expertise in handling financial transactions efficiently, such as credit card companies. Payment intermediaries largely pass costs through and thus have no reason to exclude potentially costly patients, deny coverage, or second-guess payment. The physicians for whom the PI works, however, know that their patients will see the net costs of their coverage. These costs reflect the physicians' fees and practice styles; to maintain their patient base, the physicians will have to convince their patients that their quality is worth more than what coverage through another physician would cost. Because under SecureChoice the underlying claims data (with suitable confidentiality safeguards) will be in the public domain, PIs and others will offer to advise physicians how to improve their quality and efficiency. Patients may choose to trade larger co-payments for smaller monthly premiums, but with the UCP covering most costs, the magnitudes involved will be manageable for most people; equity issues are addressed separately.

The current alternatives to single-payer proposals typically focus on various ways to get people into competing health plans. This is often done by encouraging (or mandating) that employers provide coverage or by imposing an individual mandate that everyone select a plan, perhaps with significant subsidies to help those with low incomes. Nearly all proposals retain Medicare, with its mix of fee-for-service-oriented single-payer coverage and optional Medicare Advantage HMO-type plans, as well as the patchwork of Medicaid and safety net programs for the poor and other groups. Although the political viability of these options varies, most *could* get the majority of people some type of coverage. Either by design or timidity, however, none address how to improve the delivery of care once people have coverage. This is what distinguishes SecureChoice.

Competition among health plans is a viable solution only if each health plan *and its providers* have responsibility for only their own enrollees, as is the case for Kaiser and the other integrated HMOs.[6] While taking financial responsibility for their own enrollees, most health plans, however, rely on physicians and hospitals that also treat the patients of other plans. Any such health plan choosing to teach "its physicians" how to be more efficient is subsidizing its competitors. Because most providers are essentially paid fee-for-service, if they learn how to provide higher-quality care more efficiently, they simply reduce their own income because they cannot share in the savings reaped by the plan. In the highly dispersed and non-integrated U.S. medical care system, therefore, competition among health plans cannot improve efficiency and quality.

Instead of focusing on price-sensitive competition *among health plans* or forcing patients to "have more skin in the game" with high deductibles, SecureChoice focuses on value-sensitive patient choices *among physicians.* With the UCP covering the risk associated with major acute and chronic illnesses, the PIs can essentially let each physician be her own health plan; the premiums quoted to her patients reflect the decisions made by that physician and those others whom her patients see. Physicians do not actually bear any insurance risk in SecureChoice; they have the kinds of efficiency and quality incentives the voucher advocates would like but their competing plans cannot deliver. The patient choices among physicians are *value* sensitive, and not just *price* sensitive, because physicians will have much more flexibility in emphasizing different styles of practice, attention to patient needs, and other aspects of care that may be of value to patients. Payment intermediaries, moreover, can deliver the enhanced information and decision-support roles envisioned for large competing health plans.

SecureChoice can be financed in a variety of ways. At one extreme, nearly all health care costs can be covered through taxes to fund the UCP directly and transfer funds to the PIs for outpatient care.[7] At the other extreme, it could build on the existing employer-based system by expanding the tax subsidy for all employer and employee contributions to SecureChoice, allowing existing employer-sponsored plans to buy part or all of their coverage through SecureChoice. This option would need an individual mandate coupled with income-based subsidies to ensure that everyone is enrolled at an affordable cost. An intermediate financing strategy would use taxes to fund the UCP but make minor acute care coverage optional, albeit with income-based subsidies for the poor.

The flexibility in financing options stems partly from the focus of SecureChoice on the delivery system rather than coverage issues. It also reflects the reality that any health reform, let alone one that is based on fundamental change, will require intense political negotiations and trade-offs. On the one hand, the logic of SecureChoice incorporates the market-based incentives and small role for government that are often attractive to conservatives, but it facilitates income-based subsidies, allowing the equity with dignity that is attractive to liberals. On the other hand, SecureChoice threatens the business models of many vested interests while offering little to those who favor publicly administered systems. SecureChoice, however, provides roles and options for all of the current players. Insurers, for example, can use their expertise to become effective players in the payment intermediary market, and independent insurance brokers can advise individuals in a world of many more coverage choices. Primary care physicians will have much more freedom to practice as they choose and charge for their time and expertise, but they will need to assess more carefully the cost and quality implications of their practice styles. Specialists will negotiate new collaborative roles in hospital-based teams or as outpatient consultants.

The emphasis in SecureChoice on careful assessments of the value of various interventions may threaten the current business models of pharmaceutical and biotech firms. It therefore incorporates proposals to reduce the increased risk that innovative products may undercut market positions that these firms will no longer be able to maintain by aggressive—and perhaps misleading—marketing. The increased focus on quality requires greater attention to, and openness about, patient safety. In addition, both to offset concerns physicians have about the potential of such changes to increase their exposure to malpractice claims and to create better information and incentives for change, SecureChoice offers an alternative to current malpractice reform proposals. This alternative will reduce claims of negligence, increase warranted compensation, and lower costs while maintaining a role for malpractice attorneys.

Restructuring Provider Payments

Although SecureChoice is a comprehensive proposal, at its core is a restructuring of payments to providers—hospitals, physicians, and other health professionals. The classic dichotomy drawn by health economists and policymakers with respect to payments is between fee-for-service (FFS) and capitation. Fee-for-service transfers money from payers (insurers and/or patients) to providers for each service rendered. Capitation transfers a set amount, typically determined annually, to cover all necessary services for a population of enrollees. Fee-for-service encourages providers to offer more services; capitation encourages them to offer fewer services or avoid high-risk enrollees.[8] To counter these economic incentives, external agents attempt to ensure that all the care ordered by providers paid via fee-for-service is actually necessary and that providers paid via capitation are not underserving their enrollees. These attempts to counter economic incentives with micromanagement increase paperwork, inefficiency, and conflict. Instead, SecureChoice uses payment approaches better matching the nature of the care to be delivered in order to align incentives directly.

In contrast to the usual insurance distinctions between inpatient versus outpatient care, or medical versus mental health care, it is useful to consider four broad groupings of care, summarized in Table 2.1. These are (1) major acute and interventional episodes, (2) chronic illness management, (3) minor acute episodes, and (4) preventive care. Most types of medical care, including mental health

Table 2.1 Characteristics of Different Types of Care

	Major Acute/Interventional Episodes	Chronic Illness Management	Minor Acute Episodes	Preventive Care
Frequency	Rare events, usually very expensive	Moderately common, predictable	Relatively common, low cost	Annual expectations for specific care
Decision making	Decisions are largely "go/no go"; once "go," then technical choices are needed, usually made by physicians.	Patient preferences and involvement in care are critical.	Patients often need to initiate care.	Patients may need to be encouraged to come in.
Provider choices	Choice of providers is sometimes possible; quality may matter a great deal in such choices.	Patient comfort with and access to (1 or more) providers is important.	Ongoing connection to primary care and/or urgent care	Ongoing connection to primary care providers
Financial risk	Financial "risk of occurrence" is substantial.	Some variability in financial risk within categories	Moderate risk of occurrence of minor acute problems	Highly predictable based on age and sex

care, can be included in this categorization. Long-term care, however, should be handled separately, at least in part because it includes significant components of residential services—housing and food—in addition to medical care.

Major Acute/Interventional Care

Major acute and interventional (MA/I) care involves expensive and usually acute care episodes, typically requiring hospitalization. Examples are heart attack, stroke, premature delivery, newly diagnosed invasive cancer, and major trauma. The defining aspects are that the patient typically is in need of a complex mix of often expensive interventions to be provided within a relatively brief period of time. In most instances the need for treatment is obvious, but a patient may decide to forgo treatment, such as when a heart attack occurs in the midst of a long downhill course of congestive heart failure or the perceived risks associated with a prostatectomy are not worth the expected improvement in quality of life. In the latter case, although the problem is not acute, the intervention is costly. Some MA/I episodes are acute exacerbations of an underlying chronic condition, such as congestive heart failure.

Once a decision is made to proceed with treatment in an MA/I episode, most of the other choices are largely technical. Patient input may be solicited, but the patient and his or her family have little independent experience or expertise to help them decide exactly which tests to order, which brand of hip prosthesis to use, or which new antibiotic to try. Quality matters a great deal and may often be assessed through objective measures of outcomes. Interactions with clinicians are often brief and occur in a context of significant emotional strain. It is difficult to predict with any certainty when these MA/I episodes will occur for any individual patient, and when one does occur, there is often great variation in the resources needed to care for the patient appropriately.

Chronic Illness Management

The second category of care, chronic illness management (CIM), focuses on the ongoing management of chronic conditions, excluding those acute exacerbations of the condition resulting in hospitalization. Diabetes, hypertension, heart failure, asthma, Parkinson's, multiple sclerosis, and major depression, for example, are associated with substantial costs but in quite different ways from the major acute episodes. The ongoing nature of the chronic problem requires a partnership between clinician and patient. In most instances the clinician will recommend regimens of medications, diet changes, and other patient behaviors over an extended period of time. Periodic visits to clinicians require accessibility in terms of geography, convenience, language, and other factors. Chronic conditions are relatively common, but their exacerbations are highly variable. Once it is known that a patient has one or more of these chronic conditions, conventional insurance plans will not willingly take on risk for their costs except at premiums essentially covering those higher costs.

Minor Acute Episodes

The third category includes episodes of relatively minor acute problems. Some are self-limiting and may not even require treatment, but in many instances patients desire at least reassurance from a clinician. A key aspect of minor acute episodes is that the patient is typically responsible for initiating care. Access and timely responses to patient questions may be critical (if only for reassurance), and it may be important for the primary care clinician to know, or be able to elicit quickly, how accurate the patient (or responsible person) is in reporting symptoms and preferences. There may be substantial variability in the amount of such minor acute care needed for a specific person in a year, but the financial risk is moderate.

Preventive Care

The fourth category of care is composed of "well" or preventive care visits.[9] These are opportunities for specific interventions, such as immunizations, screening tests, and counseling. Some of these interventions are clearly beneficial; others are still being evaluated. What is important is that most are seen to be "good," either for the patient or for the general population—for instance, by reducing the spread of disease. Attention therefore needs to be focused on how to get the individual into the clinical setting. Financial and other barriers to access need to be overcome rather than erected. The financial risk associated with such care is minimal; given a person's age and sex, the cost of most recommended preventive care varies very little. Included in the preventive care category is what is now being called a medical home, which obligates a primary care clinician or clinic to keep track of a patient, be the first source of contact in answering questions, and potentially coordinate care.[10]

It is well known that the vast majority of health expenditures are accounted for by a small number of patients.[11] Although it is often difficult to predict *which* patients will need expensive care in the following year, one can target a relatively small number of conditions accounting for much of the cost and most of the variation in expenditures. Elsewhere my colleagues and I have suggested that health plans could be paid on a hybrid model using the presence of selected chronic conditions in combination with prospective predictions for other patients.[12] Such an approach could work well for health plans but not for providers or groups of providers, because it is difficult to know to which specific providers to make the extra payments. SecureChoice takes this model to a finer level of disaggregation and allows different payment approaches for each category of care.

For the major acute and interventional episodes of care, a lump sum payment analogous to that used by Medicare in its diagnosis-related group (DRG) system is appropriate. DRGs would be expanded to include not just the hospital costs but also associated professional and other services. The episode paid for by this expanded DRG (EDRG) would extend beyond the inpatient stay, including immediate preadmission care and condition-specific follow-up periods. The EDRG includes episodes that are similarly expensive to treat but may not require an inpatient stay, either because the patient is able to return home within twenty-four hours or because extensive services, such as cancer care, can be provided entirely on an outpatient basis.

Critical issues to be addressed in such an approach to bundling payments include how physicians, hospitals, and other providers will organize themselves to accept such payments. In Chapter 4 I discuss these new care delivery teams (CDTs), building on changes already under way in hospital and interventional care. Surgical fees already include "normal postoperative care," so the notion of "bundling" is not totally foreign to physicians. Within the payment for an EDRG episode, however, clinicians could be paid in various ways. Surgeons might be paid per procedure, anesthesiologists by the amount of time spent in the operating room and status of the patient, and others by the shift.

If acute exacerbations are paid separately according to EDRG episode payments, the residual risk associated with managing chronic conditions is much lower. The UCP can cover these with monthly payments varying by severity within the condition. Effective management of chronic illness, however, usually requires ongoing monitoring and testing, as well as varying levels of interventions such as pharmaceuticals and treatments that may be provided by the responsible clinician himself or herself, or by others such as subspecialists or physical therapists. Fee-for-service payments to each of these providers will allow implementation of SecureChoice with minimal disruptions to usual practice. Some clinicians or medical groups may have sufficiently large patient populations to accept direct monthly payments and then pay for other services. Most clinicians, however, will want a PI to handle that function and cover the small degree of risk remaining after accounting for the monthly payments. Patient co-payments and deductibles logically have little role in the management of ongoing chronic illnesses because the clinician needs to monitor care and recommend the necessary interventions. Patient incentives discouraging appropriate interactions are thus counterproductive.

The situation with respect to minor acute episodes warrants a somewhat different approach. In many instances such problems are self-limiting but nonetheless worrisome. Fully utilizing the clinician's expertise may depend more on facilitating careful examination, listening, and watchful waiting than on expensive tests and procedures. Payment for such care should take this into consideration. Physicians should have maximum flexibility in structuring and setting their fees. There is no reason why they could not charge for extended visits, telephone consultations, and e-mail communications. Moderate co-payments may be appropriate in some cases, for example, to ensure that patients keep appointments, but not in others if they keep patients from seeking needed care in a timely fashion. Working with the physicians who are their clients, PIs will experiment with various payment models to determine which work the best for which types of patients.

Ensuring Equity

SecureChoice will require that everyone be covered for the most expensive and risky aspects of care: MA/I, CIM, and selected preventive care. Coverage for other care need not be mandated, but many people will prefer to have it. Even if a tax-based financing scheme is used, there should be a role in the system for some payment by patients. Both premiums and out-of-pocket payments for care, however, should be eligible for income-based subsidies. These subsidies will occur "behind the scenes," with transfers from federal, and possibly state, funds reducing the amounts to be paid by enrollees and patients. Providers would not be asked to accept lower fees for the poor; indeed, they would not even know who receives a subsidy.

Summarizing the Concept

The overall flow of payments is summarized in Figure 2.1. The universal coverage pool is funded through some policy-determined combination of taxes and tax-subsidized employer contributions. The UCP directly pays care delivery teams for major acute and interventional care through expanded DRG payments. These EDRG payments are similar to the DRG system Medicare uses just to pay for

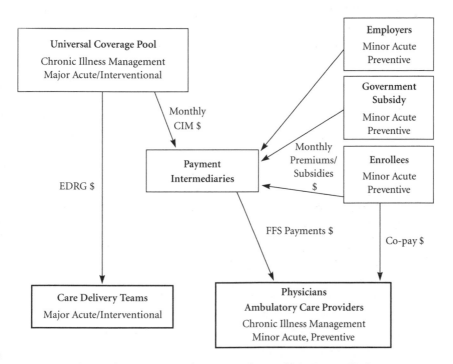

Figure 2.1 Overview of Payment Flows within SecureChoice

hospital care, but they include both physician-related and other services involved in the episode of care. Monthly the UCP also sends funds to each payment intermediary on behalf of its enrollees to cover the costs of chronic illness management. These payments are risk-adjusted according to the conditions of those patients. These payments from the UCP account for almost two-thirds of all costs and essentially eliminate the selection problems that make voluntary coverage impossible.

The payment intermediaries combine the CIM payments from the UCP with premiums received from employers and enrollees and income-based subsidies from government. The PIs pay physicians and other ambulatory care providers, primarily on a fee-for-service basis, for all of the other services needed for chronic illness management, minor acute care, and preventive care. These payments from the PI are supplemented by co-payments based on the voluntary coverage package for minor acute and preventive care chosen by the patient.[13]

Clinicians in this system will have incentives to demand information about which tests, procedures, drugs, and other interventions are most effective in treating their patients. With such information they can improve quality and/or lower costs (attracting more patients), maintain quality and overall costs but increase their own fees, or achieve some combination of these changes. PIs will compete for the physicians' business by offering them low-cost claims administration and information on how to improve their clinical practice choices. Patients will be able to choose among the full range of physicians, but if they choose physicians with more expensive practice styles, their premiums will be higher. Premiums, however, will not reflect underlying health risk because of the UCP.

There will be a role for government, albeit a limited one. The UCP will be universal, but it need not be government operated, and government will be involved in far fewer decisions than under the current Medicare program. Government will do what it does well: collect taxes, redistribute resources for the poor, and assure that the patient information collected is handled confidentially and securely, and is made available in a transparent fashion to those who need it. Antitrust enforcement will be necessary, but otherwise far fewer regulations will have to be administered than currently. The Food and Drug Administration (FDA) will continue to assess the safety and efficacy of new drugs, but many other players will provide detailed assessments of how well drugs and other interventions actually work in practice. Rather than relying on well-intentioned but underfinanced government agencies to ensure good behavior by the players, the system is designed to be transparent and creates powerful private interests that check and balance one another.

Other health plan proposals guaranteeing savings usually rely on fee constraints or administrative regulations. History has repeatedly proved such assumptions false. Market mechanisms are more difficult to subvert. The challenge is to renounce blind faith in market solutions and instead structure market incentives to achieve the desired outcomes. SecureChoice is designed to do just that. It rewards care that is efficient and responsive to patients. It rewards medical innovations that save money or provide new value. It creates informed patients and clinicians, giving them the power to make choices that matter. It is purposefully structured to achieve better outcomes both now and in the long term.

Assumptions, Values, and Design Principles

The restructured health care system offered here rests on certain underlying assumptions and values that are incorporated in a set of "design principles." Some arise from my understanding of how the health care system currently functions according to the interplay of economic, political, and social factors. Others are based on my fundamental values, such as the importance of individual preferences in health care. All affect, both consciously and unconsciously, the chapters that follow. Rather than leaving them ambiguous, or highlighting them repeatedly throughout the text, I discuss them here.

An example of how assumptions, values, and design principles come together is useful. Some nations rely on expertise housed in politically independent health departments (relatively separate from the political ministries of health) to assess new technologies. The British National Institute for Clinical Excellence (NICE) undertakes comprehensive assessments of new drugs to determine whether they will be provided by the National Health Service.[14] Such an agency to make neutral assessments of new technologies has been proposed by many in the United States. Although I find it conceptually a good idea, I am not comfortable in relying on such an approach, not because I doubt the need for or the technical ability of such an agency, but because I believe it will not succeed.

In the 1990s, under congressional mandate, the U.S. Agency for Health Care Policy and Research supported a researcher to review the published evidence for the effectiveness of a certain type of back surgery. When the scientist's review found little evidence for the superiority of surgery, at the behest of the manufacturers of surgical screws, two members of the House of Representatives almost succeeded in having Congress defund the agency.[15] Given my assumption that our political structure and the low degree of independence and authority granted civil servants will not be changed by health reform, and my belief that an effective system will need to challenge the special interests of certain powerful stakeholders, I need to find an alternative approach. Thus one design principle would be greater reliance on transparency in information and independent assessment by multiple bodies less vulnerable to political influence.

Assumptions

The first assumption is that health care is characterized by inherent uncertainty. Attempts to deal with this uncertainty underlie many of the problems in the current system. Uncertainty cannot be eliminated, given our current level of knowledge and technology, but we can deal with it more creatively and effectively. Although colloquially we say it is uncertain whether a given person will experience a health problem, this is more accurately a matter of statistical risk. Uncertainty occurs when the outcome cannot be known in advance and merely accumulating more cases does not help. People experience health problems in various ways, and it is generally up to clinicians to assign them a diagnosis, often with a good deal of uncertainty. Minimizing uncertainty may not always be the best strategy; invasive tests carry risks to the patient that sometimes exceed the benefits of a more certain diagnosis.[16] Uncertainty is not just a statistical problem; it may cause people to react in ways that are inconsistent with expectations for rational behavior.[17]

Clinicians often have several treatment options, none of which guarantees a cure, and each of which carries potential physical side effects and emotional costs. Each likely also has different economic costs that may be hidden by insurance. Determining when and how such economic costs should be included in either a patient's or a society's decision making is a major aspect of my proposal. Economists often assume that consumers seek to maximize their own well-being by making rational choices among various options, taking into account the costs of each option and their own budget constraints. A rational choice model of behavior that may work for some breakfast cereals is less applicable to a decision between bypass surgery and angioplasty. The lack of good price data and uncertainty with respect to outcomes is only part of the problem. How it feels to have one's chest split open and be on a bypass pump can be known only through experience; taste-testing and repeated purchases are rarely possible in medical care.

In the context of uncertainty, choices in health care should, I believe, reflect each individual's values and preferences, both for treatment and for additional information. While some people may want more information, others may prefer to have their choices guided by their physician.[18]

The second assumption relates to the appropriate role of economic principles and analysis in shaping health policy. Although the vast majority of economists believe that solutions based on truly competitive markets achieve the most efficient allocation of resources, few markets meet the criteria economists require for them to be considered competitive. Markets, moreover, do little to promote equity. In addition, economic incentives have effects only over time as contracts are revised, new people are hired, or firms eventually go out of business. A policy may be leading to the desired changes, but if it does not prove sufficiently effective before the next election, it may be repealed. It is critical to consider the institutional framework—political, legal, contractual, and organizational—in which economic incentives are embedded. Political players sometimes focus not on directly appropriating money but on favorably altering the rules of the economic game. Few would propose returning to a pre-FDA world without any assessment of drug safety and efficacy. Nevertheless, the precise rules under which drugs can be marketed, the indications for which they can and should be used, and the methods for evaluating alternatives can create or eliminate market advantages for various manufacturers. Economic interests frequently tout the benefits of the market but quietly advance their agendas through subtle changes in regulation and enforcement. Policy choices between market and regulatory solutions need to be assessed in terms of which will best achieve the desired goals in the context of the realities of administrative and political processes.

An example of the limitations of classic economic analyses is the failure of models of physician behavior in accounting for the observed wide variations in use and quality of health care. If physicians behave as theorized and act as effective agents for their patients, there should be continuous movement toward optimal treatment. If physicians simply follow their own income-maximization incentives, there should be clinically excessive utilization whenever patients have comprehensive insurance. Neither theoretical model is well supported by empirical tests. Rather than assuming either (1) that physicians do not seek to be good agents for their patients, or (2) that they ignore economic incentives, I assume *both* tendencies coexist in a world of limited information where people develop simple, non-optimizing ways of making decisions.

The third assumption is that it is implausible that even the most far-reaching health care system reform will go beyond those laws and regulations that deal with health care. The underlying American political system built on our Constitution, values, and traditions will not change "just" to allow a better health care system. The balance of responsibilities between the states and the national government will be largely unchanged. We can expect a continuation of the ways various branches of government operate and respond to one another and the private sector.[19] Our political system differs in fundamental ways from the parliamentary democracies often held up as having model health care systems. In conjunction with "party discipline," the parliamentary system gives the majority control of both the legislative and executive branches, allowing major policy changes to be adopted and then implemented. But in the United States, for several decades both the Congress and executive branch have denigrated the ability of the federal civil service to execute policies effectively. Legislators give regulatory agencies minimal authority and keep salaries low relative to the private sector. It is not surprising, therefore, that public systems do not "work well." Absent a fundamental change in politics and political attitudes toward the role of government, a federal bureaucracy is unlikely to manage care or assess new technologies effectively.

The fourth assumption is that the real concerns about health care expenditures have less to do with the level than with the rate of growth.[20] The fear is that new technologies will continue to be developed, creating additional opportunities and demand for growth of expenditures. The substantial annual funding of research in basic science by the National Institutes of Health (NIH) assures that new knowledge will continue to be developed. Such research must then be translated into drugs and devices that can affect clinical disease and then undergo a second translation to disseminate such innovations into community practice. While I assume that science will continue to expand opportunities for innovation, I believe the direction of technological advances and applications will reflect the incentives within the system.

Values

Values are critical in any policy discussion. My goal here is to put forward a proposal allowing flexibility in design to accommodate multiple value-laden perspectives. This reflects my belief that one's values (including my own) should not be imposed on others.[21] It also reflects a preference for deferring some of the more contentious decisions till later in the debate in the hope that some consensus can be achieved.

This book is about improving and ensuring health care value for people. It does not begin with a goal of containing costs to some arbitrary fraction of gross domestic product or share of the federal budget. By focusing on ways to improve efficiency and quality in the delivery of care, however, my proposal will probably reduce the rate of growth in medical care expenditures. If it succeeds in making it easier for people to get the care they prefer, people will feel that the system is worth what it costs. That is not the case today.

Placing the individual at the center implies a reluctance to rely on averages and rules, such as denying coverage for a new treatment if its cost is greater than some amount per quality-adjusted life year (QALY). A new cancer drug may cost $50,000 to extend life by three months—probably not a good societal use of resources in terms of extending productive life.[22] Suppose, however, that those extra three months allow the matriarch of a family to witness the graduation of the first member of the clan to go to college. She may experience the satisfaction for only a short time, but her family will keep the memory for years. Our society may be better for allowing flexibility in such decisions.[23]

A second value is that there also needs to be a community or societal perspective. Privileging the individual does not imply ignoring collective effects and benefits. A system allowing people to choose low-cost, low-coverage insurance when healthy but then to demand high-cost care when sick will not work. There must be some policy constraints on what an individual can do, which may mean "infringing on individual liberties" and mandating that everyone have coverage. Individual choices can also create collective benefits: for instance, high rates of flu immunization can benefit even those who are not immunized.

Not all decisions are best left to the market and individual choices. Market decisions are dollar weighted and reflect the decisions of those who are active in the relevant market. Many of the classic public health interventions, however, represent public goods and warrant collective action. Underlying many health problems are individual behaviors such as overeating and tobacco use. Casting such risk factors in terms of individual responsibility, however, ignores powerful and effective opportunities for collective action. Tobacco taxes and legislation restricting smoking in public places has had an enormous impact, in the first case helping youth avoid becoming smokers and in the second helping smokers overcome their addiction.

A third value relates to equity. I personally favor a system with a high degree of equity, but I recognize that not all share that value. The challenge is to demonstrate that high equity can be achieved while retaining incentives for individuals, avoiding most income and class distinctions in the provision of care, and yet minimizing the direct role of government. Premiums and co-payments can be income adjusted. SecureChoice allows substantial flexibility in this adjustment, ranging from no equity adjustment, which leaves the poor to bear co-payments as large as those of the rich, to totally eliminating co-payments for those below a certain income.

Design Principles

Design principles can have a pervasive impact on the nature of a plan. When the rationale for such principles goes unstated, it is difficult for a reader to know if a change in the proposal affects critical issues or just minor aspects of the plan. Knowing the principles, however, allows one to begin the process of making changes and asking whether such changes may critically compromise the integrity of the design. Among the key design principles informing SecureChoice are (1) emphasizing incentives for decisions, (2) carefully targeting public and private roles, (3) designing for change, and (4) recognizing political factors.

The first design principle emphasizes the importance of incentives in making decisions. Medical care decisions involve a complex mix of personal preferences and technical choices. The former vary from person to person, and even vary over time for a given person. Beyond medical risks and benefits, financial costs are also relevant considerations, but all must be placed in perspective. People seem reasonably able to assess options and consider trade-offs when relatively small costs (physical and financial) are involved; the system should facilitate such personal assessments. When the costs—in money, time, emotion, or impact on health—are large, however, decision making is far more complex. Medical care decisions need to involve the patient (and sometimes his or her family) in different ways for crises than for day-to-day situations. Decisions that may literally mean the difference between life and death are emotionally fraught. Most of us would (and do) pay a supplement to our health insurance to avoid having to think about cost in such instances. In other instances, such as surgery for hip replacement, the decision can be reached after extended discussion and even sequential trials of alternative interventions; bearing some cost then may not seem so emotionally unfair. In neither case, however, are simple financial incentives such as deductibles or coinsurance clearly appropriate.

Once a decision has been made to go ahead with an intervention, numerous other decisions are necessary, ranging from the type of suture to the model of hip prosthesis. Usually the choices are left to the physician. If so, the physician should have some stake in the economic implications of the choices. The underlying principle is that when choices and trade-offs are necessary, they should be made by those best able to make them. When those choices may affect patients, they should be involved in a time and manner that allows them to have useful, informed input.

The second design principle is careful targeting of public and private roles in the system. Government can be very effective in certain roles, such as collecting funds through taxes and transferring income to meet equity goals. Government is needed to enforce certain rules of market behavior, such as antitrust laws, as well as laws and regulations necessary to protect patients and consumers from unsafe drugs or breaches of confidentiality. Government is the logical provider of public goods ranging from research and information to public health interventions. The collection of data needed for research is likely to be underfunded; if private sector firms such as insurers own segments of the data, their usefulness is often reduced substantially. Government is also critical for collective action interventions to improve health, such as passing laws that limit smoking in public places or require the labeling of fats in foods.

In recent U.S. experience, however, government has generally not been very effective as a manager of complex, dynamic programs.[24] The government regulatory process, moreover, can be hijacked by special interests for their own benefit. When the government is the purchaser and represents a substantial share of the market, low prices will lead to cries that suppliers will be put out of business; high prices will be decried as wasteful. Carefully adjusting specific prices up or down is nearly impossible given a general desire to "reduce bureaucracy," so changes are often made across the board, guaranteeing inefficiencies.

A minimalist role for government in health care payment and delivery does not necessarily mean that large corporate and professional interests should then dominate the medical care system. To the contrary, it is easier for them to exert influence when more, rather than fewer, levers of power are in government hands. Instead the system should be designed for maximum responsiveness to individual patients and providers in treatment decisions and to rely primarily on state and local governments for collective action decisions.[25] Federal protection of free and appropriate access to information and its transparency is critical.

The third design principle is that the system should be dynamic, with built-in feedback systems to accommodate change. Medical care is characterized by rapid technological change, reflecting the constantly increasing body of biomedical knowledge. The variable rate at which new technologies diffuse, however, is problematic. In some instances they spread more rapidly and widely than is justified by the benefits; in other instances clearly beneficial technologies and interventions are underutilized. Health care system design should facilitate responsiveness to innovation, regardless of its nature. In keeping with some of the previous principles, however, the "system" should avoid overreliance on "in or out" rules with respect to innovations. Producers and the patients who believe they may be helped by an innovation can bring enormous political pressure for approval. Once it is covered for limited indications, its use then tends to expand. Even if a drug or technique really is "best for everyone" at a given point in time, it is unlikely to hold that position legitimately forever. The system needs to facilitate constant improvement.

The fourth design principle takes into account the fact that the system will be enacted and will have to function in a political environment. A realistic health reform proposal must recognize the role of interest groups both in shaping legislation and in implementing policy. The SecureChoice design principle is to incorporate special interests where their expertise is most critical, preferably with a countervailing force within the system. Health plans, for example, have developed considerable expertise in extracting information from administrative data and in developing new approaches to coordinating and integrating complex chronic care. Plans could find a major new role as processors and purveyors of valuable information, working for physicians to help them improve their clinical practices.

Some argue that the best way to create countervailing power in a political system is to set and hold a tight cap on health expenditures. I do not believe that there should be a hard maximum set for the share of GDP given over to health care. If more health care actually improves the quality of life, why should it be capped at some arbitrary percentage? Alternatively, a politically determined maximum may become a minimum that is too high if changes in behavior reduce the incidence of illness. More important, a "hard cap" means that one needs a formal mechanism for assessing what new drugs, devices, and techniques will be added and which ones dropped; existing drugs, devices, and procedures are likely to be accepted en masse even though some have never been well evaluated. The details with respect to the burden of proof in future assessments will be arcane yet critical: how one trades off small gains to the many versus large gains to the few, or quantity versus quality of life, and how one assesses various pieces of information. While eschewing the notion of a target rate of growth may make the proposal difficult to "score" in the usual sense, it also eliminates the specter of a zero-sum game in which gains of one party must be offset by the losses of another.[26]

Even without a zero-sum game, no specific group should be forced to be a loser in a proposal. Those who see no place for themselves in a reformed system will use every possible means to derail the plan. This does not mean, however, that every individual player will have a guarantee of remaining at least as well off; but each should have a chance of success in a "fair game." All providers will gain increased autonomy, and high-quality providers can gain patients and income, but some providers may lose in both dimensions. Relatively speaking, health insurers will lose power but gain stability, and some will be able to do very well in restructured lines of business. Other industries will also experience change, but in keeping with the free market rhetoric most espouse, their success will reflect their ability to meet marketplace demands. The players, however, cannot as easily stack the deck as in the current environment.

In short, the underlying design principles that inform Secure-Choice are patient-oriented care responsive to patient preferences, economic incentives focused on those best able to make choices in the relevant time frame, and equity addressed in ways that maintain appropriate incentives. The new system should facilitate value-enhancing clinical and technological innovations; government's role should be designed to keep special interests from protecting themselves at the expense of patients or efficiency.

SecureChoice accomplishes this by having a universal pool to ensure coverage for all the most expensive types of care. The payment system for those types of care relies on incentives for clinicians to improve value, recognizing that patients have little expertise and are often unable to think rationally about economic choices in those situations. For minor acute problems, however, coverage need not be mandatory, and patient choice should be maximized. Much more flexibility in the design of incentives and practice patterns than is currently the case is both warranted and possible. Government must, however, ensure appropriate subsides to allow such market incentives to operate while maintaining equity.

The system should be built around the universal collection of information and transparency, with multiple assessments of the data in open and competitive ways. New technologies should be encouraged to improve clinical value even if they threaten existing stakeholders; continuous assessment of value by patients and clinicians, however, will be necessary. The current stakeholders can all have roles in the new system, but the new incentives and arrangements will require that they function more in the market than in the political arena. If they do, they—and we—can succeed.

— 3 —

Covering the Cost of Care:
Rethinking Health Insurance

Decisions related to medical care expenditures are of widely varying complexity, and are made according to the circumstances and the particular decision maker's style. Some medical expenditures are sudden and catastrophically expensive, such as a massive heart attack or bilateral stroke. For such expenditures insurance is not only appropriate but also necessary. Other major expenditures, however, are quite predictable, such as when the slow degeneration of a hip joint leads to the need for a replacement. Far more common are minor expenditures such as care for a sprained ankle or bronchitis.

Health insurance typically deals with covering—to varying degrees—costs associated with a stream of claims. Services are sometimes categorized (and coverage varies) by the sequence during the year, location and type (inpatient, outpatient, drugs), or disease category (medical versus mental). SecureChoice returns insurance to its roots in covering unpredictable major expenses and uses new categories of coverage for other types of expenses, allowing incentives to align decisions and decision makers better. Chapter 4 discusses these opportunities; this chapter addresses when insurance is necessary and when other coverage options may suffice.

Understanding Why Coverage Can't Be Voluntary

One of the core health policy debates concerns whether health insurance can be voluntary. Some who argue for universal coverage are simply reacting to the failure of the current voluntary system to cover everyone or achieve equity goals. Some who argue for maintaining voluntary coverage want as much sensitivity as possible to consumer and patient preferences or believe that market solutions are always better than government programs. This discussion steers clear of these ideologically driven arguments. It explains why coverage for major, costly episodes and for chronic illness should be mandatory and covered through a universal pool, but coverage for other categories of expenditures can be voluntary—as long as equity concerns are addressed separately. We must first understand how economists think about insurance, how what we call health insurance currently operates in the United States, and how we can rethink the role of health insurance.

For economists, the classic, idealized function of insurance is quite limited: sharing the risks of uncertain events among a group of individuals and then paying for the losses incurred by those who experience the events. Such events are predictable across large populations; for example, the probability of heart attack increases with age and heightened cholesterol levels, but it is impossible to know whether a specific person will have a heart attack in any given year. Whenever there is a low but calculable probability of a costly event, insurance allows those at risk to pay a premium slightly more than the cost of the services times the probability of the event to guarantee payment if the event occurs. Private insurance markets can function reasonably well if neither those to be insured nor those offering coverage have special knowledge concerning whether the individual's risks are significantly lower or higher than the group average on which the insurance is calculated.[1] If such special knowledge is present, it is likely to result in what is called selection. This is known as adverse selection if the insurer draws sicker people than expected for the premium and favorable selection if it insures healthier people than the premium warrants.

Insurance spreads risk across people, creating a major social benefit. This social benefit is quite apart from any equity issues; homeowners' insurance is purchased even by the very wealthy. Many situations in which, from a societal perspective, costs should be spread, however, are not insurable in a classic sense. Some conditions are highly predictable on the basis of genetic factors. For example, if one biological parent has Huntington's disease, there is a 50 percent chance that his or her offspring will inherit the condition.[2] No insurer would voluntarily enroll such a person unless the premium were at least half the anticipated costs of treatment. To do otherwise consistently would guarantee failure of the business. This is an extreme example because of its high degree of predictability, but most chronic conditions create similar problems. Once someone has diabetes, heart disease, or cancer, the likelihood is great that future health care costs will be high; so the premiums quoted by insurers will be correspondingly high. This strikes many as being unfair. Why should a patient already suffering from a chronic disease also have to pay above-average premiums?

The difficulty is not the inherent rapaciousness of insurers but the inherent selection arising from voluntary coverage. If everyone were required to be insured, the costs of expensive illnesses would be spread among the entire population covered. Those who argue against mandates need to recognize that each person, even if healthy now, could in the future develop some rare but expensive disease or experience a catastrophically disabling accident. If people eschewing coverage when healthy did not regret its absence when they became sick or disabled, if they did not ask others to provide safety net care, and if those who had bought coverage were not bothered by seeing their uninsured neighbors die in the streets, then voluntary enrollment and purchase of insurance would be a viable solution. Absent those conditions, people should not have the choice of declining coverage. Universal enrollment is the key to "risk spreading" and thus avoiding the selection problems.

Assessing the Current Configuration of "Health Insurance"

What people describe as "health insurance" today is a combination of insurance and prepayment. My employer's "health insurance plans" cover the costs of a heart attack (insurance) and multiple sclerosis (risk spreading for a chronic condition). They also pay for periodic physical examinations, dental visits, and replacing my eyeglasses every two years. These latter "coverages" are difficult to defend as insurance or risk spreading of major costs. They may improve my well-being, but they are not expensive, unpredictable events. Even in the absence of "coverage," most of my fellow workers could afford to pay for such services, especially if their wages were increased by the amount our employer would otherwise "contribute" for the coverage. From the employer's perspective, a dollar of extra wages is no more costly than a dollar of extra health benefits, so why do we see such broad "coverage" for these low-cost interventions and events?[3]

To a substantial degree the answer lies in a series of historical accidents. Compulsory health insurance in the United States was proposed in the beginning of the twentieth century; the American Medical Association House of Delegates actually supported the plan in 1917. The plan was opposed, however, by organized labor, which wanted to be able to bargain separately for such benefits. It died when the United States entered World War I with the rise of anti-German, and then anti-Bolshevik, sentiment toward anything having socialist connotations. During World War II, when wage and price controls prevented employers from increasing wages in a tight labor market, fringe benefits were judicially determined to be exempt from that legislation. Rulings by the Internal Revenue Service and subsequent legislation exempted fringe benefits from payroll and personal income taxes. The 1974 Employee Retirement Income Security Act

(ERISA) focused largely on pension regulation but also exempted health plans that are self-insured by employers from state regulation of health insurance. Taken together, these events led to a system in which the tax rules subsidize health care purchased through employers but usually not when purchased directly by individuals. ERISA, moreover, makes statewide approaches to coverage almost impossible.[4]

The result of these historical artifacts is that what is called health insurance is a mélange of insurance, shared responsibility for chronic illness, and subsidized consumption of various predictable or relatively low cost health care interventions. Subsidizing health care may be desirable for many reasons, but the ways it is done under our current system are particularly inefficient. Aside from the administrative costs associated with marketing highly tailored coverage packages through employers and to individuals, the current system uses roughly the same set of incentives (or disincentives) for all types of care. Deductibles—a potent disincentive to seeking care—are applied according to *when* a service is rendered rather than by the *nature* of the problem or by the potential clinical impact of the deductible's effect as a cost barrier. In January a deductible may keep someone from seeking attention for worrisome bloody urine or a routine check of blood glucose for ongoing diabetes management. By December, if accumulated expenses for that person have exceeded the maximum out-of-pocket cost for the year, there are no financial barriers to such visits; neither are there disincentives for possibly unnecessary imaging tests for a minor backache.

Rethinking When Insurance Is Necessary

While insurance companies focus on processing a stream of disconnected claims for services, patients and clinicians focus on treating health problems, often in the context of episodes of illness. Such episodes may be acute, with a fairly distinct beginning and end, or chronic—continuing for an ill-defined, extended period. Some acute episodes can be very expensive and unpredictable, such as a heart attack or hip fracture, and would be prime candidates for classic insurance. Some chronic illnesses are relatively low cost but may have expensive acute exacerbations, such as stroke caused by the ineffective management of hypertension. Some chronic conditions may eventually require expensive interventions to improve function, such as hip replacement, but the precise date when that function has deteriorated to the point where the intervention is needed is difficult to determine objectively. In addition to care for acute and chronic problems, insurers often pay for preventive services that fall into neither category but may avoid future expense or promote better health, such as screening for colon cancer to ensure early intervention.

Categorizing services into episodes of illness and distinguishing the nature of the episodes allows us to escape the absurdity of payment decisions based on calendar date. We can think instead about what types of episodes should be covered fully, partially, or not at all by insurance. Episodes also provide a much more useful framework for deciding where incentives for efficiency should be placed and for assessing cost and quality. Knowing the prices for individual services is not very helpful for patients or payers; knowing the overall costs of episodes resulting in good outcomes helps identify which providers the patient should seek out or which processes should be adopted by the practitioner.

Theory and logic can take one only so far in developing policy. Empirical results help test the plausibility of this alternative way of thinking about insurance and coverage. To do this, however, one needs very large samples and complete claims files so that rare but expensive events can be observed. I use data from a large sample of people with employment-based coverage to show the distribution of medical care across various categories of episodes.[5] Results would no doubt differ somewhat if we had data for people in the Medicare and Medicaid programs, probably showing higher proportions of episodes and expenditures associated with chronic conditions and their exacerbations. Nonetheless, the basic notion that episodes can be defined and usefully examined can be assessed with these data.

One classification of episodes uses location of treatment, distinguishing major (hospitalization) episodes from ambulatory care. Hospitalizations are the classic example of when insurance may be needed, as they are expensive and relatively rare. (Not all hospitalizations are unpredictable, and some ambulatory care can be just as expensive because of costly new drugs; nevertheless, this is a useful distinction.)[6] A second classification scheme distinguishes the reasons for episodes of care: chronic illness, acute illness, or preventive care. Combining these two approaches allows us to categorize people according to the types of care they require during a year. While there are quite a few combinations, the most interesting ones are based on the most expensive categories of care experienced: (1) no use; (2) preventive care only; (3) minor acute care with or without preventive care, but without a hospitalization; (4) chronic illness management with or without other ambulatory care, but without a hospitalization; (5) hospitalization for acute care with or without other ambulatory care, but without chronic illness episodes; or (6) hospitalization for a chronic condition with or without any other use.[7]

As illustrated by Figure 3.1, the small fraction (4.6 + 7.6 percent = 12.2 percent) of people experiencing a major acute or interventional episode accounts for well over half of all of the care used by this population. At the other extreme, 15 percent of people use no care billed to their insurer, and the 30.5 percent using only preventive or minor acute care account for about 8 percent of the costs. The concentration of expenditures in a small fraction of the population is well known; what is less well understood is its impact on the viability of voluntary insurance.[8]

Figure 3.2 illustrates why voluntary insurance is not a viable model. Across all people, the average expense for care was $2,491 in 2003 and $2,687 in 2004, reflecting inflation and one year of aging and changes in medical care options. If we were to ignore marketing

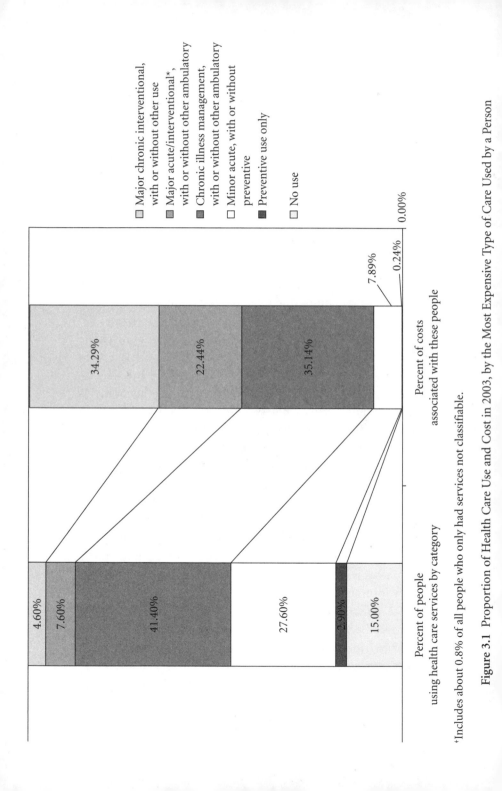

Figure 3.1 Proportion of Health Care Use and Cost in 2003, by the Most Expensive Type of Care Used by a Person

*Includes about 0.8% of all people who only had services not classifiable.

Major chronic interventional, with or without other use

Major acute/interventional*, with or without other ambulatory

Chronic illness management, with or without other ambulatory

Minor acute, with or without preventive

Preventive use only

No use

Percent of people using health care services by category

4.60%
7.60%
41.40%
27.60%
2.90%
15.00%

Percent of costs associated with these people

34.29%
22.44%
35.14%
7.89%
0.24%
0.00%

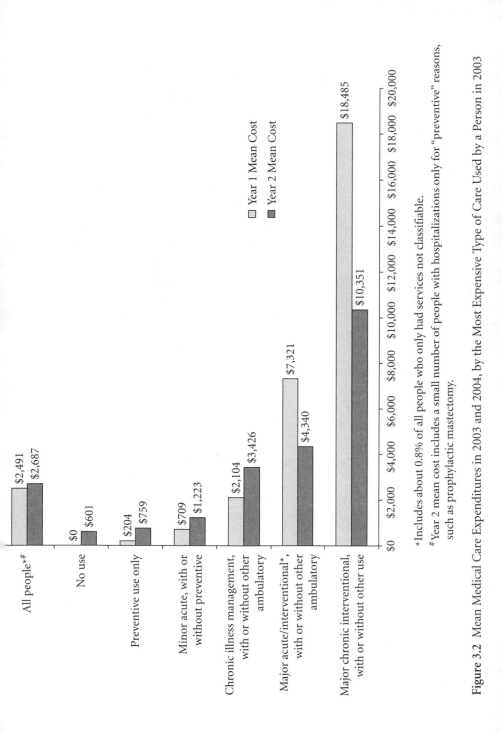

All people*#
$2,491
$2,687

No use
$0
$601

Preventive use only
$204
$759

Minor acute, with or without preventive
$709
$1,223

Chronic illness management, with or without other ambulatory
$2,104
$3,426

Major acute/interventional*, with or without other ambulatory
$7,321
$4,340

Major chronic interventional, with or without other use
$18,485
$10,351

☐ Year 1 Mean Cost
■ Year 2 Mean Cost

$0 $2,000 $4,000 $6,000 $8,000 $10,000 $12,000 $14,000 $16,000 $18,000 $20,000

*Includes about 0.8% of all people who only had services not classifiable.

#Year 2 mean cost includes a small number of people with hospitalizations only for "preventive" reasons, such as prophylactic mastectomy.

Figure 3.2 Mean Medical Care Expenditures in 2003 and 2004, by the Most Expensive Type of Care Used by a Person in 2003

and administrative expenses, a fair premium for those people would be a bit above $2,687. People who made no claims in 2003 would find that premium very expensive, especially if they knew (as do we who look retrospectively at the data) that their actual expenditures in 2004 would only be $601. An insurer able to attract such non-users could offer comprehensive coverage for a lot less than $2,700 and still make money.[9] If this selection were to occur with low-risk people joining one plan, the average cost for those left in the "non-low-risk plan" would rise.

Over two-fifths of the population depicted in Figure 3.2 might be considered temporarily lucky; although they suffered from chronic illnesses, they were not hospitalized and incurred below-average costs ($2,104 versus $2,491) in Year 1. The following year, however, their costs went up over 50 percent—to well above the overall mean ($3,426 versus $2,687). Those with chronic illnesses who also incurred a hospitalization in 2003 had expenditures nearly four times the overall average. Without a mandate, the currently (temporarily) healthy will choose not to pay average premiums to be covered, further raising the premium for everyone else, and there will be strong pressures either to exclude the chronically ill or to charge them extraordinarily high premiums.[10] These data show that any type of voluntary insurance coverage will tend to result in pricing based on risk, which is extremely detrimental to those who most need coverage. If one takes the longer view, in which people who are healthy this year may develop chronic conditions next year, then an agreement to mandate coverage makes even more sense.

Deciding What Must Be Covered and What Can Be Optional

Inherent problems of selection mean that the decision to be covered for certain types of health problems cannot be voluntary. The question then becomes: What *must* be included under a mandate, and what *may* be optional? Selection issues arise largely from chronic illnesses; much of what makes chronic illness expensive is the acute exacerbations requiring hospitalization and interventional care. It is often difficult to distinguish such exacerbations from episodes unrelated to chronic illness, however, and most people would want coverage for the latter anyway. Thus selection arguments alone mean that everyone must have coverage for the care involved in major acute and interventional episodes—regardless of the cause—and for chronic illness management. The argument for universal coverage for these episodes rests not on equity grounds or a preference for public systems, but on the predictable failure of markets to provide insurance if enrollment can be voluntary. How the coverage is to be financed, how equity can be assured, and what entities will be involved in organizing payment are issues addressed in other chapters. The next question to address is: What are the implications of ensuring mandatory coverage of major acute and chronic illness care but leaving coverage of the rest to be potentially optional?

Although some people have just one episode of care in a year, most have several. Figures 3.1 and 3.2 categorized people by the most expensive *category* of episode they experienced during 2003.[11] The same underlying data can be reconfigured to see what would happen if coverage was based on the nature of each episode. Overall, major acute or interventional care episodes (for either acute or chronic conditions) account for 4 percent of all episodes but about 34 percent of all expenditures. Another 28 percent of expenditures is associated with just the management and outpatient treatment of chronic illness. Thus almost two-thirds of all costs are accounted for by a small fraction of the population and episodes of care. Chapter 4 will show how policy focused on this concentration of resources and attention can markedly improve efficiency and quality.[12]

The vast majority of the remaining 38 percent of expenditures is due to minor acute care episodes. The costs for minor acute and preventive care is relatively low and, more important, is spread relatively evenly across the population. This is illustrated in Table 3.1, which is based on the same employed population used in the Figures 3.1 and 3.2, but focusing only on expenditures in 2003. When all health ex-

Table 3.1 Expenditures by Age and Sex for All Services and Just Those Associated with Minor Acute and Preventive Episodes

Females	All Expenditures		Only Minor Acute and Preventive Expenditures	
	Annual Expenditure	Relative to Mean for Sex	Annual Expenditure	Relative to Mean for Sex
0–17 yrs	$959	0.34	$632	0.61
18–29 yrs	$1,991	0.71	$873	0.85
30–39 yrs	$2,924	1.04	$1,105	1.07
40–49 yrs	$2,871	1.02	$1,186	1.15
50–59 yrs	$3,782	1.34	$1,384	1.34
60–64 yrs	$4,313	1.53	$1,345	1.30
65 yrs +	$5,994	2.13	$1,088	1.05
All ages	$2,812	1.00	$1,034	1.00
Males				
0–17 yrs	$1,113	0.52	$697	0.97
18–29 yrs	$950	0.44	$495	0.69
30–39 yrs	$1,285	0.60	$597	0.83
40–49 yrs	$1,920	0.90	$703	0.98
50–59 yrs	$3,145	1.47	$880	1.23
60–64 yrs	$4,247	1.98	$972	1.36
65 yrs +	$6,590	3.07	$890	1.24
All ages	$2,144	1.00	$716	1.00

Note: Based on 2003 expenditures, including outpatient pharmaceuticals, for the population in Figure 3.1.

penditures for the population included in the earlier figures are examined by age and sex, the overall means are roughly $2,800 for women and $2,150 for men, but within each gender the costs vary sixfold across age groups.[13] Focusing only on minor acute and preventive care brings the means down to about $1,000 and $700, respectively. More important, the variation across age groups for each sex is down to a factor of about two instead of a factor of six.

Most people who can afford it desire insurance against large, unpredictable expenditures for an actuarially fair premium, even including reasonable administrative costs. Whether insurance is worthwhile for small, highly predictable expenditures is less clear. I need to have my eyes examined yearly, and usually need to have my prescription modified every year or so. My employer's "insurance" plan pays for this but does not offer me the choice of cash in lieu of the plan. Someone has to pay for the administrative costs involved in processing the claims to pay my optometrist. Avoiding those administrative costs would still allow me to get my glasses *and* either (1) lower my expense, (2) increase my wages, or (3) allow my optometrist to earn more. I could pay by cash or check (with nearly no added cost) or use a credit card with a low processing fee charged to the vendor (and passed on in a higher charge). The credit card offers me the option of paying all the charges each month or lending me money to smooth out expenses over the year, for which I pay interest. As explained earlier, it is largely the result of historical accidents that these expenses are tax subsidized and included in my "health insurance" benefits.

Although some preventive care (and routine maintenance—like my glasses) may be almost totally predictable, some uncertainty is associated with most of what is included in the minor acute care category. Roughly 10 to 15 percent of the people in our dataset (depending on age and sex) experience minor acute and preventive costs twice the average for their age-sex cell, the maximum of which is $1,384 \times 2 = \$2,768$ (data not shown). This is not an enormous sum; the cost of an insurance policy with a reasonable deductible to cover such unusual expenditures would not be too high for most people (as the insurer would smooth out the unusually high cost events across all enrollees). Income-based subsidies would ease the burden for the remainder of the population.[14]

This discussion argues that, largely because of the inherent selection problems, everyone must have coverage for major acute and chronic illnesses. Contrariwise, coverage for minor acute and preventive care need not be handled through an insurance system. This does not mean, however, that the cost of *all* preventive care should be borne directly by patients. The universal coverage pool (UCP) providing the mandated coverage will have to pay for some major acute and chronic problems that might have been prevented or could be dealt with far less expensively with early detection. It makes sense for the UCP to cover such cost-saving preventive care and screening directly or indirectly. Likewise, we require that children cannot begin school without certain immunizations because it reduces the spread of disease, but many health plans do not cover those costs. This should be changed.

Making Coverage Mandatory: One Insurer or Many?

New health policy legislation could simply require that everyone buy coverage for major acute and chronic care, much as states require automobile owners to buy insurance from any carrier willing to offer them a policy.[15] That would be an enormous mistake; selection problems can occur not only when people choose to purchase coverage or not but also from the choice of health plans in which they could enroll. Some advocates argue that problems of selection can be avoided if all plans in the market are required to accept any applicant and may not disenroll anyone. Some go further and say that all the plans would have to offer the same benefits so there would be no reason for people to avoid one plan and choose another. Neither proposed solution, however, eliminates the selection problem.

When offered a choice, people select health plans not just on the basis of the financial coverage and premium, but because one offers an overall better package of service for its premium. Coverage can be the same but the "package" worse if the set of subspecialists is more limited, the drug formularies somewhat more restrictive, or the approval process more onerous. Given the highly skewed need for care, plans have incentives to look attractive for those who do not need much care and behave unresponsively for the few who require a lot of care.[16] If we seek to assure coverage for chronic illness and its exacerbations, *and* people can choose among plans, then the potential for selection is actually greater, because the choice of plan will be dominated by what patients think is better for their chronic care without any offsets for, say, better access to preventive services. A multiplicity of plans brings marketing and duplicative administrative costs, but some argue that competing health plans can better identify high-quality, low-cost providers or negotiate lower fees than a single-payer system. Markedly better ways to create efficiency and quality among providers are discussed in Chapter 4. The issue here is whether competing health plans seeking to enroll patients will (or could) undertake the complex work of encouraging efficiency and quality, or whether they would take the easier path and seek out the lower-cost enrollees.

Consider the following scenario, in which everyone is guaranteed enrollment in a set of health plans offering identical coverage for all major acute and chronic illness: as the coverage and benefits are required to be the same, the only distinguishing characteristics are the networks of physicians and hospitals offered by the plans and the premiums they charge. Suppose that one health plan, GoodCoverage, Inc., decides that in order to steer its enrollees to what it feels are more efficient or lower-cost providers, it will not include a tertiary referral center in its local network, contracting instead with other centers farther away. People living close to the excluded hospital who have chronic illnesses—and those who are worried about sudden major trauma—may decide to switch to those plans offering local tertiary care. In doing so they almost certainly lower the expected costs of GoodCoverage and raise the costs for the plans to which they switch. This is how selection occurs across health plans even with uniform benefits and guaranteed eligibility to enroll.

Risk adjustment is a technique used to measure and offset such differences in risk. The general approach is to use data collected on the health problems of all enrollees in each plan during one year, assign a value to the costs expected to be incurred in the next year associated with those health problems, and transfer money behind the scenes from the plans having lower-risk enrollees to those with higher-risk enrollees. In theory, this will compensate for risk selection across plans. In practice, the information available on last year's health status does not predict next year's expenditures nearly well enough to offset potentially very strong incentives for plans to encourage selection.

Compounding this problem is the clinical fact that selection may be good for patients even if it is bad for setting fair premiums. At its core is the reality that medical care costs are highly skewed. This means that they are highly concentrated among a small number of people even *within* specific chronic illness categories such as cystic fibrosis, congestive heart failure, or HIV/AIDS. Each of these conditions is typically a single category in a risk adjustment model, yet the clinicians treating those patients understand fine gradations in severity that are measured not by diagnoses but by clinical status indicators, such as lab test results, and not included in claims and administrative data. The average cost amount transferred by a risk adjustment system for such conditions reflects relatively low costs for many people with the condition and very high costs for a few. In many instances, most patients with such problems can be well treated by a wide range of clinicians, but if or when their condition is not responsive, they may need referral to highly specialized centers. A well-intentioned physician managing the care of such a patient enrolled in GoodCoverage might suggest that he or she switch to another plan in order to get convenient access to such specialists. With risk adjustment, the following year GoodCoverage loses the average incremental payment for the person with an expensive condition but avoids all the extremely high costs associated with his or her care. The plan gaining the patient, ExcellentCare, Inc., gets only the average cost for the category but bears the full expense. With simple diagnosis-based risk adjustment, ExcellentCare will rapidly go out of business if it does not drop specialized centers that appropriately attract those very high-cost patients.

As this scenario illustrates, we need to improve our risk assessment and risk adjustment techniques—an issue addressed in Chapter 5—but they will never be good enough to adjust payment with sufficient precision that premiums can be set a year in advance without encouraging selection.[17] Instead, money compensating for differences in risk needs to follow the patient quickly as he or she navigates the health care system. When a patient with cystic fibrosis is not responding well to community-based care and needs treatment by more specialized providers, the funding should be increased and follow the patient to the new providers.

All of this argues for a single pool—the universal coverage pool—covering the costs of major acute and chronic illnesses, rather than attempting to calculate risk adjustment amounts across competing health plans that enroll individuals. As the previous discussion points out, there is little insurance-based rationale for mandating coverage for the wide range of common minor acute and preventive care interventions. There is even less economic rationale for suggesting that such coverage, if desired, needs to be provided through a single-payer arrangement. The problem with payment is that much of the routine management of chronic illness can and should occur during visits for minor acute and preventive care. The person with diabetes and hypertension who comes in to have a sprained ankle examined should have his or her blood pressure checked and, if needed, have a blood sugar test. The challenge is to design an approach that spreads the risk for the expensive aspects of care, whether sudden or chronic, while allowing maximum flexibility and reducing the administrative costs associated with the large number of relatively low-cost interventions people may want or need.

Knitting Together a Comprehensive Package

For those Americans who are now able to obtain coverage, a major frustration is the complex set of rules regarding which health plan or carve-out is responsible, what services are covered, and how such decisions are made.[18] Not only is this problematic for patients, but also differences across patients and payers create enormous inefficiencies in the delivery of care. Integration and simplification of coverage will benefit patients, providers, and the system. From the patients' perspective, the full range of services needed during an episode should be handled in an integrated manner. Providers—physicians, hospitals, and others—should have wide flexibility in deciding what services to use but should also bear more responsibility for the choices they make (see Chapter 4). SecureChoice will shift the focus from the cost implications of each decision to overall patterns of practice, eliminating intrusive administrative interventions while retaining incentives.

The conceptual split between major acute and interventional episodes and chronic illness management on the one hand, and minor acute and preventive care on the other, relates to the types of care for which coverage should be mandatory. Everyone needs to be, either directly or indirectly, participating in the universal coverage pool for major acute and chronic illness care as well as for selected preventive services. Coverage may be optional for the remaining types of care; a person may have a third party to pay for part or all of the expenses— or not. As the patient contemplates seeing a physician on a particular day, however, it may be unclear what categories her problems fall into and whether the services will be eligible for UCP coverage. To assure better clinical care, those questions should be eliminated; the patient should not have to worry about which "plan" will pay, and the clinician should have no incentives to fragment care. Indeed the appropriate care of minor acute problems may be affected by the patient's chronic illnesses and vice versa. What may initially appear to be a minor acute problem may ultimately be identified as an underlying chronic illness. Thus, even though we need a universal pool for only roughly two-thirds of all costs and can have a wide range of "plans" for everything else, the arrangements must be as seamless as possible for both clinicians and patients.

From an economic risk perspective, although everyone needs to be covered for major acute and chronic illness care, the day-to-day payment issues are better distinguished as between major acute/interventional care and everything else. As nearly all the expenditures occurring in hospitals and similar facilities will be covered by the UCP, there can be direct payment by the UCP for those services. These payments will cover not only truly acute episodes but also the exacerbations of chronic illness requiring hospitalization or similar interventional care. Because the UCP carries the risk for both types of care, it need not distinguish the reason for the admission—vastly reducing conflict in assessing causality.

Ongoing chronic illness management, minor acute care, preventive services, and ongoing coordination, however, may involve a wide range of providers and services, sometimes with a single visit incorporating multiple problems and categories of episodes. The UCP need not be involved in such care except to make available funds to cover the costs of chronic illness management (CIM) and designated preventive care.[19] Because the UCP is universal, it spreads risk across everyone, and there is no reason for it to focus on annual enrollment. Instead it can make CIM payments on a monthly basis, reflecting the patient's current (not past) illness, and those payments can move with the patient as he or she moves among providers. What is necessary is a payment intermediary (PI) to collect the CIM payments from the UCP and any government subsidies available for those with low incomes, along with funds from the patient and any voluntary coverage he or she has purchased, and then pay providers.

The patient would pay for care obtained from all providers with a health care card (HCC), analogous to a credit card, issued by a payment intermediary. By administering the payment of those provider claims with the health care card, the PI captures data on the diagnoses associated with each service, much as is done today with Medicare and other billing systems. Relatively straightforward software allows the grouping of claims into episodes of care and classification of those episodes into chronic illness management and other reasons for treatment.[20] The PI uses this information to request monthly payments from the UCP for its enrollees with chronic illnesses, with these payments reflecting the nature and severity of the problems. These monthly payments for CIM care, as well as direct payment of major hospitalizations and similar care by the UCP, essentially eliminate any risk the PI might face from having a sicker-than-average enrollment group.

If the PI were simply to take the total costs incurred by each person and net out the CIM payments from the pool, the situation would be analogous to that of the employee using his credit card for all purchases and then having those associated with business travel covered by his employer. Even with a well-functioning pool to cover CIM and major acute/interventional care (MA/I), however, there is probably more variability in medical expenses than most people would want to bear. Thus PIs will be more than just credit card companies. They will offer to smooth out these residual costs across time and individuals, converting them into the more familiar mix of monthly premiums and per service co-payments. Although superficially similar to the current payment model, behind the scenes the PI scenario differs in fundamental ways; in particular, the PI does not attempt to organize providers or manage care. Patients will have much more flexibility in the structuring of these payments; some will choose to have large co-payments and small premiums, while others will choose no co-payments in combination with higher premiums. The new role envisioned for the PI constitutes the "choice" component of SecureChoice, and does so in ways that allow far more choice and responsibility than conventional health plans.

Providing Incentives: Direct Co-payments by Patients

A fundamental aspect of SecureChoice is that financial incentives will be placed on the parties most responsible for decisions and will be appropriately timed to affect such decisions. Some argue that co-payments should have no place in medical care, pointing to the British National Health Service and the Veterans Health Administration as systems operating largely without co-payment. Indeed, co-payments are neither necessary nor sufficient for a well-run health care system. Without them one needs a unitary authority that makes decisions as to exactly what services will be provided and how they will be organized. In the absence of unlimited budgets, such top-down decisions will always result in demand (at zero price) exceeding supply and hence explicit or implicit rationing. Whether such rationing creates health problems depends on the tightness of the overall budget, how well the available resources are allocated, and the independence and expertise of those running the system, but there will be a perception of "arbitrary bureaucratic constraints." In the American political system this is a highly sensitive charge and a critical vulnerability.

If co-payments are to have a role, it should be primarily for their incentive effects, not as a way to shift costs to the patient at the time when care is needed. In general, as will be discussed in Chapter 4, patient payments (deductibles or coinsurance) applied during a hospital episode have little or no incentive effect on the resources used during the episode. Such co-payments may reduce the likelihood of hospital or interventional care a bit, but in most cases they simply transfer a financial burden to people needing the care, who are often losing earnings and incurring other costs not covered by any insurance. Some major acute/interventional care may be discretionary— neither obviously necessary nor clearly unnecessary—and disputes over this are at the root of many insurance coverage conflicts. Joint replacement and other procedures can improve the quality of life, but at substantial cost, and there exist less invasive and costly approaches that should ordinarily be tried first. A significant co-payment, say $1,000—less than the typical out-of-pocket cost associated with a deductible and coinsurance now—might be required if such procedures occurred within a year of the diagnosis of the limitation, with the co-payment falling over time, provided less costly alternatives are explored.

Small per-visit co-payments have been used quite successfully by certain HMOs to get their patients to think about whether an ambulatory visit is necessary. A more significant co-payment may be levied for visits to the emergency department that could have been handled by same day appointments or urgent care visits.[21] Requiring co-payments for *all* ambulatory care, however, may be counterproductive. If the goal of preventive visits is to uncover problems early and address them before they get worse, there should be no financial barrier to such visits. Some have argued for "value-based benefits" that lower the co-payments—sometimes to zero—for specific treatments such as medications to control diabetes.[22] This idea should be pursued extensively and will be discussed in Chapter 4. The challenge is to design the mechanisms that will be most effective in identifying and implementing such an approach as part of a more fundamental change.

We do not have answers to the question of optional co-payment design today, largely because it has never been asked in the context of a situation in which the major costs of MA/I care are handled directly and the incremental costs of CIM are offset by another entity—the UCP. Moreover, insurers have always either used one-size-fits-all packages of coverage for specific employer-based group plans that inherently pool risk or else offered plans with the enormous selection potential inherent in individual coverage policies. Within SecureChoice, PIs will not face selection problems and will be able to explore a wide variety of co-payment options, experimenting with fixed amounts per visit or for visits of certain types, perhaps zero co-payments for selected preventive or monitoring visits, or perhaps health care reimbursement accounts. An important aspect of the co-payment issue, however, is the role of the clinician in the generation and management of such costs.

Bringing Together Patient and Physician

Although physicians strive to adapt their treatment to each patient's illness and needs, physicians also have distinctive "practice styles." Some may spend a lot of time with patients, order few tests, and use the passage of time to help assess the condition. Others try to reach a definitive diagnosis quickly, even if it requires extensive testing and often produces no change in treatment. Such commonly observed variations in practice styles would not be so problematic if (1) we knew they generated comparable outcomes, and (2) if patients decided that the differences in cost were worth whatever differences in outcomes or reassurance they created.[23] In fact, we know little about the implications of practice style variations, and the current system does not really engage the patient in decisions around practice style.

The payment intermediary will be in an excellent position to facilitate getting answers to both of these questions. Many firms can serve as PIs, and this is likely to be a highly competitive market. The natural customer for the PI is not an employer or consumer but the primary care practitioner, or PCP. The PCP is the clinician (or clinic) serving as a point of first contact for many clinical problems, the provider of much of the primary care a patient may need, a referral source, and the medical home for the patient's records. PCPs in this definition include not just physicians such as family practitioners, internists, pediatricians, and gynecologists but also nurse practitioners and physician assistants, if state scope of practice laws allow. Payment intermediaries will offer certain services that are directly valuable to PCPs—processing bills and providing information—and in doing so, create an enrollment venue. There is no reason for the PI market to be structured around employers, although employers may still pay for much of that coverage, as will be described in Chapter 6. Competition will not be focused on PIs' touting their coverage options to individuals, for they are difficult to market to and relatively uninformed.

Employer-based retirement programs offer a useful example of how the PI function might work in SecureChoice. Fidelity, Vanguard, Schwab, and many other firms offer employers 401(k) plans for their employees with an enormously wide range of investment options, most of which are quite comparable. They compete for the employer's business by offering low administrative costs and good information tools, as well as enough investment choices to satisfy the

needs of each individual enrollee in the 401(k). There is no reason for employers to have multiple 401(k) administrators; employers switch administrators from time to time with little impact
on their employees' retirement investment choices. Likewise there is
no reason for a PCP to need more than one PI to process claims.
SecureChoice would require that PIs use uniform protocols to collect
information from PCPs, making it easy for a PCP to switch from one
PI to another to facilitate competition. PIs will develop a broad range
of coverage plans to be offered to the patients signing up with a PCP;
PIs failing to do so will lose business to those that make themselves
more attractive.

As a natural by-product of the bill-paying process and the receipt
of monthly payments from the UCP for chronic illness management,
the PI will know the cost of each PCP's practice patterns, controlling
for the mix of patients.[24] The PI can then price the premium for the
patients *signing up with that PCP* according to the expected net costs,
given that clinician's practice pattern and the type of coverage the patient wants. Because the UCP carries the risk associated with MA/I
episodes and transfers payments for CIM care to the PI, these premiums reflect the differential costs associated with the decisions of
those clinicians and the patient-based incentives inherent in the coverage chosen. This patient- and provider-based premium maximizes
the "choice" aspect of SecureChoice.

In the current system, insurers set their premiums on the basis of
costs averaged across all providers. People choosing physicians who
order many tests pay no more in premiums than those choosing physicians who primarily take careful histories and then monitor symptoms. Co-payments and deductibles are intended to affect patient decisions at the time of care, but it is unlikely that a patient concerned
about a health problem and seeking advice will engage in careful
benefit-cost analyses with his or her physician. Instead the exchange
is likely to begin, "What do you think I should do, Doctor?" Practice
pattern studies show that the answer depends, at least in part, on the
physician.

Instead of averaging the costs of variable practices across all physicians, the PIs will reflect the costs of differential practice patterns in the net provider-based premiums paid by patients. (I use the term "provider-based premiums" when not specifically accounting for the influence of patient preferences on co-payments and deductibles.) Because the UCP covers roughly two-thirds of all costs, and nearly all of the costs associated with ongoing health problems, such premium differentials will not reflect differences in health status across patients. With the implications of their own practice patterns reflected in the premiums paid by their patients, PCPs will demand better information from the PIs on quality and costs in order to keep their premiums competitive. The initial reaction of PCPs with above-average premiums will be to claim that their quality of care is worth it—and some patients will ask for the evidence of this. The next likely reaction will be for the PCPs to ask PIs to compare their practice patterns with those of lower-cost PCPs of comparable quality. They will ask whether the differences are due to fee levels, less frequent use of certain tests and procedures, or different patterns of referral to specialists.

In some cases PIs might report that better and less expensive care is associated with certain *patient* incentives. Outcomes may be the same and premiums lower when covering certain medications without co-payments leads patients to adhere to their drug regimens. Paying physicians for telephone and e-mail consultations may lower overall costs, perhaps most markedly when combined with per-visit co-payments. When premiums vary with practice style, more quality indicators will be collected to show what makes a difference. For example, physical outcomes may be no better for patients seeing physicians who emphasize testing and imaging, but the patients may be much more reassured—and that may be worth the extra cost to them.

Figure 3.3 summarizes the various insurance and related aspects of SecureChoice, postponing for the moment the question of how the system is financed and providers paid (the subject of other chap-

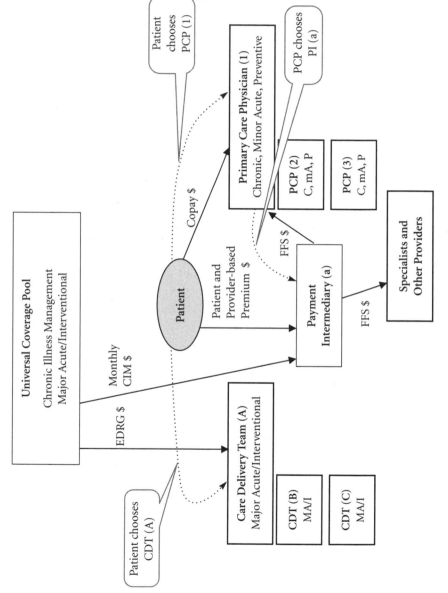

Figure 3.3 Payments to Providers

ters). As already discussed, major acute and chronic illness care, the most expensive aspects of health care expenditures and the ones at the root of selection problems arising from making coverage voluntary, are dealt with through the UCP. Coverage for minor acute and (most) preventive care need not be mandated. The UCP can pay for the major acute and interventional care directly because these are typically short episodes with highly concentrated costs owed to a small number of providers. A care delivery team (CDT) composed of physicians and a hospital will be given a bundled payment based on an expanded DRG (EDRG) for each admission. Patients can select among different CDTs for their care. The ongoing costs of chronic illness management (CIM) are also covered by the UCP, but this care is provided by a highly diverse mix of clinicians over extended periods of time; CIM care often occurs in conjunction with minor acute and preventive care, and patients should have well-designed incentives to participate appropriately in such care. Payment intermediaries simply reorganize funds received from the UCP for CIM care reflecting the health risks associated with each patient, and from patients, employers, and government subsidies for premiums to cover minor acute and preventive care. The PIs do this with patient- and provider-based premiums reflecting the choices patients make in terms of the coverage they desire in combination with the fees and practice patterns of the clinicians the patients choose. The patient may select any primary care physician, and the PCP will already have chosen a PI to handle the flow of funds.

Linking the UCP- and Provider-Based Premium Components of SecureChoice

SecureChoice calls for mandated (or tax-financed) coverage through a universal pool for major acute and chronic illnesses; everything else is handled though voluntary enrollment in plans with patient- and provider-based premiums for minor acute care.[25] The question is whether there should be financial linkages between the two programs. Consider a flu shot costing about $60 that should be delivered annually. This is a cost affordable by nearly all, and the annual use is highly predictable; under a classic economic framework there is little rationale for it to be covered by "insurance." A flu shot, however, protects not only the individual but also others by reducing the spread of the disease, so there is a public health argument for eliminating a price that may deter some people from getting the shot; indeed, people might even be paid to be immunized. Likewise, a screening exam with the potential for detecting a problem that can be easily treated in an early stage may save the UCP from having to spend substantially more in hospital care in the future. A record-keeping service making it much easier for the UCP to assess health across individuals in an area may also warrant subsidy.

Thus there are efficiency arguments that SecureChoice should ensure that certain preventive services are fully covered and that each patient will have a medical home—either a clinician or care system— taking responsibility for tracking the person's health over time, maintaining records, and serving as an initial point of contact for advice and referral. Difficulties arise, however, in deciding exactly what preventive services should be covered. For example, screening for breast cancer can catch the disease early, but recent evidence suggests that computer-aided detection is not only costly in itself but also significantly less accurate than conventional interpretation.[26] Interest groups argue vigorously for complete coverage of their particular services and products, often in the absence of definitive studies confirming their value.

The UCP may decide that certain preventive services should be covered within the provider-based plans because they either serve a public health function or will save the UCP money in the future. It can work out various arrangements with the PIs to include coverage for such services in their plans, perhaps even excluding them from any co-payments. PIs may press for an expansion of such transfers, but the UCP will demand good evidence that specific items to be covered, such as computer-aided mammograms, really justify the cost. Chapter 5 describes how natural variability in the practice and use of such services will provide important evidence as to their worth.

The PIs and UCP will also develop financial linkages as a result of the variations in use of inpatient and other expensive services covered in full by the UCP. Although PIs are not at risk for such care, some will quickly notice that the patients they cover are associated with certain PCPs having lower-than-expected use of such interventions. This may be because their physicians have practice styles including careful outpatient monitoring that reduce the rate of acute exacerbations of chronic illness, or use watchful waiting for certain minor acute problems rather than interventions. These PIs will argue on behalf of their PCPs for transfers from the UCP to help compensate them for their additional effort. Although this represents an additional initial cost for the UCP, identifying the clinician behaviors associated with more efficient care will allow the UCP to create incentives for other PIs to pass on to those PCPs with *higher*-than-average use in order to bring it down. Sometimes what is passed on will just be better information for the PCPs; sometimes it will be translated into patient incentives, such as co-payments that would be required if an initial trial of more conservative care is to be bypassed.[27]

Ensuring Secure Coverage with Maximum Choice

It is highly desirable that coverage be seamless and financial incentives be placed appropriately. In SecureChoice a universal pool covers the costs associated with most of the expensive aspects of care: inpatient and similar episodes. The pool also provides coverage for chronic illness, the aspect of the current system that results in selection problems, health plans trying to avoid risk, and skyrocketing premiums for those chronically ill people who are able to get coverage. A universal pool is not needed for the remainder of care, but some preventive and related services may nonetheless be covered indirectly by the UCP. Individuals (and perhaps their employers) are likely to pay for those remaining services through some combination of premiums and co-payments, with the specific mix of incentives decided upon by the enrollee, not some external carrier, employer, or government body. The system will be designed to collect and provide key decision makers—patients and physicians—with relevant information on quality, costs, and trade-offs. Not everyone will make the same decisions; the system is purposefully designed to support diversity and learn from it. From the patient's perspective, the medical care system will not be radically altered. But much will have changed behind the scenes, as will be discussed in the next chapters.

— 4 —

Organizing Care and Paying Providers

Medical care has typically relied on fee-for-service (FFS) pricing. In part this is because it is often difficult for a physician to know exactly what a patient needs when beginning care. With FFS, physicians have no reason to stint on care they provide or order. This may result in better outcomes if "more" is better than "less," but this is not always the case.[1] It is unusual for consumers, let alone patients, to have the experience to ascertain accurately whether their hired expert's skills really are superior.[2] Quality is not just "in the eye of the (average) beholder" but is often reflected in how well unusual problems are dealt with and whether good outcomes are achieved in unpredictable and possibly never-before-experienced situations. Medical care quality may be impossible to determine on a case-by-case basis, but it can be more readily assessed by looking at large numbers of cases.

The previous chapter focused on when insurance should be mandatory and when it can be optional. Insurance, however, largely addresses who will pay for care once a problem occurs—what is sometimes called occurrence risk. Chapter 3 introduced the notion of organizing medical services into episodes of care as a way to estimate the cost associated with various occurrences. The question to be addressed here is how to structure the actual payment to providers for that care. The uncertainty associated with the resources needed to achieve high-quality care can be termed "production risk." This recognizes that care cannot be delivered in a purely cookbook fashion. Skill, flexibility, and an ability to deal with the unknown is important. Fee-for-service and strict economic separation of providers is traditionally used in medicine, at least in part because it insulates the clinicians from all production risk. By doing so, however, it reduces incentives to be more efficient. For example, it is more costly for hospitals to stock hip prostheses produced by every manufacturer than to develop a preferred list. There is no reason for the orthopedists practicing at the hospital (who are simply paid for what they do and have no involvement in the costs they generate) to decide collectively on a preferred list. Creating the appropriate incentives for clinicians and other providers is the best way to increase the efficiency with which care is delivered without assuming an all-knowing oversight system.

There are many differences between major acute and interventional (MA/I) care and the other types of episodes (chronic illness management, minor acute, and preventive) typically addressed in ambulatory care settings. This leads to the possibility of different payment approaches described in the next two sections. The final section addresses a series of supplementary but complex issues about these different approaches to the organization of care and payment.

Paying for Major Acute and Interventional Care

Major acute and interventional episodes incur not only the cost of hospitalization but also the cost of related and similar care. "Related care" refers to the services of all the professionals—physicians, respiratory therapists, psychologists, and others—who may be involved in the patient's care for that episode. This includes tests and procedures provided on an outpatient basis just before the patient is admitted— for example, MRIs scheduled before a surgical admission to help the surgeon know exactly how to undertake the procedure. Likewise, certain services after discharge, such as checking on how a wound is healing, are considered part of the episode, as are readmissions for complications.

A single episode can be quite complex. For example, a person experiencing severe chest pain may go to an urgent care setting, be referred to an emergency department for more definitive assessment, and then admitted to the hospital for care. The workup may show the need for open-heart surgery to do a coronary artery bypass graft, which may require a transfer to another facility. Complications recognized after discharge may result in a third admission. Transfers and complications will certainly be troublesome for the patient and are costly to the health care system. Although they may have been unavoidable, a restructured payment system should create incentives for the various parties to see what can be done to improve both quality and efficiency.

MA/I episodes should not be limited to those including a hospital stay but also include those offering comparable services relying only on what are called outpatient facilities. Many surgical procedures can be performed in operating rooms that may or may not be part of a hospital; if the patient is in the facility less than twenty-four hours, the treatment is currently considered—and paid for as—an outpatient procedure. Using an "if it looks like a duck . . ." criterion, I include such episodes in the MA/I category. Procedures so minor that they can be done in almost any physician's office, such as simple suturing of a cut, do not meet this criterion.

What Care Delivery Teams Will Do

Inpatient care involves a complex mix of physician and other clinical services along with services provided by a hospital and its employees. Currently Medicare pays hospitals a lump sum for each patient according to the patient's diagnosis-related group (DRG) designation (or surgical procedure). Physicians providing care in the hospital for these patients bill separately. This separation adds billing costs, but more important, federal laws prohibit any gainsharing between physicians and hospitals. Gainsharing occurs when a party—typically a hospital—shares some of its gains or otherwise rewards physicians not in its direct employ. Two important pieces of federal legislation, often referred to as Stark I and II after their author, Congressman Pete Stark, prohibit gainsharing. The underlying concern this legislation was designed to address is the potential for hospitals to reward physicians either for steering patients to their facility or for admitting patients for care that is unnecessary. Many states also have anti-kickback or anti-fee-splitting laws to preclude gainsharing between physicians. Because of this legislation, a hospital cannot legally reward surgeons who schedule their elective cases on days when there is excess capacity or reward orthopedic surgeons who agree to reduce the number of different brands of prostheses they use.

SecureChoice will incorporate new legislation allowing physicians and hospitals (or other facilities) to form care delivery teams (CDTs) to receive the episode payments for major acute or interventional care.[3] The CDT framework is flexible in terms of operation and governance. CDTs can range from a comprehensive entity, such as an integrated delivery system like Kaiser, to a collaboration of separate physicians and one or more facilities. Most, however, will focus on episodes of inpatient care and their equivalents to accept part of the production risk associated with MA/I episodes. CDTs may use a variety of internal arrangements to pay for the services they must provide, including FFS, salary, subcontracts, and various incentive programs. These are discussed later in this chapter.

Physicians and the facilities at which they care for patients currently have a symbiotic relationship; the CDT is intended to facilitate efficiency and quality within that setting. It is important, however, that the CDT be responsible, either directly or through referrals (which it coordinates and for which it takes financial responsibility), for all the care a patient may need within an MA/I episode. A hospital may partner with multiple CDTs whose patient populations do not overlap, such as orthopedics and obstetrics.[4] Hospitals should not have arrangements with two CDTs that could be responsible for the same types of episodes. A hospital involved with two CDTs caring for similar patients (for instance, in cardiology) could become embroiled in arguments about which CDT has the sickest patients within a payment category and how revenues are to be split. More important, outcome-focused assessments of quality will typically not be able to determine whether good (or poor) outcomes for the first CDT's patients (as compared with those of the second) are due to the care delivered by the physicians in each CDT or to care received from the hospital's staff that may be common to both CDTs.[5]

Although hospitals should not become members of multiple CDTs treating similar patients, a comparable restriction may not be necessary for all physicians. Attribution of quality measures underlies the rationale for not allowing hospitals to have similar patients in multiple CDTs. In most surgical cases, however, the surgeon is clearly identifiable and is typically held responsible. The patients of a surgeon operating as part of CDT-D in Hospital D on Monday, Wednesday, and Friday and CDT-E in Hospital E on the other days can be easily tracked. Other physicians, such as radiologists or inpatient medical specialists, may be deeply involved in the care of patients, but usually in combination with many other clinicians. It is unlikely that cross-CDT quality measures would attempt to identify the influence of specific clinicians in those specialties. The effects of their combined care will be assessed at the CDT level, and there is little reason to preclude their involvement in multiple CDTs.[6]

Not all CDTs will involve hospitals; for instance, ophthalmologists may form a CDT to perform eye procedures. Specialty outpatient surgical centers already exist, but separate fees are paid for the facility and the physician. Currently an important loophole in Medicare's gainsharing prohibitions means that there are no restrictions on a physician's assessing a patient, recommending a procedure, and then performing it in a facility he or she owns, as long as the facility is not a hospital.

Following the intent of the anti-kickback provisions in precluding incentives for unnecessary admissions, physicians involved in CDTs should not be able to encourage a patient to be admitted. Instead of there being a barrier between physicians and hospitals (or other facilities), the barrier should be between those deciding whether a patient requires admission and those deciding which services are provided during the admission.[7] The barrier should prevent the CDT from attempting to induce admissions, but it should not get in the way of good patient care. CDT physicians will obviously be able to decide that a patient is not a good candidate for surgery, or that their facility is not the best place for that patient to be treated. PCPs will not be the only physicians deciding whether a patient should be admitted; other physician specialists will serve in that role, including some surgeons and others who no longer want to be in the operating room. To see how this would work, consider a patient with a knee problem. Today she is likely to be referred by her PCP to an orthopedic surgeon, who will both assess her need for a knee replacement and do the subsequent surgery—a situation that may encourage intervention rather than watchful waiting. To reduce the incentive for overly aggressive interventional care, under SecureChoice the PCP would first refer the patient to an orthopedist who serves as a diagnostic expert, focusing on when surgery is most beneficial and when watchful waiting is appropriate. When a decision is made to go ahead, a referral is made to a surgeon in a CDT to undertake the procedure. The surgeon will then decide whether to perform the procedure and exactly what approach to use. To facilitate consultation between the ambulatory-based clinicians—who may know the patient the best—and the members of the CDT, the UCP will directly pay for consultations, either in person in the facility or by telephone, at the same rates usually charged for office visits and consultations.

How to Expand and Improve the DRG Model

Medicare's experience with diagnosis-related groups informs the design of how to pay the CDTs. Medicare pays a fixed amount to each hospital for each admission based on the DRG category.[8] The DRG is determined according to presenting symptoms for the patient's hospital admission, with adjustments for comorbidities and complications. The UCP will build on this concept, creating expanded DRGs

(EDRGs) for major acute and interventional episodes. EDRGs will include all professional and other costs associated with the episode as well as appropriate preadmission and postdischarge care. Follow-up care in short-term rehabilitation or other settings and readmissions for complications should be bundled into the initial payment. The guiding principle is to offer incentives for the CDT to provide the most appropriate care for the patient, regardless of setting.

The switch away from simple, independent fee-for-service will be new for most physicians, so it is important that they perceive the system as being fair. Under SecureChoice the UCP will do several things to ensure both the perception and the reality of fairness in payment. The Medicare DRG approach uses diagnosis and procedure information for classification of patients. This generally works well, but the care of some patients is much more complex than for others with the same diagnosis because of the stage of the disease. The EDRG classification system will be open to including such measures in its risk categories for both payment and outcomes measurement. Rather than holding to an arbitrary budget, the UCP will commit to pay CDTs what is needed for superior-quality care—that which is obtained in CDTs with outcomes above the median. In practice this means that the UCP will put into place methods to assess outcomes across CDTs by EDRG, review the resources used by CDTs achieving better-than-average outcomes, and pay every CDT an amount that will cover the costs implied by the resources used by CDTs achieving that superior level of care.[9] (Chapter 5 discusses how the information will be collected to implement this system.) The second "fairness" policy is that, unlike the current Medicare program, which precludes providers from charging more than Medicare deems allowable, SecureChoice explicitly permits CDTs and other providers to charge more than what the UCP determines is necessary to deliver superior care. Instead of a regulatory approach, SecureChoice uses market tools and patient assessments to give providers incentives to be efficient and cost-conscious. Chapter 6 addresses these issues in more detail.

Medicare DRG payments have been in place for several decades, and hospitals have managed to adapt to them. Although the payment levels for individual DRGs may not be precisely correct, and hospitals often complain that the overall amounts are too low, most hospitals are able to balance gains and losses across patients in a specific DRG category as well as across DRGs. Specific problems in adding professional and other costs to the amount bundled into specific EDRGs will require careful examination of the data and demonstration projects. Chapter 9 addresses these implementation issues along with how CDTs are likely to be formed.

Why It's Not Just the Mean Payment: Variance Also Matters

Risk adjustment will be needed to help the CDTs address the uncertainties of production risk that come with being paid a fixed amount for an episode of care. This is analogous to the problem faced by a contractor with a fixed-price contract; unless some mechanism is provided to deal with such uncertainty, quality may be compromised. EDRGs are supposed to hold CDTs financially responsible for the things they can plausibly control but not for the things that are out of their control, such as the arrival of patients at their CDT who are substantially sicker than average. SecureChoice will incorporate a process addressing this concern.

Currently some Medicare hospital stays are very long, generating costs far exceeding the average amount included in the DRG payment. It might take years of below-average costs to allow a hospital to recover the losses from even a few such cases. Medicare, therefore, has an "outlier" program to provide extra payments for admissions far exceeding the average cost for a particular type of case. Serious concerns, however, have been raised about some hospitals' being too aggressive in their claims for outlier payments.[10] More problematic than potentially fraudulent payments for outlier cases is the failure to learn how to manage cases better so as to prevent patients from requiring very long stays or expensive interventions.

Medicare pays (in a relatively passive way) for outlier cases out of its overall budget. In contrast, the UCP will not directly cover outlier cases but will suggest that the CDTs buy reinsurance for outlier expenses from independent entities.[11] The average cost of such premiums will be bundled into the EDRG payments from the UCP. The private reinsurers will pay for the outlier cases out of the premiums they charge the CDTs, so they will have strong incentives to explore patterns of claims for outlier cases. They will probably initially focus on certain CDTs with high rates of outlier cases and increase the premiums for them. Those CDTs believing that they have low rates of outlier cases will seek out reinsurers offering "preferred risk" coverage. This turns selection from a problem into a solution to help identify what leads to outlier cases, creating an opportunity for researchers and consultants to learn and disseminate practices that will result in better care at lower cost.

Certain CDTs will be serving as referral centers, appropriately attracting more complex cases *within* the EDRG, but all CDTs may feel (or claim) that they are located in the town of Lake Wobegon, with all their cases more complex than average. Geographic patterns of admissions will initially help identify cases likely to have been referred. Reinsurers will ask for better and more specific documentation of what may have led to the referral. Such data and observations of referrals may lead to further refinement of the EDRG classifications.[12] (An example of this in the current Medicare system was the recognition that the "re-do" of a knee replacement is a far more complex procedure than an initial knee replacement.) Some CDTs will have identified more effective ways of managing such cases. These lessons should be widely disseminated and may allow a reduction in referrals supported by better, more accessible care.[13]

How CDTs Might Work

The bundling of payment within each EDRG category and the focus on overall outcomes will give those involved in the CDT the freedom to organize themselves to achieve the best quality of care in the most efficient manner possible.[14] Several changes over the last few years have altered clinical practice in ways that work well with this new payment and organization model.

The care of hospitalized patients has traditionally been overseen by their personal physicians or surgeons. Other physicians, such as radiologists and anesthesiologists, might be involved but were rarely selected by the patient. Today, inpatient medical care is increasingly managed on a twenty-four-hour basis by hospitalists—physicians who work only in the inpatient setting. Hospitalists make up a relatively new medical specialty in the United States, although the model has been commonplace in Europe for decades. Typically working in teams, they provide twenty-four-hour, on-site expertise to respond rapidly to changes in a patient's status. Because they specialize in caring for the sickest patients, they develop expertise in exactly which other specialists to call upon to achieve optimal care.[15]

As patient stays have become ever shorter and more interventions are undertaken in outpatient settings, primary care physicians are likely to have only an occasional patient in the hospital on any given day, making traditional early morning rounds increasingly disruptive of their schedules. Medicare's refusal to pay for visits by both a hospitalist and the patient's usual physician has further attenuated the link between outpatient clinicians and inpatient care.

Although the increased use of hospitalists offers many opportunities for improved quality and efficiency in inpatient care, a potential problem area is in the transfer of information. Information transfers are needed from the community-based clinician to the hospitalist as the patient comes into the facility and from the hospitalist to the community-based physician upon discharge. Shared electronic medical records can help in this regard, but informal communication may also be valuable. The patient's PCP may be the one person who knows how best to "read" the patient, especially when emotionally difficult decisions need to be made. Having the PCP available during the stay may also increase the patient's perception of a caring health system. Although the CDT will be precluded from including PCPs in its gainsharing arrangements, the revised legislation will allow the

UCP to pay for inpatient visits by PCPs, as long as the fee for time does not exceed the PCP's comparable fee for office visits.

Many surgical procedures are being shifted from general hospitals to facilities specializing in a narrow range of procedures, such as orthopedics or cardiovascular procedures. Specialized hospitals have incentives to organize themselves efficiently and to be responsive to the needs of a relatively narrow set of patients, but some allege that such facilities "cherry-pick" the simplest cases within their purview.[16] Specialized facilities can easily become CDTs; in many instances the facilities are already owned by the physicians using them. There are, however, three important areas of concern with these arrangements. One is ensuring that these organizations take responsibility for all the costs implicitly encompassed by their EDRG payments.[17] A second is ensuring that the providers involved in such CDTs are isolated economically from those who decide whether the procedure needs to be done. This will be addressed as part of the modification of the gain-sharing prohibitions. The third is ensuring that the quality and cost measures used to assess CDTs are equally appropriate for specialized and general facilities.

The underlying concern is that some CDTs will specialize in the easier cases within an EDRG category—perhaps patients for whom the intervention may not even be necessary. Such cases may be less expensive to treat and may also have relatively good outcomes. Simple application of outcome measures would initially identify these CDTs as being superior. One automatic check on such behavior would be requests from the UCP and others to learn about the processes employed by such CDTs to achieve their unusually good outcomes. Most CDTs would be honored to be selected to help set the standard for others; those declining to share their methods may find themselves under more careful scrutiny and audit to detect potential fraud associated with unnecessary interventions on healthy patients.

The increased flexibility and responsibility given to CDTs allows providers to decide what resources are needed to achieve superior care. Currently, when someone else is paying for imaging, there is no reason for a surgeon not to routinely request a repeat scan just before surgery, even if it is necessary in only a small fraction of cases. Observing the resource use patterns of those CDTs achieving the best outcomes will help determine when such tests are needed, perhaps with the advice of the radiologists in the CDT.[18] Likewise, responsibility for postdischarge care will improve both resource allocation and quality as assessed at the end of such care. Not all the professionals involved in the care for which the CDT is responsible, however, need be part of the CDT. Some services, such as rehabilitation care, may be provided through contracts with the CDT.

CDTs may use a variety of mechanisms to allocate payments internally. Some clinicians, such as hospitalists, may prefer a base salary because they are "on" for fixed periods of time, caring for a broad range of patients. Surgeons, by contrast, may prefer an internal fee-for-service arrangement reflecting exactly what they do. If the hospital or facility is part of the CDT, it may want to provide internal incentives to subgroups of clinicians for certain contributions. Orthopedic surgeons may share incentives to evaluate the mix of prostheses the CDT needs to stock; hospitalists may help design the drug formulary and share in the savings that result from more appropriate prescribing and reductions in drug interactions. CDTs will need to design incentives appropriately so as not to overemphasize cost containment at the expense of quality or malpractice risk. Physicians can adjust their compensation mechanisms to reward investing more time in their assessment, planning, and thinking, thereby allowing them to reduce the use of costly nonphysician services such as imaging tests. Fewer imaging tests, however, need not mean less income for radiologists, because they may be compensated for consulting with other physicians to determine when tests are likely to provide little information.

Ambulatory Care Organization and Payment

The inpatient setting provides a natural nexus in which physicians, other clinicians, and facilities repeatedly bring together resources to bear on the treatment of patients. The large number of patients treated in a typical hospital allows CDTs to serve as effective *organizations* coordinating the care for individual patients. Ambulatory care, however, is not provided in such an organized setting. Over 55 percent of physicians practice in groups of nine physicians or fewer, and most groups represent just a single specialty.[19] Large group practices offering a full range of specialties with integrated electronic health records exist in relatively few parts of the country. Where they do exist, they could be an effective analogue to the hospital-focused CDT, accepting episode-based payment and transmitting incentives for quality and efficiency to the participating clinicians.[20] Regardless of the benefits of large groups, some patients do not want to restrict themselves to physicians formally connected in a medical group or partnership. By analogy, some people do their shopping in a single department store, others browse throughout a single mall, and yet others prefer to visit all the shops in the downtown area. There is no clearly "best" way to shop—or get medical care. If today's ambulatory care practice arrangements—where and how clinicians do business—are taken as the starting point, what else should be changed, what maintained, and what avoided?

What to Change in Ambulatory Care

The complex coverage rules currently imposed by the multiplicity of payers and plans add administrative costs and reduce clinical effectiveness. Although a patient may need to interact with just one plan if there are no carve-out carriers, providers may have to deal with literally hundreds. Large group practices can automate the billing process, but even the most efficient expend considerable resources just to get paid. Conflicting clinical, coverage, and payment rules mean that clinicians cannot discern consistent, useful signals. Many health insurers "carve out" and hand off coverage for drugs and mental health care to other carriers with their own formularies and preferred networks of providers. From the clinician's perspective, even if a given drug or therapist is best for several patients with a certain problem, such differences in coverage may mean that different drugs or therapists will need to be used for each patient.

The insensitivity of patients to differences in resource use is a key feature of the current system that needs to be changed. Clinicians use widely disparate varieties of treatments and resources to achieve what appear to be similar outcomes. By quoting the same premium to all enrollees in an area, however, conventional insurance averages practice styles across physicians. More expensive care might be worth more, but patients lack information on quality as well as the cost implications of different practice patterns. The only incentives patients now have to choose among physicians are the small differences in co-payments they would incur, but there is no way for them to know in advance what those differences in costs might add up to over the space of a year. With SecureChoice, the provider-based premiums offered through the payment intermediaries will change these incentives.

What to Maintain (and Enhance)

Any new system should maintain (or enhance) the patient's ability to choose among clinicians without imposing payer-controlled restrictions on access. Likewise, physicians should have maximum flexibility in making referrals and deciding what treatment options would be best for a specific patient with a given problem. Choice is good; informed choice is better. Patients and clinicians need much more—and more accessible—information to guide their choices. Furthermore, given the rapid changes in science and medical technology, this information needs to be constantly updated.

It is not clear what types of practice organization are best suited to the new environment. Current evidence suggests that integrated group practices can achieve the economies of scale needed for keeping complex electronic health records and for effective practice management. In a system with much simpler bill-paying processes and rapidly changing technology, however, a highly structured system may not be optimal. For example, with advances in imaging, the "virtual colonoscopy" may reduce the need for gastroenterologists and increase the need for radiologists, shifting the preferred mix of specialists within a group practice. Virtual linkages (electronic, financial, and professional) among small independent groups of practitioners may be better than larger but less nimble organizations. A payment system should continually encourage the design of better systems.

What to Avoid

A new system should minimize the ability of powerful interests to further their own goals at the expense of others. Payers should not have power to set fees, either to increase their own profits or to achieve an arbitrary budget constraint. Likewise, antitrust laws must be enforced to keep providers from colluding to increase their fees through market power or political pressure. Interest groups should not be permitted to use more subtle tools, such as the design of specific practice guidelines, to protect their own market niche under the guise of improving quality. Given the many ways in which effective government activity in the United States is hobbled and subject to political pressures, these concerns argue for more of a market-based approach than a regulated one.

How SecureChoice Defines "Ambulatory Care"

Ambulatory care includes everything except major acute/interventional (MA/I) episodes, but this is not a very helpful definition. There are situations, moreover, in which sharp boundaries between the two should be blurred. The three major categories included in ambulatory care under SecureChoice—chronic illness management (CIM), minor acute episodes, and preventive care—offer a more useful basis for detail, definition, and distinction. CIM incorporates all the services needed for the ongoing monitoring, care, and management of chronic illness. This includes not just medical visits but also the tests needed to monitor progress, medications and assistive devices, and the services of nonphysician professionals. These could be provided in the clinician's office, at home, through electronic communications, or by other means. CIM applies equally to mental and physical illnesses.[21]

Minor acute episodes are the typical types of problems that lead people to seek care in outpatient settings or by communicating with their primary care provider. All the necessary services for these problems would be included in ambulatory care. Preventive care includes not just the "routine" physical exam but also appropriate immunizations and screening tests for early detection. It also includes preventive services, such as smoking cessation programs and exercise encouragement programs. Not included in preventive care, however, are primary prevention efforts, such as reducing the advertising of highly sugared cereals to children, instituting zoning changes to make neighborhoods more walkable, or increasing taxes on tobacco, all of which are discussed in Chapter 7.

Determining what belongs in the ambulatory care category for financing purposes, however, cannot be done on a service-by-service basis but needs to be based on the reason for the service. An image obtained with an MRI physically located in a hospital building in response to a visit for back pain would be considered part of a minor acute episode; an MRI image performed in an outpatient setting to guide a surgeon in preparation for a major procedure would be part of an EDRG paid to the CDT. What might begin as a simple office visit for a headache may lead to discovering a brain tumor. Such ex post categorization is not new. Medicare faced a similar problem when it developed the DRG system to pay hospitals on the basis of the reason for admitting the patient. In many instances the patient presents with ill-defined symptoms, and it is only after extensive testing and observation in the hospital that a diagnosis can be determined.

Ex post determination of coverage is a significant problem in the current system when it means that providers face the risk of not being paid by an insurer for care they have delivered in good faith. If payment is denied, the provider must then seek payment from the patient (an unpleasant process for both parties) or forgo the income. The focus on the precise justification for each payment for each patient reflects how the current insurance system is organized around employment-based groups. Insurers compete on the basis of being able to cut claims costs; they want to assure each employer that they are paying no more than absolutely necessary for each of its enrollees. Most medical care, however, offers substantial benefits to the patient; ex post claims denial simply shifts the cost to the patient and adds administrative costs for claims adjudication. Accepting and paying for occasional errors may consume far fewer overall resources. Fraud can be addressed much more simply and less expensively by examining patterns of payment and focusing on aberrations.[22] How appropriateness in payment will be assessed is discussed later in this chapter.

How Ambulatory Care Providers Will Be Paid

Inpatient episodes involve physicians, other clinicians, and organizations in a team effort that can serve as the nucleus of a CDT, but other than group practices, there is no comparable grouping of ambulatory care clinicians who always work together. The payment intermediary (PI) concept permits the blending of funds for chronic illness management and for other ambulatory care, but it does not specify how those funds are paid to providers. Provider-based premiums allow differences in practice style to be reflected in premiums that are organized around, but are not necessarily the responsibility of, primary care providers.

Most ambulatory care is currently paid on a fee-for-service basis, so this is a good place to begin. With FFS, providers bear risk only with respect to how much it costs them to deliver a specific service; they complain primarily when they feel that the fees they can charge insurers are inadequate. Under SecureChoice, PIs will be prepared to pay providers FFS, and there would be no arbitrary constraints on fees for either PCPs or referral clinicians. Instead the PCPs who observe the implications of fees and practice styles in the premiums charged their patients will ask questions about fee levels, practice styles, and partial alternatives to FFS. Such alternatives will be driven by what works best to create value for patients and providers, and will reflect creative solutions to a wide variety of problems and opportunities.

With today's FFS system, a patient with a back problem may be referred to an orthopedist, who may order various imaging studies to be performed with equipment in his office. The patient may then be referred to a physical therapy facility, perhaps also partially owned by the orthopedist. The orthopedist's net income in this example is a mix of fees for services he provides as well as earnings from ownership of other services. Some patients certainly benefit from each of these services; others may improve with no care or with simple physical therapy alone. With SecureChoice, PCPs will have much more interest in the cost implications of the various ways their patients can be treated. Some may approach orthopedists who they believe provide high-quality care and discuss different payment arrangements. These may compensate the orthopedist for his or her expertise in deciding whether imaging is needed or just a referral to the physical therapist, who will be trained to know when a referral back to the orthopedist is warranted. Fees for time spent (with patients and in consultation with other professionals) may be higher in this new model, but overall costs may be far lower. It is not just cost that matters; many interventions and diagnostic tests are not totally benign. The rapid growth in imaging is now believed by some to increase the incidence of cancers.[23]

A different approach may be developed for the management of chronic illness. Some specialists may be willing to accept the CIM payment from the UCP as covering all the services they provide as well as what they order for their patients. In this manner they accept much more of the financial risk, but they also may reap greater rewards by more efficiently caring for their patients. Over time, specialists offering better care at lower cost will attract more referrals from PCPs; not all the payment models will be FFS, but all will be voluntary and mutually acceptable to those involved.

How Care Is Organized around a Medical Home

People will select a "medical home," usually a primary care provider, to keep track of their care and to be a usual source of first contact and referral. From a clinical perspective, having a medical home is desirable because it means that one clinician maintains the patient's medical records. In the context of SecureChoice the medical home is also the focus of the provider-based coverage and premiums quoted by the PI. In its simplest form the PI might just pay the bills of all the providers seen by each patient for whom it is coordinating payment. The medical home is not a "gatekeeper," and providers—PCPs, specialists, and facilities—can set their own fees and determine their own preferred practices. Depending on the co-payment options selected on enrollment, some of these costs will be charged back to the patient. After monthly risk-adjusted chronic illness management payments received from the UCP are accounted for, the rest eventually gets converted to premiums.

Provider-based premiums shift much of the incentive for monitoring practices and fees to the PCPs, who are not well equipped to do so, but they can ask their PIs for help. Fee differentials may account for overall premium variability; or some specialists may have more efficient practice styles. It is also possible, however, that an occasional specialist may be doing things unnecessarily, or even billing for services not rendered. Unlike the current situation, in which insurers attempt to assess whether *each* claim should be paid, the PIs will have access to all claims and will thus be able to examine patterns of care. It is certainly the case that some patients presenting with back problems may need an MRI; it is also almost certainly the case that not every patient needs one. Seeing the claims for *all* patients makes it easy to distinguish the latter and trigger a more careful review in the small number of such aberrant practices.

The PI charges a fee composed of several parts, which may or may not be passed on to the patient. One is a fee for processing each bill from each provider, analogous to the small amount charged by credit card companies (even for those customers who pay their bills in full each month), and for requesting CIM payments from the UCP. A second component is associated with a small degree of insurance needed to offer a fixed-in-advance premium for enrollees to smooth out the fluctuations in their use of minor acute care. A third component rewards the PI for analyzing the patterns of claims, thereby identifying chronic illnesses. This last component—the analytics—can also be performed by third parties hired directly by the PCP or else made available through the PI.

How to Ensure Choice in Covering Families

A key component of the ambulatory care aspect of SecureChoice is the provider-based premium allowing people to choose their medical home and how they will pay for their care and then seeing the cost implications of those choices. Coverage has traditionally been focused on families (which helps reduce somewhat the risk of adverse selection) and employer-based contributions. The role of the latter is discussed in Chapter 6; but SecureChoice allows each person in a family to have a different medical home (with different associated PIs) and coverage options. Adding one more type of intermediary allows this flexibility—and enhances patient confidentiality—with little administrative burden. Figure 4.1 illustrates how this will work.

Choosing a medical home implicitly associates each patient with a single PI. The PI issues a health care card to each person it covers for all his or her medical and health-related needs. On a monthly basis the PI sends each enrollee a statement itemizing the care received, the fees paid his or her providers, and the co-payments and monthly pre-

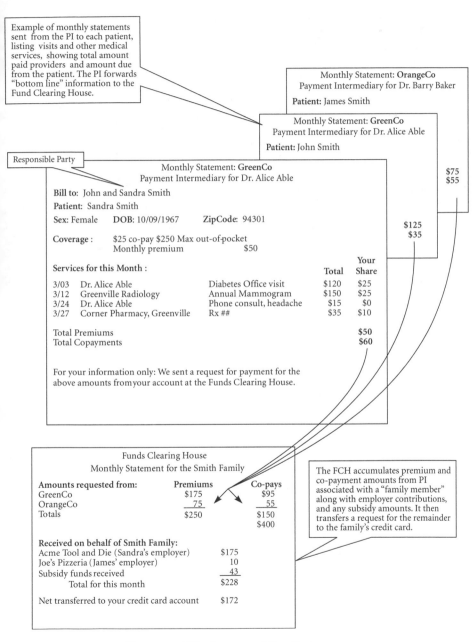

Example of monthly statements sent from the PI to each patient, listing visits and other medical services, showing total amount paid providers and amount due from the patient. The PI forwards "bottom line" information to the Fund Clearing House.

Monthly Statement: **OrangeCo**
Payment Intermediary for Dr. Barry Baker

Patient: James Smith

$75
$55

Monthly Statement: **GreenCo**
Payment Intermediary for Dr. Alice Able

Patient: John Smith

$125
$35

Responsible Party

Monthly Statement: **GreenCo**
Payment Intermediary for Dr. Alice Able

Bill to: John and Sandra Smith

Patient: Sandra Smith

Sex: Female   **DOB:** 10/09/1967   **ZipCode:** 94301

Coverage : $25 co-pay $250 Max out-of-pocket
Monthly premium $50

Services for this Month :

			Total	Your Share
3/03	Dr. Alice Able	Diabetes Office visit	$120	$25
3/12	Greenville Radiology	Annual Mammogram	$150	$25
3/24	Dr. Alice Able	Phone consult, headache	$15	$0
3/27	Corner Pharmacy, Greenville	Rx ##	$35	$10

Total Premiums $50
Total Copayments $60

For your information only: We sent a request for payment for the above amounts from your account at the Funds Clearing House.

Funds Clearing House
Monthly Statement for the Smith Family

Amounts requested from:	Premiums	Co-pays
GreenCo	$175	$95
OrangeCo	75	55
Totals	$250	$150
		$400

The FCH accumulates premium and co-payment amounts from PI associated with a "family member" along with employer contributions, and any subsidy amounts. It then transfers a request for the remainder to the family's credit card.

Received on behalf of Smith Family:
Acme Tool and Die (Sandra's employer)	$175
Joe's Pizzeria (James' employer)	10
Subsidy funds received	43
Total for this month	$228

Net transferred to your credit card account $172

Figure 4.1 Bills, Payers, and Family Accounts

mium due from the enrollee. In Figure 4.1, Sandra Smith has chosen Dr. Able as her PCP, and Dr. Able uses the PI services of GreenCo. Sandra's monthly premium is $50, and in March she used $310 in medical care that under her plan was associated with $60 in co-payments. John, her husband, sees another PCP, who also happens to use GreenCo, but he has selected a different coverage option. James, their son, sees yet another PCP, who is associated with OrangeCo. To protect patient confidentiality, each PI sends the monthly statement to each patient individually.[24] The family members, however, pool their financial resources to pay for their coverage.

The family has a single account with the Funds Clearing House (FCH), which serves as an intermediary between enrollees, payers, and PIs. The FCH is the mechanism through which different PIs interact. Each month the PIs submit to the FCH the monthly premium and co-payment amounts for each person, without any details about the types or reasons for the visits—thereby enhancing patient confidentiality. The FCH pays the PIs on a monthly basis and receives into the account whatever employer contributions are being made on behalf of family members. Income-based subsidy payments (see Chapter 6) may also flow into the account. The remaining balance is transferred to the family's credit card account.[25] The FCH will probably be a private entity collectively owned by the PIs to facilitate their transactions. It will adhere, however, to all federal privacy and confidentiality rules.

Stepping Back and Letting the System Work

Our current system devotes enormous amounts of time to ensuring that all parties are playing exactly "by the rules" because it has misaligned incentives. Getting the incentives right will allow government largely to step back and let the players adapt to the markedly different environment. Physicians will have enormous freedom to practice and charge as they choose, but those decisions will be reflected directly in the premiums paid by their own patients, who can best assess whether the extra cost is worth it. With the major aspects of medical care covered by the UCP, the differential costs borne by patients largely reflect differences in practice style, not in their health.

This fundamental shift in focus obviates many of the troublesome details in conventional health plan proposals. It matters not whether physicians choose to bill for telephone calls and e-mail messages or for forty-five-minute office visits. Some patients may prefer physicians who provide a lot of "face time," while others may prefer those who are quick to order the latest test. Rather than rely on contentious and interest-group-dominated national panels to decide exactly which approach is better, patients will make their own choices. PIs will price out the implications; external assessments (see Chapter 5) will demonstrate whether there are differences in quality. An important aspect of this incentive-based strategy is that it permits nearly all the data to be available with suitable safeguards (see Chapter 5) and allows various assessments by many independent analysts to shed light on performance. In essence, SecureChoice is modeled on the openness of the Web, using this as part of its self-correcting mechanism.

Focusing on Patterns

SecureChoice relies on patterns and averages rather than on adjudication of individual bills. Not only is this much simpler administratively, but also it explicitly recognizes the inherent uncertainties in medical care diagnosis, coding, and treatment. Errors, even those that may push an episode into a category paid for by the UCP, can be easily tolerated as long as they are infrequent and random. If they become common, they will be detected by means of statistical screens. Audits can then determine whether the "errors" were indeed innocent or reflect a pattern of fraud.

With the UCP providing monthly payments for chronic conditions, it might appear that there will be strong incentives for providers and PIs to identify every chronic condition possible. Not all chronic conditions, however, are equally costly to manage, and costs vary with severity *within* a condition, such as diabetes, depression, or HIV infection.[26] The extra CIM payment for the mild categories of some chronic conditions will be nominal but will nonetheless trigger computer searches for the tests and interventions needed to manage such conditions to keep them from progressing. Without such evidence, the initial code for a chronic condition will appear to be an error, or the physician will appear to be undertreating the problem. Clinicians with what seems to be unusually effective management of cases, that is, who order fewer than the usual number of tests and assessments, will be invited to share their expertise—either informing their colleagues of new and better ways to manage care or exposing themselves to audit.

Payment determinations are most problematic in "boundary" issues, such as between minor acute as opposed to chronic illness management or between ambulatory and inpatient care. The distinction is often associated not just with the simple change of a code but with frequently expensive tests to arrive at the appropriate diagnosis. Making PCPs indirectly responsible for the costs incurred by their patients creates financial incentives to underuse expensive imaging and other tests, potentially harming patients. Given the small number of patients seen by the typical PCP, the health consequences of such underuse are unlikely to be statistically detectable at the physician level. National data will help identify the appropriate trade-off between higher test rates (which result in few missed cases but many "false positives," putting people at risk for potentially harmful follow-up procedures) and overly conservative testing in which nearly everyone identified needs care, but many are identified too late.[27] These figures will inform the "expected number of tests" associated with superior quality. The UCP will reimburse the PI for tests associated with what ultimately is identified as a true chronic illness or MA/I episode. Just as the UCP may mandate or subsidize certain preventive services, it will incorporate the expected cost of *true negatives* in the age-sex amounts for each enrollee.[28] The clinicians responsible for the test centers—imaging, laboratory, or otherwise—

see thousands of tests over the course of a year from many PCPs. With appropriate communication from the PCP as to what indications the patient had before the test and whether the test results were later confirmed, they can offer valuable input for future practice as to whether the particular test is indicated for a similar patient. The radiologist or pathologist can be paid as a consultant to help determine whether a test should be done in the first place.

Similar arrangements will develop along the boundary between ambulatory management of an episode and admission for major interventions. Patients are often admitted to the hospital for assessment of a problem. On the one hand, these "rule-out" admissions allow patients to be monitored appropriately in a setting in which they may suddenly need to be treated. On the other hand, hospitals are inherently dangerous places, and unnecessary admissions should be avoided. Unlike in the situation we have currently, PCPs and those specialists managing a patient's chronic illness care would not directly admit and care for patients in a hospital; instead they would coordinate the admission with the CDT responsible for the case. The EDRG payments from the UCP can be set to pay differentially as appropriate for "real cases" and "rule-outs," reflecting the typical costs for each type of case. Since the EDRGs may still provide an incentive for too many admissions, the UCP can provide feedback, and perhaps eventually financial rewards, to CDTs that move toward an optimal mix of the two, accounting for the population-based rates of the illness. As indicated in Chapter 3, if PIs notice that their PCPs have lower-than-average admission rates but superior outcomes for their patients once admitted, they will begin to negotiate with the UCP for a transfer of funds to offset the better outpatient care they are arguably receiving.

Increasing Variability in Practice Organization

Most of this discussion has focused on the modal form of care delivery, the solo or very small group of practitioners in a single specialty. This, however, is just one point along a continuum. At one extreme are the current prepaid group practices and other HMOs that accept an annual premium and full risk for all the care their enrollees may require. As seen in numerous studies, some of these organizations provide high-quality care at comparable or lower cost than FFS, partly because they align the incentives and organizational systems appropriately.[29] Whether integrated delivery systems or independent practices linked by information will be superior overall may become clear over time, but it is more likely that the two approaches will continue to coexist, each with advantages and disadvantages, and each learning from the other.

Setting appropriate overall capitation amounts for integrated HMOs has been problematic because of the need to adjust for differences in risk across enrollees. The UCP could just pay such plans for the major acute/interventional episodes and chronic illness management costs as it pays other providers, and the HMOs could price their net premium taking that into account. This, however, undercompensates HMOs that are more effective than FFS in avoiding acute exacerbations or in preventing chronic illness—two innovative areas that *should* be encouraged. The selection issues that bedevil current voucher schemes are less problematic when patients can change into or out of an HMO only by changing physicians. The UCP could also require that as a condition of accepting full capitation, health plans will have to agree to more sophisticated risk adjustment to offset potential gains (or losses) due to selection.

At the other extreme of the continuum are innovations such as limited primary care provider settings located in retail stores such as WalMart. Often staffed by nurse practitioners (NPs) and focusing on a limited range of services, these settings have been opposed by some physician groups as potentially providing poor-quality care. Although physicians' fear of competition is probably at the root of such claims, it is plausible that further fragmentation of care may cause problems in coordination. Alternatively, more convenient and timely access may improve care, especially if medical records are shared and referrals improved. This argues that flexibility, rather than further restrictions in licensing, is appropriate, and that the emphasis should be on overall quality and cost.

One problematic area with respect to the organization of care is in the realm of state licensure of professionals and their scope of practice. Some states limit what certain groups of professionals can do—usually with the rationale of protecting the health of the public, but often with little evidence and with the effect of protecting the economic power of certain professional groups. Nurse practitioners are a case in point. Twenty-five states and the District of Columbia allow NPs to practice without physician supervision; in seventeen jurisdictions they can write prescriptions (including for controlled substances) without any physician involvement.[30] Conversely, other states limit what NPs can do. SecureChoice is envisioned as the result of federal legislation and would not infringe on constitutionally protected state powers. The ready availability of data on costs and outcomes, however, would allow a better-informed debate on the state level about the wisdom of such state restrictions on practice arrangements.

Organizing Care to Meet Patient Demand

SecureChoice guarantees coverage for the care that is most expensive and difficult to insure, but many other health reform proposals offer this. Uniquely, SecureChoice incorporates fundamental changes in the ways providers are paid in order to allow them more flexibility in how they organize and deliver care while encouraging greater efficiency and value in the care they provide. Building on the DRG model developed by Medicare, the EDRGs paid for by the universal coverage pool give care delivery teams flexibility and incentives to be internally efficient. Entities offering CDTs reinsurance to reduce their production risk will identify and share the processes that result in better, more efficient care. If a CDT wants to charge more than what the UCP calculates is needed by other CDTs to provide superior care, it is free to do so, as long as patients are willing to pay the differential.

Ambulatory care is currently far less structured around organizations than is inpatient care, so SecureChoice builds on the existing FFS system, but with provider-based premiums to create incentives for more efficient, quality-responsive care. The payment intermediaries help primary care providers assess practice styles and fees, sharing information from those who have developed best practices. Statistical monitoring, rather than expensive reviews of each claim, can capture the rare occasions of fraudulent behavior. FFS is likely to be just the starting point for some clinicians who may find they prefer certain types of bundled payment or alternative organizational forms.

This is a radical proposal designed to alter markedly the way care is delivered. In the context of rapid scientific and technological change, it uses a market approach—structured in a productive way—to offer efficient responses to widely varying patient preferences. Getting the incentives right is one necessity; getting the information is the other.

— 5 —

Choices:
Harnessing Data to Inform Decisions

This chapter concentrates on a key aspect of how SecureChoice works to change practice and improve value: by collecting data, converting it to information, and using it to inform decision making. Contrary to the movie *Field of Dreams,* we cannot assume that "if you build it, they will come" with respect to health information technology. Most people these days suffer from information overload. Our challenge is to structure the health system so that (1) people demand information to help them make decisions, (2) information can be delivered to the right people at the right time to inform decisions, and (3) the combination of better information and incentives leads to continuous improvement. In essence the motto needs to be, "If they demand it, you will build it—and then they will come."

Turning Data into Information

Paradoxically, the practice of medicine is simultaneously overwhelmed by data and starved for information. Measurements are taken, codes applied, forms filled out, and transactions processed, but much of the data implicit in these processes is used just once—or sometimes not at all. In part this is because paper transactions and records still predominate; it is also because electronic transactions often use inconsistent codes or fail to be linkable across systems. The administrative simplifications of SecureChoice will deal with both of these problems. All data transfers among organizations will be electronic, using unique patient and provider identifiers that allow data to be linked in multiple ways. As will be discussed later in this chapter, the data flow will enhance the confidentiality of patient information while facilitating transparency and data analysis.

To convert data into information, one needs not only (1) access to the data but also (2) a conceptual framework to organize the data and (3) decision makers who request information. Linked medical data organized by hair color and astrological sign would not be much more informative than the current claims files sequenced by insurer and billing date. A more useful organizing principle is to cluster claims and other data into episodes of care, which are characterized by the specific reason for the episode, the patient, and the principal provider.[1] If the people providing the data do not care how it is used, the underlying data and organization will degrade over time in reliability and value. If, however, people use the data to inform decisions, they will press for continued improvements in coding and enhancements to organization and analysis.

Information derived in this manner will be used at various levels and by various players. Although clinically relevant information available at the time of care can be enormously valuable, it will be years, if not decades, before electronic health records are implemented for everyone. Electronic billing is a much more feasible near-term goal and facilitates SecureChoice's use of a universal coverage pool (UCP) for inpatient care and payment intermediaries (PIs) for ambulatory care. Such administrative data, sometimes with clinically relevant measures routinely collected in the care of patients, will be placed in secure relational databases after having been stripped of sensitive patient identifiers. The initial use of these data will be for payment and premiums. (See Figure 5.1.) Patients will use premium and other information in choosing their primary care providers (PCPs) and in deciding among various treatment options during an episode of care. Specialists, care delivery teams (CDTs), and PCPs

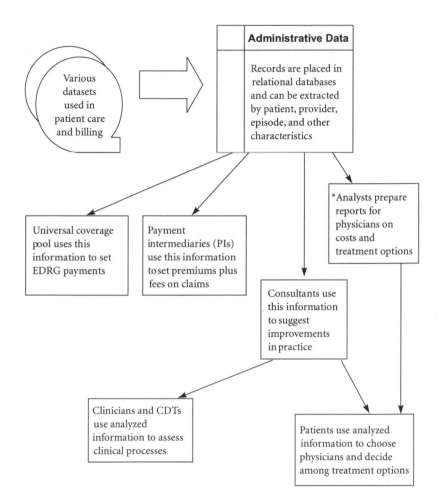

*Analysts have access to these raw data without identifiers to report on costs, quality, and other questions. Many of these reports will be placed in the public domain. Even if privately commissioned, the underlying methods need to be transparent and made public as a condition of being granted access to the data.

Figure 5.1 From Data to Information to User

will seek new information derived from analyses of these data to help improve their care processes.

People will make better-informed choices, first as consumers choosing where they will get their medical care, and then as patients deciding which treatments they prefer. Although one could argue that both types of decisions should involve quality and cost measures, this is true only at the most general level. SecureChoice is structured so that economic choices are primarily moved to the time when people choose among PCPs and the practice styles with which they are associated. Quality and cost issues may be important considerations in selecting a PCP, but these are likely to be based on rather general and sometimes hypothetical needs. When people are ill and have to choose among different treatment options, SecureChoice places the economic factors in the background; these are implicit in the practices of the clinicians already chosen. Quality measures, especially in conjunction with individual values and preferences, however, may be very important in choosing a particular course of treatment. The final sections of the chapter discuss how the database will be built and managed, and how data will be converted to information.

Informing Consumer Choices

For decades, health reform proposals have argued for greater consumer choice and competition in health care. Alain Enthoven and others encourage choices among competing health plans offered through a sponsor, such as an employer or Medicare.[2] In these proposals, sponsors play the role of a well-informed "super-consumer" to decide which benefits to include in the package and, ideally, to "risk-adjust" payments to plans so the premiums reflect differences in efficiency rather than enrollee health status. Others, such as researchers at the conservative Heritage Foundation, argue for individual responsibility for coverage and plan choice, eliminating the role of the sponsor.[3]

With SecureChoice, the universal pool bears all the important insurance risk (that is, for all major acute and chronic care), and enrollment in this part of the plan is mandated or provided through taxes. (Chapter 6 discusses these financing options.) Before people become patients—that is, before they face choices about specific medical care interventions—they may be termed consumers, and they have two major decisions to make: (1) how financially involved they want to be in the costs of their care not covered by the pool (for instance, minor acute episodes), and (2) what type of practice style they would prefer their physicians to have. The two decisions are intertwined; practice style will impact cost, and coverage can affect practice style. In part because people are accustomed to thinking about "coverage" questions in the abstract, it is easier to begin there.

With employer-sponsored health plans, or proposals that offer consumers choices among plans, the plans package together specific benefits and often preselected networks of providers. Standardized coverage packages reduce the problems associated with adverse and favorable selection (see Chapter 3), and consumers typically have a limited number of plans to choose from in any locality. SecureChoice allows far more choice in the coverage options and provider networks for ambulatory care.

Choosing a Coverage Option for Minor Acute Care

There is ample evidence that deductibles, co-payments, and coinsurance affect the use of medical care.[4] The UCP pays directly for major acute and interventional episodes and offsets the costs of chronic illness with monthly CIM transfers to the payment intermediaries. For minor acute episodes, many people will prefer to have some type of coverage to smooth out the random expenses, not all of which are trivial in cost. Some people with sufficient resources will choose no coverage for minor acute care, preferring to make such medical decisions while assessing their economic implications. Others, perhaps with similar resources but preferring not to make economic decisions when ill (even with a minor acute problem), will opt for complete coverage although this implies higher overall cost. After suffering a bad ankle sprain while playing soccer, a young stockbroker may feel comfortable deciding whether to follow her physician's recommendation to have a CT scan at an out-of-pocket cost of $700 (possibly bargaining down the price with the imaging center in the process).[5] Her professor brother in a similar situation may be glad he chose to pay a higher monthly premium and bear only the small per-visit co-payment in a plan covering the cost of an optional CT scan. His higher premium reflects not just the expected costs of the CT scan but also the fact that, with his costs nearly fully covered, he is less likely to forgo the scan and is unlikely to shop around for the lowest-priced imaging center. How would each—as consumers making choices among types of coverage—decide which coverage to choose?

Current health insurance options focus on differences in deductibles, coinsurance, and the maximum they will pay out of pocket for covered services. From an economic perspective, the maximum out-of-pocket (MOOP) figure is critical because it implicitly caps the risk borne by the patient. The figures quoted in current insurance policies, however, are highly misleading because they refer to the maximum out-of-pocket expenses required by the plan *for covered benefits,* that is, deductibles and co-payments. Services not covered by the plan or fees in excess of covered amounts are not included in what is protected by the MOOP. With SecureChoice the consumer will have more choices, better information, and fewer surprises.

The "fewer surprises" aspect is a fundamental feature of Secure-Choice: benefits depend on the nature of the health problem, not the services rendered. A patient will not suddenly find that a specific drug or treatment (except for those that are experimental) is not covered or that a physician's fees in excess of an undisclosed amount will not be paid by the plan and have become their responsibility. The implications of various coverage and provider choices are rolled into premiums that can be assessed calmly by people in their consumer roles. Uncertainty is still present, but is limited primarily to the types of medical problems a patient will face and how much care will be needed.

How will this new approach work? There are actually three decisions facing the consumer: (1) the general type of coverage he or she desires for ambulatory care, (2) the specific primary care provider to serve as a medical home, and (3) further adjustments to coverage based on the specific PCP and his or her PI. These decisions can be made sequentially, much as someone wanting a new vehicle first decides whether it will be an SUV, a family sedan, or a two-seater. Once the general category of vehicle is selected, the customer can research different brands to narrow the search down to manufacturers, and then go to dealers to try out different models. At the last step, the customer decides which options to include in the car.

Selecting the General Type of Coverage Package

Decisions about the general scope of coverage a consumer may desire can be assessed with Web-based tools allowing people to examine the implications of different choices. Consumers will enter their age, sex, and zip code as well as a list of their major chronic conditions.[6] The consumer could select, for example, the co-payment levels for office visits and prescriptions, and the maximum out-of-pocket expenses in a year. The Web site will then show the monthly premium and the chances that the out-of-pocket expenditures will be within certain ranges, such as less than $500, $500–$1,000, and so on. Customers could lower the maximum out-of-pocket exposure to whatever level they feel is acceptable and see the implications for premiums; alternatively they could see the savings if they were willing to accept more risk, such as a one in a hundred chance of having to spend over $2,000 during the year, but with a firm maximum of $3,000.[7] By altering the coverage parameters, the consumer can identify the coverage and premium combination that is best for him or her. For those less engaged in the process of "shopping" for coverage, the site would offer as a default the coverage option most frequently chosen by people in the same age-sex category.

These estimates would be derived from analyses of accumulated claims data of millions of enrollees who collectively have tried out an enormous range of combinations of coverage. Actuarial expertise and simulation models will fill any remaining gaps and provide reasonably good estimates of the implications of various coverage choices. The location information, however, simply scales the values to reflect roughly what coverage costs in the customer's locality. The results of this first-level search would be analogous to what the potential car customer considers in deciding between an SUV or a family sedan. The actual premiums will depend on coverage choices *and* the physician chosen.

Creating Informed Price Sensitivity

Today some insurers quote premiums with estimated out-of-pocket costs based on a typical person in a geographic area. These estimates, however, are independent of the physician and his or her practice style. Apart from minor differences in co-payments, the enrollee would pay the same for physicians varying twofold or more in the costs incurred in caring for their patients, even adjusted for illnesses. With the provider-based premiums of SecureChoice, the implicit practice styles and fees of the clinicians will be reflected in what the consumer pays. Most people currently select a clinician for their routine care and then, as health problems develop, ask for referrals. Patients occasionally use services or providers not recommended by their primary care provider; some patients seek most of their care outside the PCP's usual referral pool. The provider-based premium does not require formal provider networks, as do current preferred provider organizations (PPOs) or HMOs, but builds instead on observed patterns of patients and sets prices accordingly.

Choosing a Medical Home

The second stage in choosing coverage is for the consumer to select a primary care provider as his or her "medical home." The medical home is responsible for maintaining patients' medical records and contact information, with providers receiving small monthly payments from both the UCP and the patient. These payments assure (1) that the patient is still comfortable with the medical home, and (2) that the PCP keeps track of where the patient is located. The choice of medical home reflects a combined assessment of costs, practice style, and perceived quality. The measures of practice style and quality available for clinicians in a local area will be discussed later in this chapter. To facilitate comparisons across PCPs, the consumer would go to a Web site displaying PCPs in his or her local area.[8] Using information on the coverage option chosen at the first stage, the site would show the annual premium for such coverage associated with each PCP, along with a wide variety of quality measures. The data for these comparisons would come from the PIs, who would be required to price the premiums and offer such standard "benchmark" coverage packages.[9] These benchmark premiums would be drawn from the Web sites of each PI, but would then be arranged by third parties and presented in conjunction with quality measures. In many ways this is similar to being able to go to a Web site such as CNET that allows one to examine a class of products and select some for specific comparison, then provides links to both the manufacturer for more details and to vendors for purchase.

Customizing the Coverage Package

PCPs will have selected the payment intermediary that will handle the claims of their patients, and some PIs may have developed innovative coverage and payment options. Once the consumer has selected a PCP, a link to the PI facilitates the third step: further customization of the coverage package. For example, a PI may experiment with an option that pays clinicians for telephone and e-mail consultations while allowing patients to avoid the nominal co-payment on the first five communications per year. An obstetrician, for example, may work closely with a midwife or Lamaze coach and bundle those services into the "standard" prenatal package, using a nonstandard charge code. In conjunction with a number of its PCPs, a PI may offer a coverage package that includes cash rewards for important behavior changes, such as beginning and continuing in exercise programs, or quitting smoking and staying off cigarettes. The consumer can examine such options and see whether they seem worth trying.

The premiums quoted for various coverage options at this stage largely reflect the PI's experience with the claims history of patients who choose each particular PCP as their medical home. This claims experience includes the services not just of the PCP but of all the providers used by those patients. The costs rolled into the premiums net out the monthly CIM payments from the UCP. The PI will know, however, whether patients of that PCP incur greater or lesser expenses than the payouts the UCP offers based on PCPs providing superior-quality care. To offer more precise premium estimates—which will also help patients choose among PCPs—the consumer can grant the prospective PI permission to access information from the UCP as to the precise coding of the chronic illnesses for which it is paying.[10] The PI has no reason to prefer or avoid patients with any of various illnesses because it largely passes on the expected costs to the patient. Where the PI does take on some risk is in averaging out the random fluctuations in costs; this will be priced according to the PCP's other patients' own experience and actuarial analysis of large volumes of data. The PI is required to break out in its quotes what proportions of its premiums are paid out to providers as opposed to claims processing and profits. Although the PI is chosen by the PCP, making this information transparent will help keep these costs low.

Patient intermediaries will have strong incentives to develop creative solutions for their clients—the clinicians serving as the medical homes. Many now see e-mail and telephone communication with patients as cutting into their fee-for-service revenue. Patients, by contrast, may value such modes of communication because they promote quick answers to simple problems without the cost (and bother) of an office visit. Innovative PIs will develop ways for clinicians to charge for such communications. Likewise, appropriate payment may revive house calls, which provide convenience for patients and an opportunity for clinicians to assess how the home environment is affecting the patient's health.[11] The PIs, in turn, will spread these ideas to other clinicians who may find them valuable.

There are opportunities for patients to "game" any system. Suppose quoted premiums are low because most patients of a particular PCP get care from a narrow range of providers with conservative practice styles. Since patients do not require approvals (in other words, the PCP does not have to function as gatekeeper), an opportunistic patient may choose a medical home with low premiums and then behave unlike most of the other patients, seeking care from clinically aggressive, high-cost specialists. The resulting pattern of claims cannot easily be distinguished from that of a patient with significant (but subtle) medical problems genuinely needing care by such providers. As long as such opportunistic behavior is uncommon, it will not have much impact on the overall premium for the medical home. If there are many patients "gaming" the system, however, the premiums quoted by the PI will rise, and the PCP may ask why that is the case. With some focused analysis of the claims patterns, the PI will be able to report that a small segment of the PCP's patients seem to be routinely going to more expensive practitioners. The PCP may request that the PI design and offer two coverage options, one resembling a PPO network based on the conservative providers usually used (or used with formal referrals) and the other without constraints.[12] Premiums for the second plan would rise relative to the first. Gaming can never be eliminated, but the system can be designed to be self-correcting.

PIs and independent consultants will also offer analytic tools so clinicians can understand why their premiums are higher than those of other physicians who provide care of apparently comparable quality. For example, Dr. Jones may be surprised to learn from his PI that 35 percent of his patients seen for an ankle sprain have imaging tests, compared with 15 percent for comparable patients of other physicians, with no evidence of any difference in repeat visits for the problem. Likewise he may learn that many of his colleagues first try a course of a generic antibiotic before prescribing the latest drug. The PI may even identify for him the types of cases for which the new brand-name drug *is* preferentially used as a first-line treatment by his colleagues. Information of this type currently exists in the medical literature, and occasionally enters some of the hundreds of clinical guidelines, but is often lost in the deluge of new research. Dr. Jones can choose to change his practice style on the basis of such information (or not). Either way, his patients' premiums will reflect whatever practice style he actively or passively adopts. What is new under SecureChoice is the ability of physicians to see their own practice compared with that of colleagues who are providing high-quality care at lower cost. Because patients will directly bear the implications of such decisions, and some may have discussions with their PCPs about costs and quality, there will be a demand for information about what works and how much it costs.

Measuring and Reporting Quality

Costs (or premiums) are easy to measure, but quality reporting is far more complicated. For the same medical condition there may be multiple measures of quality, and these measures may be differentially important to various physicians and patients. Furthermore, the small number of cases seen by most physicians limits the statistical reliability of reports. A single measure of quality for a public "scorecard" is an impossible goal, especially if it needs to be approved by a widely diverse set of interest groups. There is no reason in an era of Web-based information, however, why we should have to decide on a single measure or even a limited number of measurements, but we must be clear about the different purposes for which quality measures may be used.

Quality measures are central to SecureChoice. Payments from the UCP are based on the resources used by providers achieving superior outcomes for their patients. When choosing clinicians and care delivery teams, patients may want to know about the quality of care they provide. Patients may also want to know about the implications of various treatment options in order to decide what course of care is best. Clinicians will want information on how to achieve better outcomes more efficiently. Each of these uses involves quality in different ways, sometimes relying on markedly different types of measures. In some instances there may be a single scale on which quality is measured; in other instances there may be many dimensions, and reasonable people may disagree on the relative importance of those dimensions.

Quality Measures for Determining Payment by the UCP

Quality measures are commonly distinguished by whether they refer to outcomes or processes. Patients tend to be most interested in outcomes of care such as mortality or return to usual activities, which are relatively easy for a layperson to understand. Clinicians, however, know that even well-cared-for patients occasionally have bad outcomes, often because of other underlying problems (comorbidities) that are out of the control of the clinicians involved. Clinicians prefer process measures that assess whether the appropriate things were done in given situations, for example, whether a patient discharged after a heart attack was prescribed the appropriate medications. When well-specified, process measures hold the clinician accountable only for things under his or her control. Moreover, a low score on a process measure directly points the clinician to what should be improved. Finding out that one's patients have a high rate of poor outcomes—even after all the possible comorbidities or risk factors are taken into account—still gives the clinician no clue about how to improve.[13]

Quality and payment are directly linked in UCP decisions, so it will be critical that the UCP use transparent and agreed-upon measures. SecureChoice rests on a public commitment that the UCP will provide the resources needed for superior care. Therefore the measures of superior care should be those that make sense to the public—and typically these will be outcome measures. Some outcomes are objective and easily measured, such as survival rates thirty days after a heart attack. Not all medical care, however, is provided in situations in which death is a common outcome. Knee replacements are intended to improve function, and death after such a procedure should be very rare, so its quality measures might be based on functional status, such as the ability to walk two blocks without pain.

An important early task for the UCP will be to convene "risk model panels" composed of clinicians, patients, and researchers to agree on relevant and meaningful outcome measures for the EDRGs used to pay CDTs and for the major chronic conditions represented in CIM payments. For EDRGs, the goal of the panels is to identify one outcome for each episode group that (1) best characterizes what patients feel is a reasonable indicator of quality, and (2) is sufficiently proximate to the inpatient or similar episode so that it largely reflects the care provided by the CDT. Clinicians and researchers will need to determine exactly how to measure such outcomes. They will also need to identify potential risk factors not under the control of the CDTs that may explain the observed outcomes. Researchers and experts in administrative processes will need to determine how to collect the data in a comprehensive and timely manner. This task is complicated but not impossible. The UCP will fund the staff work and analysis needed to develop the models. New York, Pennsylvania, and California have been measuring and reporting outcomes, in some cases for well over a decade.[14]

There is far less experience with outcomes measurement for

chronic illness management, but both patient-reported and clinically measured indicators should be considered. Patient reports of functional status are obvious candidates for some conditions, such as arthritis, and have been in use for years for research purposes. Indices may be needed for some conditions that have acute exacerbations as well as chronic limitations, such as congestive heart failure and asthma. Certain conditions, such as hypertension, are "silent" but have well-defined indicators such as blood pressure.

The challenge with a focus on outcomes is achieving appropriate risk adjustment so that clinicians do not try to avoid the most difficult cases in order to "look good." Several features of how outcomes will be used in SecureChoice reduce this concern. The most important is that the UCP will use these outcome scores simply to identify the CDTs and clinicians who achieve superior quality in order to measure their resource use. As superior care would be that in the top half of the outcome distribution, it does not matter whether a CDT or clinician is in the top or fifth decile. It also doesn't matter much for the resource use measures whether a few CDTs above and below the median might switch places. Precise risk adjustment may matter a good deal for fine determinations of scoring but not for this purpose.[15]

Initially, many EDRGs will not have available usable outcome measures or risk adjustment models. The risk model panels provide a mechanism for addressing this. One way to speed their agreement on measures will be to set the default payment levels at the resource requirements of the middle 60 percent of CDTs for the EDRG, omitting those in the top and bottom fifth of the *resource* distribution. This contrasts with the current approach by Medicare, which essentially bases DRG payments at the mean. Some clinicians and hospitals will argue that the highest quality occurs in settings using the most resources. They will press for and help develop usable and acceptable outcome measures, at which point the UCP will transition to the "above the median" approach.

Whereas the outcomes measures should be decided on early in the implementation of SecureChoice, the risk adjustment can get better year by year.[16] Providers often argue that even the best risk models do not account fully for subtle patient factors and point to anecdotal evidence that high-risk patients have been turned away by clinicians fearing they will look bad if a complication or death occurs. Even if true, this does not necessarily mean that the risk models were inadequate. Those clinicians may have recognized that the risk models implicitly assume all clinicians are of equal quality and the only factors that matter are patient based. It is more plausible that all physicians in a category such as cardiovascular surgeons can (or should) be able to provide high-quality care to uncomplicated cases, but only a select few are good enough to handle the most complicated cases. If so, the referrals elsewhere may simply mean that the risk models are working very well and keeping the high-risk cases from the less expert practitioners. It is also possible that the models really do omit some key risk factors. To address this concern, the risk model panels may allow each CDT to *prospectively* exclude up to a certain percentage of cases it believes are at higher risk than would be assessed by the risk models.[17]

The purpose to which the UCP-sponsored outcome measures are used may also increase their acceptability. If quality measures are used neither to exclude clinicians from practice nor to pillory them in the press for apparently poor quality, there is far less reason to waste energy attempting to find the perfect measure.[18] The problem of poorly designed "report cards" is already with us. The increased transparency in data described later in this chapter will not preclude various assessments from occurring. It is likely, however, that with ever more privately sponsored measures becoming available, people will either ignore them all or develop more effective ways of identifying those that are trustworthy.[19] Reports on quality prepared by the UCP, moreover, should focus on identifying those CDTs whose outcomes are statistically reliably *better* than expected. Most studies of the effects of public reporting show that few patients take note of the findings and even fewer use them to change their sources of care.

Public reporting does, however, seem to tap into the professional ethic and change overall practice as physicians and organizations learn what they can do better. Even more valuable is specific information on how they can improve.

Quality Measures for Clinician-Based Improvement

Suppose clinicians who have developed a practice style with which they are comfortable are presented with evidence that other clinicians handle similar cases equally well using fewer resources. In some instances this information will be based on reports from the UCP about how the clinician's risk-adjusted outcome scores compare with those of other (unidentified) clinicians. In other cases it may be in response to the clinician's PI explaining why the premiums it is quoting for that clinician's patients are higher than those it quotes for other clinicians in the same area. The likely reaction in either situation is that the quality of care provided by other clinicians is somehow worse. PIs will be pressured to show with "hard data" that this is not the case. Initially statistics are likely to be drawn from the readily available claims data, such as whether the patients of the physicians using lower levels of resources have more subsequent visits, suggesting that the problem was unresolved. If that does not indicate lesser quality, the next response is to argue that more resource-intensive management avoids the rare but serious complication, and that many of the low-resource physicians were just lucky because they had fewer cases. The PI can aggregate findings across all physicians to test this hypothesis. Risk models may also be challenged, and the PI may respond with an offer to collect additional clinical information and recalibrate the models.

These steps recapitulate what good researchers have already done for a very limited number of measures; the technical expertise to do more of this work is available. What is currently missing is (1) the demand for these assessments from practicing clinicians, and (2) readily available data. As discussed later on, multiple groups focusing on selected problems but working from shared databases can do numerous assessments in parallel. In the long run, statistically valid data should be publicly disclosed to ensure that findings are taken seriously by clinicians. It is preferred, however, that those doing the assessments first supply confidential practice comparison reports to providers, allow them time to challenge data and analytic methods, and give them the opportunity to improve their practices before provider-specific results are made public. The media and consumers will become attuned to the fact that random events will result in even high-quality providers' occasionally having an unusual number of poor outcomes; only consistent patterns are truly problematic.

Some clinicians will tentatively accept that they may have poor outcomes warranting improvement. Many more will feel that they have average (or better) outcomes but admit that they may be overusing resources. Both groups will probably begin by asking their PIs to provide data on how the processes in their practices differ from those with similar patient outcomes but using fewer overall resources. These questions are essentially process measures analogous to current guidelines, but they need not be "blessed" by formal committees relying on tightly controlled trial evidence. Instead they will reflect what appears to work best in actual practice.[20]

Yet another step holds even more promise. On behalf of their physicians and their patients, PIs or independent quality assessment and improvement experts will ask the physicians apparently exhibiting low cost and high quality to allow research teams to observe their practices to see precisely what works so well. In many cases the identified physicians will not even think of themselves as doing anything special. Being selected is both an honor and a way for physicians to help push forward medical care, so refusals will likely be rare. Those who refuse to share their superior processes may confront skeptics wondering whether these providers are hiding something.[21]

Some clinicians may respond too aggressively to the practice style data, potentially cutting into the margin of safety. As the vast majority of the measures will be based on routinely collected data, such overshooting will quickly become apparent. The pressure for continuous assessments of quality will come from the practitioners, not the PIs or the government. The initial working assumption of SecureChoice is that clinicians are primarily interested in functioning as professionals in the care of their patients and that the new payment methodologies are designed to facilitate rather than hinder such behavior. Ensuring better information and transparency will allow the vast majority of well-meaning clinicians to do so; it will also catch the occasional "bad apple."

Some assessments will show that the best outcomes are achieved only with more resources. New medical technologies move into practice at varying rates, with some clinicians being early adopters and others lagging behind. The continuing assessments will quickly pick up the early adopters as having more expensive practice styles, but they may also achieve demonstrably better quality. If so, this will provide strong evidence in favor of rapid adoption of that innovation. Many new technologies yield higher quality for some patients, albeit at higher cost. The challenge is in deciding when those technologies should be applied and when they need not be used, which is where these feedback systems will be most useful.

Quality Measures Informing the Choice of Providers

Detailed process indicators can be helpful not only to clinicians in improving the quality of the care they provide but also in helping them make referrals for specialized services.[22] When people are choosing a primary care practitioner as a new medical home, however, they are likely to be more interested in summary measures of provider quality. The challenge here arises from the fact that people differ in what they think are the most important aspects of quality. SecureChoice recognizes such differences and is designed to maximize the ability of people to choose the providers who best meet their preferences. The opportunity and weight given patient preferences is probably greatest in the choice of PCPs and least in the selection of a specialist physician or CDT for a major acute problem when delay may be life-threatening. A PCP who understands the patient's preferences can serve as a suitable proxy in making such referral decisions.

When considering patient preferences with respect to the choice of practitioner rather than for specific treatments (the latter situation is discussed in the next section), we need to take into account a variety of quality dimensions. Some may relate to "objective" indicators, such as outcome measures or adherence to process guidelines associated with high quality. Others may relate to geographic or language accessibility of the practitioner and interpersonal style. The problem with the first set of measures is that there will be many specific indicators—for example, one for each major EDRG grouping for CDTs—and the person is unlikely to know in advance which EDRG group will be most relevant to his or her care in the future. Independent Web sites would allow people to produce customized assessments of this broad set of quality scores by applying their own weights. There may be default weights across conditions reflecting the age- and sex-specific likelihood that the person will need such care: single men are unlikely to be concerned about scores for maternity care. Some people may have particular concerns about certain types of care or conditions, and Web sites are sure to develop that will make it easy to focus on those areas. Once the indicators have been selected, there are many ways to weight the scores. Some people may give the most weight to measures that assess how well providers do in life-threatening cases. Others may want to be assured that none of the specialists score significantly below average in quality, and then seek out the PCPs within that set who refer to clinicians with the best communication skills.[23]

The SecureChoice approach guarantees access to a wide range of such measures; there is no single entity that determines which of these measures is best for any one person—or even that people need to use such assessments at all. The various condition-specific or specialist/CDT–specific outcome and process measures could be ig-nored, or used in a general way to help in the choice of one's PCP, or in discussions with that PCP about the providers to be used for the care of specific problems. This is similar to the ways one might re-view the many different magazines regarding choices of cars before actually going out for a test drive; the recommendations of *Consumer Reports* may differ from those of *Road and Track*.

Once patients decide how they would assess the providers to whom they may be referred, patients will typically focus on choosing a PCP to serve as their medical home. There will certainly be objec-tive measures for primary care; many already exist and are being im-plemented for both acute and chronic conditions. Beyond indicators such as the timely screening and monitoring of diabetes, routinely collected measures will track how well test results were used to alter care or how effectively the diabetes was controlled. Patient assess-ments of the processes of care will also be important, ranging from reports on the median time to first available appointment or office waiting time to ratings of how well providers communicate infor-mation. The health insurer WellPoint recently announced a partner-ship with Zagat to survey a million WellPoint members on their assessments of trust, communication, availability, and office environ-ment.[24] Other firms may present clinicians with a set of case scenar-ios that could be handled in a number of ways—from aggressive test-ing to watchful waiting. Their written responses to that survey will help potential patients understand the differences in how they ap-proach clinical care.

It is likely that just a small minority of patients will use such tools to make their decisions. Many will use the time-honored albeit im-precise method of simply asking one's neighbors. Most patients, moreover, do not change physicians unless they must. This is charac-teristic of most markets. Nevertheless, even if a relatively small frac-tion of consumers changed in response to appropriate quality and price incentives, that would have a substantial impact on producer behavior.

Quality and Choice of Treatment

There is constant tension in medicine between treatment decisions reflecting "averages" based on scientific evidence and each patient's uniqueness. Even when there are published studies, few experiences exactly parallel the clinical trajectories described in the research. Researchers understand the importance of variability across individuals and design studies to provide the best possible tests of their interventions. The statistical methods used are typically focused on averages, however, rather than the distribution of results. Most people are not very adept at understanding even simple probabilities or averages; to help them make informed decisions, much more data and more sophisticated decision support tools are needed.

What patients require is information about the implications of each of the viable clinical alternatives facing them. Such data go far beyond simple measures such as the life expectancy under each option, but may extend to the fraction of people with short-, medium-, and long-term survival. Patients will want to know how it feels to be treated in each of the options, preferably in the words of others who have experienced the treatments. Irrevocable choices between treatment strategies A and B are markedly different from situations in which treatment A can be followed, if necessary, by B. Moreover, unless patients are being offered care in settings and circumstances exactly like those of the research studies on which the findings are based, they need to know how similar patients have fared in the provider settings actually being considered.

Decision support tools are critical to realizing the potential of such information. Even well-trained researchers find it difficult to organize, summarize, and assess information. When people under emotional strain are facing complex treatment choices that directly affect their survival or quality of life, rational thinking may not be possible. The tools for such situations are not yet available for a broad range of problems, but they are being developed.[25] New methods, ranging from better graphic presentations of statistical data to video game scenarios, are likely to be developed to help patients understand the implications of certain choices.

Additionally, a specific patient's values and preferences may differ from those of the "average person" and from those of "society" in general.[26] Colonoscopy may be more effective than sigmoidoscopy as a screening measure in detecting potential colon cancer. Both require the same preparation, but colonoscopy requires the use of anesthesia and carries a somewhat higher risk of immediate complications. Even when a clinician offers a clear recommendation for colonoscopy, a patient who fears anesthesia may opt for sigmoidoscopy. Some patients believing that the onset of cancer is preordained and unpreventable may reject both procedures.

The problems of how to inform and engage patients better in their own care are present in the current system. Innovations in SecureChoice will help by making it easier for patients to select clinicians who support, rather than are uncomfortable with, high degrees of patient involvement. When people choose a PCP, those wanting more direct involvement will be looking for information on how clinicians react to such engagement; clinician responses to hypothetical scenarios will offer much insight in this regard. Patient assessments are likely to reflect how good the match is rather than whether involvement is necessarily better or worse. Such engagement will likely facilitate a wide range of innovations for decision support. Because SecureChoice changes how data are collected, organized, shared, and used, the information base for decision making will be markedly enhanced.

Building and Managing the Database

There has been robust discussion about the promise of electronic health records (EHRs) for improved patient care. Organizations such as Kaiser Permanente have spent billions on such systems, and there is evidence that it can be used to great advantage. The transition cost, however, is substantial, and debates over the "best" system will not be settled soon. As a payment and reporting system, SecureChoice does not require a national EHR, thereby making it far easier to implement. SecureChoice, however, will increase the value that can be added by improved decision making in patient care, thereby enhancing the business case for EHR adoption.

An effective EHR system must be able to access a patient's complete medical record instantaneously. As soon as a worrisome new lab result becomes available, the responsible physician should be alerted to the findings. EHR systems, moreover, must include identifiable and often sensitive patient information. The data needed to implement the quality and cost measures described here do not require a full-blown EHR system and can be based instead on "static" data, downloaded periodically from "live" systems. The data must be linkable across patients and providers, but coded identifiers can be substituted for real names, allowing far more security than in a universally available, live EHR system.

A well-functioning information system requires more than just hardware and software; without apparent value to the providers and the people who enter the data, such tools will go unused, or people will "just go through the motions" without ensuring that the data are meaningful. Two approaches to making the information system worthwhile are (1) piggybacking the early quality measures onto claims for payment, and (2) adding clinical measures to help clinicians manage the care of their patients. Many of the initial quality measures can be developed from information that is already present in established claims administration systems. Some clinicians and researchers have criticized outcome studies that use hospital and other administrative data. When enhanced with a small number of easily accessed variables, however, the resulting risk models have been found to be nearly as accurate as those based on far more extensive (and expensive) databases.[27] Some supplemental data, such as blood pressure and pulse rate, should be routinely collected at each visit. Other data may need to be added only for patients with certain conditions (for example, blood sugar levels for diabetics). In many instances laboratory results are already transmitted electronically to the physician's office. Capturing and transmitting these data, not necessarily on a real-time basis, is within the reach of even most paper-based practices. The quality of coding and entry is always a concern, but as Medicare discovered when it implemented DRG payment for hospitals, coding improved once it made a difference in payment and quality assessment.

Routine quality measures are most meaningful for problems seen frequently, such as chronic illnesses. Part of providing a medical home for people with these problems is maintaining an electronic registry and record of their care. Monthly CIM payments from the UCP will offset the costs of these systems.[28] Registry data can be used to alert clinicians if a patient with diabetes has not come in for a routine blood test or eye exam. By linking data across providers, the PI can let a PCP know that the patient actually had an eye exam elsewhere.[29] As the data become routinely available, practitioners will adapt their workflow to incorporate the information in their day-to-day care. Questions from engaged patients will add to the usefulness of the data during the clinical encounter.

Owning, Analyzing, and Disseminating Information

If the technology needed to do this quality measurement is readily available, one might reasonably ask why it has not been integrated with our current system. Lack of incentives and the presence of proprietary interests are the major explanations. Although clinicians have an interest in improving their quality of care and in making better-informed referrals, they have little information to help them do so. Health plans are pressured to improve quality, but as currently organized the market does not reward quality-enhancing expenditures. Suppose an insurer such as Blue Cross developed effective guidelines and training programs for clinicians to identify high-quality specialists for referrals. It would be both unfeasible and unethical to require physicians to use this information solely for their Blue Cross patients; thus Blue Cross would have invested substantial sums to improve quality with many of the benefits reaped by its competitors.[30] Each carrier has similar incentives, so there will be no change unless an external force, such as a business coalition, requires collective action.[31]

Even if the "will" is present, the data are not, in spite of the enormous amount of data collected by the American health care system. This apparent contradiction arises from how data are "owned" and used. Physical medical records are owned by the provider storing them. The personal data *within* the records, however, belong to the patient and, if identifiable, generally cannot be used without the patient's authorization. Medical and other information may be transferred among organizations as part of the delivery of, or payment for, services without express permission from the patient. De-identified data, however, can be shared and used for other purposes, such as research, without patient authorization.[32]

To be used to inform decisions, data must be organized and presented in sufficient detail and in a manner that reflects the choices to be addressed by decision makers. Generic statements such as "Hospital A has higher quality than Hospital B" are not very useful. One wants to know whether outcomes for patients with condition X are better in Hospital A, and the clinicians at Hospital B will want to know what accounted for those differences. Once one focuses on patients with particular problems, the number of cases shrinks markedly. As discussed earlier, patients tend to be interested in outcomes, but fair and statistically reliable assessments of outcomes require good measures of risk factors across many patients. Most research has focused on inpatient care, at least in part because hospitals are well organized to collect and code diagnostic information. Yet hospitals rarely keep track of how well their patients fare after discharge, although researchers often link death certificate information to assess postdischarge survival. Except for patients with terminal conditions, death should be a rare event, so a great many patients are needed if differences in outcomes are to be reliably assessed; to extract useful information, one needs as much data as can be collected.

Claims and billing data can help in this regard. Although few patients die after a discretionary procedure, many more may require unusual amounts of postdischarge care, and some may continue to need care because the surgery did not resolve the problem. Such postdischarge patterns of use can be detected in claims data. Although medical data are "owned" by the patient, billing records and claims information are owned by the payers. Claims data can be valuable because they bring together in a single place data from potentially millions of patients and hundreds of thousands of providers. Unfortunately, even the largest such dataset, that of Medicare, accounts for only a fraction of the patients seen by any physician; each of the private insurers has a far smaller share. Because individual physicians see fewer patients by orders of magnitude than do hospitals, it is critical for the development of physician-specific outcome and cost measures that all potential data be analyzed. Although SecureChoice assumes that each practitioner has only one PI, it provides mechanisms whereby data across all PIs are shared. Some insurers currently fear that if their claims files were available to competitors, they might identify pricing and other business practices that could place the insurer at a disadvantage. With SecureChoice combining data from all PIs, however, that problem will be eliminated.

SecureChoice will entail relatively minor changes in laws and regulations regarding data ownership and use. Identifiable patient information will still belong to the patient, but de-identified medical information would belong to the public—not the PIs—and would be releasable (as now) after review by a privacy oversight board. Similar rules would apply to claims and other administrative data; but before release, information on fees paid by the PIs would be removed, along with the identity of the PI. This reduces the ability of providers to collude in fee setting or the opportunity for competing PIs to "steal" one another's innovations in networks and incentives.[33] Researchers will be able to access data through a single review and approval process, but they would be directly subject to penalties for purposeful release of sensitive information, and their organizations would be held accountable for creating secure information systems.[34]

Linking Data and Enhancing Security

Each person will receive from the UCP a unique health identification number (HIN) for use only in medical records and billing. This will happen when people initially enroll in SecureChoice, either directly or through a participating employment-based health plan. People who have not yet enrolled despite the individual mandate to do so will be assigned this HIN when they first seek care. The HIN replaces one's Social Security number (SSN) as a health care identifier; since the SSN is currently used for various financial and other transactions, using a different number enhances the confidence patients have that their medical information will not be misappropriated by hackers and identity thieves.

The securely managed datasets derived from SecureChoice records should be freely available to researchers pursuing any legitimate project, but with an important proviso. Because the underlying data files are seen as belonging to the public, researchers who develop marketable analytic tools (such as risk adjustment models or computer programs that better assess variations in treatment trajectories) should be required to make them available under a nonexclusive license.[35]

Collecting data quickly, inexpensively, and securely will continue to be a challenge, but the integrated payment system should help. The premiums the PI quotes for the PCP's patients are based on the costs of all the ambulatory care provided to those patients. The PCP therefore has a strong interest in ensuring the ability of PIs to provide timely and accurate information on the use of services, even (1) those that occur within a deductible, or (2) those that are not covered, such as over-the-counter medications. The former are important because they may predict use later in the year; information on the latter will help guide practice patterns and quality of care information, such as alerting clinicians to drug interactions or allergies.

PIs will probably give each of their enrollees a health care card (HCC) that functions like a credit card for payment purposes. Patients would receive a discount of 5 to 10 percent for all health-related purchases on the HCC not eligible for coverage. For those purchases covered through the PI, the share due from the patient for co-payments and the like is transferred to the patient's usual credit card through the Funds Clearing House described in Chapter 4.[36] The HCC allows a far simpler, paperless transaction system for payment. All providers will know that they need only the HCC in order to bill for care. In our current system, possession of a health insurer's card does not mean that the person is still covered, and even when it does, the insurer needs to check the exact extent of coverage before authorizing payment. Providers currently may have to input a wide variety of information that may differ for each insurer, and then still not be assured of payment.

SecureChoice allows providers to deal with a single PI as their entry point for payment. Their PI will provide the secure systems for electronically transmitting the billing information associated with the patient's visit. Immediate checks on transmission will verify the plausibility of diagnosis and procedure codes and input the fees determined by the provider. Errors identified at that point can be corrected immediately. The information is then transmitted to an automated clearing house (ACH), which forwards it to the PI issuing the patient's HCC, charging that PI for the visit. The ACH simply serves as a convenient way for the PIs to communicate with one another and net out transactions. Its functions are modeled after similar functions for clearing checks. The provider's PI receives payment via the ACH and then credits his or her bank account.

Figure 5.2 reflects the situation in which a patient, Sandra Smith, who has chosen Dr. Alice Able as her PCP, elects to see Dr. Barry Baker for some care. Sandra provides her HCC, which includes her health identification number. Dr. Baker's office electronically connects to his PI, OrangeCo, and transmits information about what treatment Sandra received for which diagnoses. Before Sandra leaves the office, OrangeCo checks the data for consistency. It can append Dr. Baker's usual fees and transmit the information to the ACH that night. The ACH looks up Sandra's current PI—the one used by Dr.

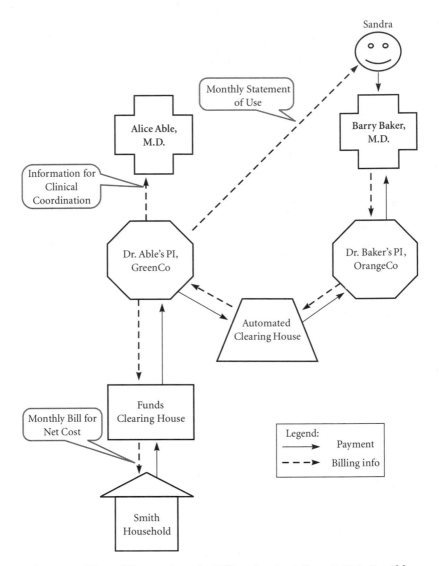

Figure 5.2 Flow of Transactions for Billing: Sandra, Whose PCP Is Dr. Able, Has a Visit to Dr. Baker

Able, GreenCo—and transmits the information along with a request for payment. Millions of such transactions occur each night involving dozens or more PIs. The ACH calculates the net amounts due each and transfers money among their accounts. The next morning Dr. Baker has a deposit in his bank account from OrangeCo for Sandra's visit. GreenCo processes Sandra's information and calculates what co-payments she owes, including 95 percent of the costs of uncovered services such as over-the-counter drugs she may have bought at the pharmacy. Sandra has given permission for GreenCo to share information with her PCP about any services she receives from other providers. Though far from a complete electronic health record, this billing information will help Dr. Able manage Sandra's care. The total of those costs, along with Sandra's monthly premium, is transmitted to the Funds Clearing House shortly after the end of the month. The FCH takes account of other sources of payment, such as employer-based contributions and subsidies, and charges the remainder to the credit card for the party taking responsibility for the Smith household.

The ACH simply serves as a convenient way for the PIs to communicate with one another and net out transactions. The transactional relationship between the PIs and the FCH, however, is more important. Both of the PIs in this example need to know Sandra's diagnoses and procedures in order to handle the transactions, and they can do this through her HIN; they do not even need to have her real name and address attached to the transaction information. When GreenCo submits its monthly statements to Sandra regarding her care, it could even do so via Dr. Able, who knows Sandra's address. GreenCo submits its billing information to the FCH by way of an account linked to the party responsible for Sandra's payments—an account number that may receive charges from one or more PIs on behalf of one or more patients. The FCH receives only financial information from the PIs and needs only a Social Security or tax identification number in order to request income-based subsidies.

Using the Data to Inform Decisions

Data collected through this process will serve multiple purposes, some of which replace existing single-purpose data collection efforts and others of which are entirely new. Just as the development of the Web spawned previously unimagined applications of newly available information, the existence of comprehensive files for research and analysis will generate novel applications that cannot be specified at present.

The immediate uses of the data will be for payment, coordination of clinical care, and premium setting. Standard billing practices of clinicians in fee-for-service will require few modifications—largely the use of the HIN as a unique patient identifier. Most bills are already submitted electronically and require diagnosis and service or procedure codes. Laboratory and imaging studies are often transmitted electronically to the physicians ordering the tests. Some "low-tech" measures, such as height, weight, and blood pressure, are not routinely coded electronically, but these can be easily added without the need for a full-scale electronic health record (EHR). Clinicians will be able to keep track of such information in simple databases that can be housed on desktop computers, and PIs will facilitate some low-level computerization and linkage. As EHRs become more common, applications using their data will proliferate, and versions will be developed with adequate functionality for smaller-scale applications. The first partial applications will probably be registry-based modules to track key clinical measures for patients with selected chronic conditions such as asthma, diabetes, and congestive heart failure. With on-line access, patients may securely add their own assessments as to how they are functioning, and indications of worsening status may be used to alert the clinician managing the patient's care.

This information system will offer significant additional "public good" benefits beyond the simplification of billing. It will greatly enhance post-release surveillance to capture problems associated with new drugs and devices that cannot be assessed during preapproval clinical trials.[37] (This surveillance need not be limited to early adoption of *new* drugs and devices, but could be used for the assessment of those that have been on the market for years or decades.) The existence of unexpected differences in outcomes or side effects does not imply a causal relationship; various research methodologies, however, can explore this question of causality. These "monitoring functions" will be undertaken by the FDA, researchers, and others with the skills to do so; the consolidation of data makes it feasible for this to happen.

The system will also directly inform payment. Payments from the UCP will cover the cost of resources used by those providers with better-than-average outcomes within each EDRG category. Even though CDTs may use various forms of internal incentives and sharing arrangements among their clinicians and facilities, a claims-like billing system will continue to capture procedures and diagnoses. Some facilities currently have detailed accounting systems to estimate and manage resource use. Others will add similar capabilities to manage their costs effectively. The largest component of inpatient costs is wages and benefits; exploration of various types of staffing patterns is to be expected and encouraged. The pool will adjust the labor components of its payments to CDTs on the basis of local wage costs.[38]

A "Smart" Payment System

Health reform proposals developed by economists typically rely on prices and incentives—tools that work reasonably well in the rest of the economy. Market-based solutions have equity problems, but assuring that all people can be covered can minimize these problems. The Achilles' heel of such proposals is that the efficiency claims for prices and incentives rely on the ability of consumers to assess the quality of the products and services they purchase and to bear the costs of those decisions. As described in Chapter 3, the inherent risk in the need for medical care requires insurance, but the uncertainty as to the specifically appropriate care required for a given patient means that providers will not bear the production risk. Chapter 4 showed how the UCP will address the risk of occurrence and how provider-based premiums can bring appropriately scaled incentives to clinicians and patients.

Reorganizing the flow of data and converting it into useful information is what allows these incentives to work and makes Secure-Choice a "smart" payment system. The "smartness" arises not because new pipelines are built to transmit data or because new software is developed to replace paper medical records, but because clinicians and patients will demand better information; the underlying infrastructure will then allow those demands to be met. By offering to pay whatever is needed for care of superior—rather than just average, or any—quality, the UCP creates incentives for clinicians to press for the development and use of risk-adjusted outcome measures. They will also ask various sources for help in identifying those processes that yield better outcomes with fewer resources. SecureChoice offers enrollees enormous flexibility in their coverage and choice of providers. Many people will be happy with what they currently have, but some will demand better information to choose among coverage options and providers. As in most markets, improvements in price and quality will be driven not by having all consumers acting at once, but by relatively small numbers making changes at the margin. SecureChoice will provide the information needed to facilitate such behavior. It will also support better-informed choices by patients among clinical options, and will help clinicians assess and improve their own practices. All of this can be accomplished with a far simpler and more efficient set of administrative processes that also enhance the security and privacy of patient information.

— 6 —

Financing SecureChoice

As health reform has risen on the political agenda, people have focused on the costs of various proposals. Most estimates are projected over five or sometimes ten years, in keeping with congressional guidelines for "scoring" legislation. It is important to have a common set of rules for assessing proposals, but short horizons work against fundamental changes designed to yield long-term savings. Estimates typically assume that present trends will continue, except when the proposals highlight their own changes. Some claim offsetting expenditures with savings from illness prevention, even though many analysts see prevention as improving health but not necessarily lowering costs. In short, the "bottom line" estimates are limited in scope and not very helpful in evaluating major changes to the health care system.

Even if the methods for assessing proposals are biased, some ballpark estimates are nonetheless needed in order to join the discussion, and this chapter begins with one. In an environment in which tax increases are seen by some as political suicide, the discussion starts with whether SecureChoice must be tax based or whether it can be built on the existing system of tax incentives for employers; I argue that either financing method can be used. This leads to a discussion of how to achieve equity if one relies on mandates rather than taxes. A further argument is made that it is better to explicitly have two levels of coverage—Gold and Platinum—while dealing directly with equity concerns.

Estimating Overall Cost

With a few exceptions, the net effect of the incentives incorporated within SecureChoice are cost-reducing, or at worst cost neutral. This is true despite substantial reductions in coinsurance and deductibles for patients. As discussed in Chapter 3, most medical costs are incurred during expensive inpatient care and complex chronic illness management, when patient-focused financial incentives have little impact. Given reasonable estimates of deductibles, coinsurance, and maximum out-of-pocket limits, about a quarter of all expenditures for people under age sixty-five occur when patients' cumulative costs have exceeded this maximum and then bear no incremental financial cost.[1] As pointed out in Chapter 3, almost another three-fifths of expenditures are incurred when patients are responsible for only twenty cents of every additional dollar. Patients have little financial stake in the treatment costs implied by these decisions, but for most providers, additional services mean additional revenues, and there is no reward for reducing overall cost. SecureChoice changes this balance, focusing on incentives for clinicians and thereby encouraging them to be more discerning in their use of resources—both directly and indirectly.

SecureChoice eschews fee constraints, a popular but ineffective means of controlling costs. Under the usual "scoring" approaches, eliminating fee constraints will appear to fuel medical expenditure inflation. The opposite, however, is likely to occur under Secure-Choice because of its provider-based premiums. Clinicians who simply raise their fees without otherwise altering their practice patterns will discover—along with their patients—that the annual premiums quoted for their care will rise dollar for dollar. Patient resistance to such increases may be more effective than what appears to clinicians to be arbitrary fee constraints, particularly because fees are only a small component of cost increases. Currently, if fees are constrained, clinicians can increase their income by performing more tests, procedures, and other services that also generate additional costs above the net profit to the clinician. With SecureChoice, clinicians can increase their income with less patient resistance if they increase their fees for time spent with the patient and offset this by ordering fewer tests and being more discriminating in their choice of medications.

SecureChoice rejects the usual approach to coverage based on service and sequence during the year, focusing instead on coverage for different types of medical needs—with a mandated UCP for major acute, interventional, and chronic illness management and a portion of preventive care. Coverage for other services will be voluntary and will use varying mixes of "insurance" and out-of-pocket payments. Although this entirely different structure makes it difficult to estimate overall costs, a "back of the envelope" calculation is informative: we can ask whether current insurance payments would be sufficient to cover fully the costs included in the UCP.

There are two ways to estimate this for the commercially insured population. Data from the Medical Expenditure Panel Survey (MEPS) for 2003 indicate that out-of-pocket costs, including the costs for medical care not included in the benefit package, was 35 percent for people aged eighteen to sixty-four and 30.5 percent for those under the age of eighteen.[2] The data referred to in Chapter 3 show that minor acute care episodes (the care not covered by the UCP) account for 34 percent of all costs—roughly the same amount.[3] A second way to approximate cost is to examine what would have been the patient's responsibility under a typical conventional plan with a $500 deductible, 20 percent coinsurance, and a $2,500 maximum out-of-pocket charge for the year. Applying this coverage structure to all the claims in this population indicates that patients would be responsible for approximately 28 percent of all costs (excluding dental, long-term care, and prescription drugs), again in the same ballpark. Thus, at least for a commercially insured population, providing total coverage for all hospitalizations, major interventions, and chronic illness (and even many preventive services) would cost roughly as much as current coverage does now. That is, if all insurer payments were redirected to the areas of major cost (and prevention) and no insurance payments were directed to minor acute care, the amount borne by the patient would be no more than it is now, and probably less. The actual costs borne by patients under SecureChoice are likely to be lower because insurance would focus on only 39 percent of the episodes—markedly reducing the administrative costs associated with processing many small bills. In practice, the medium-term savings are likely to be far greater because of the simplification in enrollment, premium collection, and claims processing with universal coverage and provider-based premiums.

These data are based on the costs for insured people, so one may argue it is not surprising that one could reallocate how their coverage is distributed. The question in the current political debates is how to pay for the uninsured, but this is largely a red herring. Few people in the United States are denied hospitalization or emergency department care because of lack of coverage. They are treated either in safety net facilities supported by tax funds or by other providers, with their charges largely written off as bad debt.[4] Either way, "somewhere in the system" funds are found to pay the physicians and other staff who provide many of the services needed by the uninsured. The primary problem of care for the uninsured is not a lack of resources but the way those resources are funded and organized.[5] The current patchwork approach covers the most expensive types of care for the poor. Because they often do not have coverage—or sufficient coverage for ambulatory care—they often do not receive effective early intervention and treatment for their chronic illnesses, thereby increasing overall cost.

These rough estimates suggest that a comprehensively redesigned system is likely to be no more—and probably less—expensive than our current one. The savings implied by the increased focus on value will be even greater over time. If we accept for the moment that overall costs in the near term are likely to be similar (or less) than what we as a nation spend now, the next questions people typically raise are what the relative roles of government versus the private sector should be, and whether achieving universal coverage requires a tax-financed system. Most people see the two questions as equivalent, but in fact the issues are separable.

A totally tax-based system can achieve universal coverage by instituting a unitary single-payer system or by giving everyone a voucher to enroll in a privately managed plan. Alternatively, legislation could mandate that everyone purchase coverage (as with car insurance), and people could choose their own plans or buy into a government-run option. The limitation of the mandate approach is that the cost of coverage may be out of reach for many people, but this can be addressed with various types of subsidies or special programs. Choosing the "best" financing approach is primarily a policy and political choice, not a technical one. If we were designing a system from scratch, equitable and simple tax-based financing would probably be best. Given the political challenges of raising taxes sufficiently and the complications of making the transition from our current employer-based system, SecureChoice is designed to work either way.

Arguments for Tax-Based Financing

There are two major reasons for tax-based financing of medical care. One is equity: many people see health care as a fundamental right. A just society would not let people who cannot afford to buy insurance suffer or die. Nor should high co-payments be a barrier to care for the poor. Our current imperfect approach to financing seems to arise from attempts to address this concern. Medicaid provides coverage for segments of the very poor; other safety net programs (for instance, Federally Qualified Community Health Centers, other community clinics, public hospitals) provide fragmented care for the poor who do not qualify for Medicaid because of eligibility requirements, whether based on income, family structure, or citizenship.

Medicaid's functioning, however, exposes several key flaws in policies targeted to the problems of the poor. The program has stringent eligibility criteria and avoids any pretense that its fees and rules should be such that providers will be as happy to care for Medicaid patients as they are for "private" ones. Medicaid's roots are in a welfare program model—offering services for those deemed to be the deserving poor—rather than the social solidarity model common in western Europe. The solidarity model envisions a program that is the same for all people, building on a shared identity. Medicare approximates such a model, offering what is essentially universal coverage for the elderly through a largely publicly funded system linked to payroll taxes. Although Medicare has significant gaps that are filled for most people by either Medicaid or employer-sponsored (or sometimes privately purchased) supplements, it maintains the symbolic value of a unitary, uniform program.

The second argument for an entirely tax-based system is simplicity or efficiency. The typical way this argument runs, however, confounds (1) the administrative costs of the highly inefficient claims payment and adjudication system we have at present with (2) the additional costs of marketing, underwriting, and enrollment by private insurers. Medicare still has to process claims (it contracts with conventional insurers to do so), but it does not have to deal with the second category of costs associated with marketing. Although tax collection is not free, it is certainly less costly than collecting and processing monthly premiums.[6]

SecureChoice's universal coverage pool eliminates underwriting; its provider-based premiums with payment intermediaries in the background eliminate marketing costs. If the political stars could align long enough to allow sufficient taxes to finance everything, surely lesser sums could be found to provide income-based subsidies for part of the population. The question is whether it would be worth the incremental political cost to go to a fully tax-based system. SecureChoice involves a fundamental change in the way providers are paid and incentives operate. Replacing the current employment-based model would eliminate $209 billion in tax deductions and raise nominal taxes by an additional $380 billion.[7] Changes of this magnitude would focus attention on the redistributive effects of whatever tax changes are contemplated and not on the more substantive changes necessary in payment and delivery.[8]

Even if the politics of a tax increase were not an issue, the way our system works suggests that a tax-based system might not be optimal. Legal and political factors require that a publicly financed system be uniform. Centralized decision making for payment and coverage has certain advantages in reducing duplication of effort, but it makes it far easier for interest groups to concentrate their efforts on getting what they want. Political influence reflects more than just health providers' economic interests. Expending federal funds for abortion has been forbidden since 1976.[9] Congressional efforts to intervene in the Terri Schiavo case suggest that a centralized program may allow passionate but narrow majorities to impose their will on the care actually delivered.[10]

These issues are less salient in many western European systems. Our congressional system offers more points of leverage for interest groups to exercise power through individual members of Congress than does a parliamentary system. Parliamentary systems also tend to have stronger and more insulated civil service–based government agencies able to hire and retain highly skilled people. On the other side, since the War for Independence many Americans have seen being free of government restrictions as an important value—sometimes trumping whether government is the only way to achieve certain significant benefits.

A Mixed System of Financing

The problems of insurability and "free-ridership" discussed in Chapter 3 mean that coverage for major acute/interventional episodes and chronic illness management cannot be voluntary. Universality can be assured if the government either provides coverage directly or mandates that each person prove he or she has such coverage. The following discussion focuses on the latter path, with (1) the (political) constraint that the federal government does not outlaw the sponsorship of private coverage by employers, (2) the goal that all, or nearly all, payments rapidly move to the simplified system described in Chapter 5, and (3) the recognition that many employers do not currently offer comprehensive, or any, coverage.

The Universal Coverage Pool

To recap, the new universal coverage pool would be established to offer (directly or indirectly) coverage for major acute/interventional and chronic illness care. The UCP should be a semi-independent agency, much like the Federal Reserve, with a broad charter and insulated from the political micromanagement to which the Centers for Medicare and Medicaid Services are subject. The UCP will be charged with directly covering or reinsuring the costs of all medically necessary care in the major acute and interventional, chronic illness management, and preventive categories.[11] Under a tax-financed approach, the UCP would receive its funds from the federal government much as Medicare does today. In a mandated system, it balances its own budget by setting premiums for coverage and reinsurance to cover its payouts and nominal operating costs.

To minimize direct involvement in coverage decisions (and hence its sensitivity to political pressures), the UCP will be required to set payments per episode based on what it would cost in each local area to pay for the services needed to achieve nationally superior outcomes.[12] Providers will have broad discretion in the mix and number of services they use. This implies that the UCP is primarily involved in collecting and assessing data on patient outcomes, resource use, and input costs rather than deciding exactly what services will be paid for or at what rates. As described in Chapter 5, outcome measures are to be derived partly from administrative files supplemented by patients' assessments of their care according to standardized measures. Resource use and fee information comes from claims files. Local labor costs will be reported routinely by care delivery teams, or CDTs.

The UCP will cover nearly all the costs associated with major acute and chronic illness care. Some providers achieving the best outcomes may use various types of co-payments to engage patients appropriately in their care, and these revenues would be subtracted from what the UCP pays. Also excluded from UCP coverage would be two categories of services: highly discretionary interventions, such as cosmetic surgery, and experimental treatments, which will be paid from another financing stream, discussed later.

Using these data, the UCP offers various types of payment or reinsurance. If people enroll directly in the UCP through a payment intermediary, it will pay for all (or most) of their care.[13] Alternatively, people can continue with their employment-based coverage, and the UCP will stand ready to reinsure those plans. The expanded diagnosis-related group categories (EDRGs) used to pay CDTs are geographically adjusted amounts that reflect what care should cost. EDRG payments incorporate physician and other professional costs associated with the episode.[14] Unlike hourly workers of a given skill level, professionals may use greater skill and knowledge to achieve excellent outcomes in fewer hours or with fewer "redos." Even if the overall cost of the care they provide may be lower, these more highly skilled professionals *should* receive a higher hourly rate than similar professionals who are not as "expert." The UCP payment, moreover, is not a ceiling; a CDT may charge its patients more than what the UCP pays, and pay participating clinicians whatever it must to retain their services. If that CDT is in the top half of the quality distribution, its higher implicit resource use will be reflected in the calculation of what the UCP pays all CDTs the next year. Increases in labor and professional compensation costs reflecting geographic patterns directly adjust what the UCP pays CDTs in that area.

In contrast to the ways that Medicare constrains payments through its budgetary authority, this adjustment mechanism appears to lack cost control.[15] To some degree that is intentional. The mandate of the UCP is to ensure that the system provides high-quality care, letting market mechanisms determine how much people value that care rather than relying on congressionally set budget constraints. With prospectively fixed payments each year per EDRG, CDTs have incentives to economize on the resources they use, and ongoing quality assessments encourage them to improve quality continually. If new techniques, drugs, and equipment result in better outcomes, the annual adjustments by the UCP will reflect the costs of those innovations; internal incentives, however, will keep CDTs from overusing those services. Shortages of labor and professionals will be reflected in higher compensation rates covered automatically in the adjustments from the UCP. CDTs are not limited in what they can charge patients, but provider fee increases may meet resistance from two quarters: directly from patients and indirectly from the physicians serving as their medical homes (because such increases will be reflected in their patients' premiums).[16]

The UCP as Reinsurer of Conventional Plans under a Mandate System

Under the mandate option, the UCP collaborates with conventional insurers in two ways. First, it can pay for all inpatient and other major acute and interventional (MA/I) care *on an episode basis* on behalf of the insurer. A conventional plan such as Aetna may subcontract with the UCP to pay CDTs whenever an MA/I episode occurs among Aetna's enrollees. In this case Aetna carries the risk of occurrence and uses the UCP to provide incentives for the CDT to manage care effectively. The UCP covers its costs by pricing this MA/I payment reinsurance with a small markup over what it pays the CDTs. Bundled payments generate significant administrative cost savings over what insurers, hospitals, and physicians are incurring now, so it is unlikely that private payers will be able to beat the UCP's payment level.[17] The UCP will require that insurers desiring to contract in this way do so for a whole line of business in an area; it won't allow the insurer to keep the simple cases and pass on the complex ones. It is advantageous for the UCP to offer this simple reinsurance option because clinicians will change their behavior more quickly as a larger fraction of their patients are paid through a CDT.

In a second reinsurance option, the UCP offers to accept responsibility for *all* the chronic illness management (CIM) and (MA/I) care needed by persons covered by a conventional plan. Rather than simply offering the conventional insurance plan access to a bundled rate whenever an MA/I episode occurs, in this reinsurance model the UCP accepts the risk of occurrence for the categories of events accounting for over 60 percent of all medical costs for the non-elderly. As with the MA/I-only reinsurance, the UCP pays the CDTs on an EDRG basis. The UCP, however, will offer the bundled MA/I and CIM reinsurance only to insurers that function as payment intermediaries with physicians acting as medical homes and for whom provider-based premiums are calculated. The UCP will also require that the coverage offered by the insurers (that it is reinsuring) meet its minimum benefit package requirements for preventive services and for information sharing.[18]

The UCP offers its MA/I + CIM reinsurance package on an age-sex-location basis, requiring that plans seeking reinsurance buy it for all their enrollees in an area. This provision reduces the ability of insurers to dump high-cost contracts onto the UCP. Some insurers might find market niches (within those age-sex cells) in which they attract high-cost enrollees, "pass them off" to the UCP as average, and charge overall premiums just a bit above average. This is a risk the UCP will accept in order to build its market share, and while it may allow a few clever health plans to make excess profits in the short run, it is unlikely to be a long-term problem.

The MA/I + CIM reinsurance package offered by the UCP opens up the coverage market for many small employers who do not currently offer health benefits.[19] At present the premiums small employers are quoted reflect the occasional high costs of chronic or acute patients without the ability to average those costs over large numbers of employees. Moreover, because premiums for small employers are often underwritten—requiring health exams or other exclusions—significant marketing and administrative costs are added to the benefits actually paid. Those costs would disappear with the reinsurance offered by the UCP. More important, the same logic applies to individual enrollment. The UCP's ability to offer MA/I + CIM reinsurance to any PI will allow organizations functioning as PIs to accept all comers without having to worry about their underlying risk of needing expensive care. It will also make it difficult for health plans to make money on risk selection and then pass the risk on to the UCP.[20] In essence, the willingness of the UCP to offer MA/I + CIM reinsurance coverage to any PI at age-sex-location-specific rates means there is no longer a need for employers to sponsor specific plans.

Building on the Employment-Based System of Coverage

There would be no reason to tie coverage to employment if one were designing a health insurance system from scratch. Employment-based health insurance benefits, however, are deeply embedded in the U.S. labor market. Some employers use their "fringe benefits" to retain employees and have structured compensation packages that differ substantially from what they would offer if wages were the only focus. Unions have often emphasized such fringe benefits in their bargaining. Even if a tax-funded system were politically achievable, any plausible transition plan would have the UCP operating side by side with employer-based coverage. The challenge is to eliminate most of the problems of employment-based coverage quickly while gaining the advantages of both universal coverage and consistent incentives.

Although the current tax system offers significant subsidies to employer contributions for health insurance, many employers do not offer it, and some employees who are eligible for coverage do not enroll. The individual mandate embodied in SecureChoice requires that everyone have coverage for MA/I and CIM care. This mandate can be met by enrolling directly in the UCP via a PI, or indirectly through an employer-sponsored plan that offers equivalent coverage.

The provider-based coverage options described in Chapter 5 all include full coverage of MA/I and CIM costs, thereby eliminating most of the opportunities for selection strategies. By offering to reinsure the most expensive aspects of care and charge simple demographically based premiums, the UCP eliminates the selection spiral that bedevils small employer coverage. Tax subsidies for employer-based contributions will be available for all employers—large and small. More important, there is no requirement that employers "contribute" enough for employees to choose coverage voluntarily; the mandate guarantees enrollment, and the Funds Clearing House mechanism described in Chapter 5 allows workers to pool even small amounts of contributions across family members. Premiums, moreover, will be scaled to age, markedly reducing the incentives the young have for avoiding coverage.[21]

Uncoupling employer *contributions* from employer *sponsorship of specific plans* eliminates a major source of inefficiency. The ERISA legislation allowing each employer to design its own health benefits creates the administrative complexity that drives up costs and makes it difficult for clinicians to practice effectively. SecureChoice does not require repeal of ERISA; instead the mandate version expands the employer's tax exemption to all payments made by an employer either directly or at the behest of an employee to a PI for UCP-approved coverage. Most well-paid employees already have good employer-paid health insurance; many also avail themselves of salary reduction plans to get tax subsidies for out-of-pocket costs. Secure-Choice will expand these benefits to all workers; low-wage earners may not gain much in avoiding the income tax, but this change allows them to avoid the 15.3 percent combined payroll tax on such contributions.

Employers currently offering health insurance will have two

choices. First, they could maintain their current health plans as long as they meet the requirement to cover all major acute and chronic illnesses, thereby fulfilling the individual mandate for those who enroll. Such insurance plans and HMOs could continue to do business as they do now. Most conventional carriers are likely to convert over time to operating as payment intermediaries. Because conventional carriers have been unable to provide incentives for clinicians to practice efficiently, their only cost-containing tool is fee constraints, but providers will be unwilling to accept lower fees and more constraints when they have patients with PI-based coverage. Some HMOs will actively manage care and compete effectively with the PIs working with less organized sets of providers.

Alternatively, employers could convert their contributions for coverage into payments to PIs on behalf of employees and dependents. To avoid selection problems, the UCP will not offer its reinsurance if enrollees can go back and forth between an employer-sponsored plan and contributions for coverage through a PI. Once they are in SecureChoice for more than ninety days, they cannot move back into the employer's plan. Employers typically contribute a fixed amount per eligible worker in a class (for example, hourly employees opting for single coverage) irrespective of demographic factors, so the net premium for an employee reflects the costs of everyone in his or her group. The twenty-two-year-old may decline coverage claiming he would enroll if the premium were scaled to his age. To turn this around, if his employer offers contributions for coverage through PIs, the twenty-two-year-old cannot claim the average contribution. Instead, employers would convert their total contributions into age-sex-location-adjusted amounts, paralleling what the PIs will be charging.[22] This offers the employee a contribution roughly actuarially proportional to what coverage would cost from a PI. In many instances employer contributions may be enough to offset the cost of covering not just MA/I, CIM, and preventive care but also part or all of the expense of minor acute care. Some employers with rich benefit packages may expand their menu of options, allowing the employee to divert part of the tax-privileged contribution into additional retirement savings or long-term care insurance.[23]

If SecureChoice is implemented with an individual mandate building on employer-based contributions, several adjustments can be anticipated for various categories of people currently without employer-based coverage. These include (1) those working for employers offering plans but do not enroll, (2) those working for employers *not* offering coverage, or not offering coverage for people in their employment status, and (3) the self-employed.

Large employers typically offer coverage, but as the employee's share of the premium increases, some decline coverage. The employer "saves" the contribution it would have made, but the average cost of the plan *per enrollee* typically increases. Workers in such settings will push either for their age-sex-location-based "share" of the contribution via transfers to a PI or for a comparable benefit that they can use in other ways.[24] Small employers are particularly vulnerable to selective enrollment, and insurers typically do not offer coverage unless most workers enroll. Given the underwriting and marketing costs associated with small employer coverage, most small employers currently offering plans will likely eliminate those plans and make the contributions to individual coverage through PIs, probably increasing the effective coverage for the enrollees.

In the second category are people working for employers without health plans or without coverage for certain groups. For example, some employers offer no benefits for those who work less than 50 percent time. Others engage workers as independent contractors rather than as employees and pay no benefits. Labor market theory suggests that occupations and job categories not eligible for health insurance will have some increase in compensation to offset that loss, but in practice many of these people have both low wages and no benefits. These workers, along with the truly self-employed—the third category—currently have to obtain coverage in the "individual enrollee" market with even greater underwriting and marketing costs than the small employer market.

If we rely on an individual mandate, SecureChoice will minimally intrude on this wide range of employment arrangements. Employers could scale benefits to total effort—offering 20 percent of the usual contribution for a 20 percent–time employee. The UCP will allow employers that do not cover certain classes of workers to make contributions on their behalf for individual PI coverage while keeping their other workers in employer-sponsored plans. The Funds Clearing House allows individuals to pool contributions from various sources while expanding the tax subsidy currently available only to those in employer-sponsored plans.

Creating a Seamless System: Incorporating Medicare and Medicaid

Ideally, SecureChoice will eventually include everyone, subsuming both Medicare and Medicaid. Many of the current health reform proposals leave those programs in place, focusing instead on people without coverage. Chapter 9 addresses implementation issues, suggesting that Medicare may actually "lead" in this regard. Forcing Medicare beneficiaries into a markedly new program, however, is politically fraught. Medicare is often described as the "third rail" of politics, destroying anyone who attempts to touch it. The elderly are politically powerful, vulnerable to medical care costs, and often averse to any change that may involve uncertainty. This does not mean, however, that a SecureChoice Medicare option may not be advantageous to both the elderly and the Congress.

Medicare enrolls nearly all the population aged sixty-five and over, but this coverage is far from complete. It requires substantial copayments and deductibles, and some services are not covered. The vast majority of enrollees have supplemental coverage to fill these gaps, which is costly to them and even more costly to the Medicare program.[25] The budget caps imposed by Congress and the executive branch to deal with mounting costs have largely been achieved by overall fee reductions. This makes Medicare participation unattractive to primary care physicians. Although Medicare involves many co-payments, it assures enrollees of "no surprises" by forbidding "balance billing" by providers who feel that Medicare rates are insufficient. SecureChoice, with its flexibility in fees, is likely to be more attractive to providers than Medicare.

From the perspective of Congress, Medicare is an enormous threat to budgetary flexibility, but there is at least the façade of budgetary control. On the one hand, shifting management of the program to SecureChoice, with *its* notion that payment levels should be based on whatever it takes to provide superior care and its willingness to allow providers to charge patients more than the UCP pays, threatens both the budget control and "no surprises" objectives. On the other hand, there is ample evidence over the long term that Medicare does not have the tools or incentive structure to slow the rate of growth in costs; fee constraints imposed to keep budgetary costs down, moreover, seem to be affecting beneficiary access.

The purchase of supplemental coverage by most beneficiaries, either directly or through their former employers, offers an opportunity for them to switch voluntarily into the UCP, just as the Medicare Advantage program currently offers people the choice of an HMO option or classic fee-for-service Medicare. Payment intermediaries would simply offer an analogous Medicare option. Medicare will transfer an age-sex-location-specific amount to the UCP for each enrollee who opts for SecureChoice.[26] It is not clear whether this would be enough to cover fully the MA/I and CIM costs; empirical work needs to be done to determine whether giving up the current low Medicare fees would be offset by more efficient practice styles offered through the PI plans. The PIs would then add residual costs into their plans for minor acute coverage and offer these as substitutes for the standard Medicare supplemental plans. An analogous option could be offered by employers supplementing their retirees' Medicare benefits.

It is likely that those beneficiaries with relatively conservative physicians will be able to get comprehensive coverage for substantially less than the existing Medicare supplemental premiums. Adverse selection could be problematic if people are able to move back and forth between Medicare and SecureChoice. It would be best if people were allowed to switch coverage only once while they lived in the same geographic area, although they might be permitted to switch back once within ninety days of trying SecureChoice. Switching among physicians and PI plans within SecureChoice, however, would be constrained to once a year. This choice option will require a substantial educational effort. In some ways it will be more complex than the implementation of Medicare Part D, but in other ways it will be simpler because SecureChoice will not be just for the elderly. The PI concept is markedly different from Medicare supplemental plans, but it has the similarity of being an add-on to a universal plan. Offering SecureChoice as an alternative to Medicare will threaten the perception that Medicare is a unitary program. This perception, however, is already challenged by Medicare Advantage; the SecureChoice strategy, moreover, substitutes true universality for age segment universality.

The situation for Medicaid and other programs for the poor is more complex. Unlike Medicare beneficiaries, people in these programs pay little or nothing for their care, so creating financial incentives to join is problematic. Providers, moreover, are often markedly underpaid by these programs and are geographically concentrated, so a switch to mainstream fees may be both expensive and logistically difficult. Because these are often seen as welfare-like programs, however, they have none of the "third rail" aura of Medicare. There may be more political opportunity for significant changes in Medicaid without offering options to individuals.

Most people picture Medicaid in terms of low-income women and children. This does reflect the majority of *people* covered by Medicaid but not the *distribution of expenditures:* 70 percent of Medicaid's medical expenditures are for the disabled and elderly.[27] A coordinated approach to delivering chronic illness care may yield substantial improvements in both cost and quality. The budgetary implications of rolling Medicaid into a unitary system are complicated. Most observers feel that Medicaid is the payer with the lowest fees—at least for ambulatory care. Medicaid hospital rates are also low, but these losses are offset partially by federal "disproportionate share adjustments" and for public safety net hospitals by direct subsidies from local government. Low ambulatory fees limit access to care (as many providers do not accept Medicaid) and result in the overuse of expensive emergency departments for minor illnesses. Delayed care also results in hospitalizations that could have been prevented had access been better. From an overall perspective, rolling Medicaid into SecureChoice will almost certainly improve quality; total costs may be either higher or lower. In the short run, however, there will very likely be a need for additional "on budget" funds.

Other broad-based programs for the poor, such as State Child Health Insurance Programs (SCHIP), should be brought into the system.[28] Most of the people covered under these programs use a relatively low level of services and are thus inexpensive to cover. These arguments do not necessarily apply to certain narrowly focused programs that provide services to people with serious mental illness and major disabilities, or to those who face language, geographic, and other (nonfinancial) barriers to access. For these populations, merely offering comprehensive coverage may not be enough; special outreach programs are needed. For the vast majority of people without health insurance, however, SecureChoice will work well, but the cost of the premiums and co-payments may be a barrier.

Achieving Equity While Using Patient Incentives

Individual differences in values and preferences argue against the inherent uniformity of a single-payer approach; using incentives to guide choices argues for some personal responsibility for premiums and co-payments. Dollar-based incentives, however, mean that the premium differentials and co-payments sufficient for a middle-income person to think twice about a decision may create barriers so high for the low-income person that care is jeopardized. It does not make sense to require a $20 co-payment for amoxicillin to treat strep throat if it leads a low-income mother to split the prescription between two children, thereby reducing its clinical effectiveness. Eliminating all co-payments for specific categories of people, however, will bring back the problems of Medicaid: hard-edged rules for eligibility and lower-than-reasonable fees for providers of their care.

The Funds Clearing House allows SecureChoice to address the equity problem in a different way. The FCH will establish accounts on behalf of each "responsible person"—the person identified as being financially responsible for patient or enrollee payments for *all* the members of a family. Employers contributing to health coverage send their payments to the FCH account designated by each employee. Multiple employers can pay into the same account. Likewise, the coverage costs associated with multiple individuals can be linked to that single account, much as several people can now share family insurance coverage. Each person in a "family" can choose a different medical home and coverage, yet all can be linked to the same responsible party. People in a real family need not all use the same responsible party; after a divorce one parent may still have responsibility for a child's coverage even though the child lives with the other parent.[29]

The FCH also provides an effective mechanism for achieving equity. The FCH passes on to a new Federal Health Equity Agency (FHEA) the tax identification numbers of all the people listed on the account, if the responsible party requests a subsidy.[30] By querying the Internal Revenue Service, the FHEA is able to determine if the incomes of the people on the account are low enough to be eligible for subsidy, and if so, the appropriate subsidy rate. Subsidies will be scaled to income, adjusted for the number of people covered in the account. Above a certain figure there is no subsidy, and below a certain amount co-payments would be so nominal as to be primarily of symbolic value. Even symbolic payments may be important, however, both as incentives to help influence appropriate care and as a way for all to feel that they are operating under the same system.

The Federal Health Equity Agency coordinates and provides the income-based subsidies to the Funds Clearing House. In contrast to the FCH, which may be a private firm operating under contract to the UCP, the FHEA will be a government agency with codes of confidentiality comparable to those of the Internal Revenue Service, from which it seeks limited information about subsidy eligibility. Funds for the agency would come partly from a redirection of existing federal outlays for Medicaid and other programs for the poor, as well as state and local contributions to such programs and to safety net providers. State generosity in funding such programs (as well as their share of Medicaid) varies, and states may supplement the federal funds flowing into the FHEA for their residents. This mechanism allows the magnitude of the subsidy to be adjusted, further addressing equity concerns. Analysis of de-identified linked data from the FHEA, FCH, and UCP allows independent assessments of whether federal subsidies are so low that people are not seeking care when appropriate.[31]

Although there are several entities involved, the overall system is much simpler than our current fragmentation. Instead of having complicated and demeaning eligibility determinations for various programs (like Medicaid), the FHEA makes electronic queries directly to the IRS. All fee and other payments are processed through the same clearing house and PIs as for people not receiving subsidies. Eliminating state and local program bureaucracies will free funds to subsidize care. More important, everyone is in the same system with scaled incentives that operate proportionately for all. Providers do not know whether their patients are covering their payments through the FCH with employer contributions, the family inheritance, or FHEA subsidies. Low-income people do not have to worry about suddenly becoming ineligible for all subsidies if their incomes rise a little, as subsidies are slowly reduced as income increases.[32]

Every system has flaws. IRS data lag substantially, so some people whose incomes increase may be inappropriately subsidized, and those who lose income may be in jeopardy. This could be addressed by projecting income on the basis of quarterly payroll tax submissions. Accounts can be trued up later, however, much as people's withholding payments may not exactly match their tax bill. As with the income tax, rule enforcement by occasional audit is far more cost-effective than case-by-case eligibility determination.

There is substantial flexibility in deciding who is eligible for subsidies and the subsidy rates. The FCH can provide the FHEA with the individual tax identification number (ITIN) or Social Security number of each person on the account. The IRS issues ITINs to individuals required to have a U.S. taxpayer identification number but who are not eligible to obtain a Social Security number. ITINs are issued regardless of immigration status because both resident and nonresident aliens may have U.S. tax return and payment responsibilities under the Internal Revenue Code.[33] This allows subsidies for coverage based on presence in the United States and some minimum levels of employment income, probably reducing the amount of "off-the-books" work by immigrants.

Even extensive equity-based subsidies will not eliminate the need for certain safety net providers. Some people, especially the homeless and those with serious mental illness, may not associate with a medical home or may find a health care card to be meaningless. Likewise, some populations with language and other problems may be best cared for by dedicated provider groups with extensive outreach services. Federally Qualified Community Health Centers, community clinics, and other such programs should continue to be funded. Substantial parts of their costs may be covered though the new system, but special grants and/or line-item budgets will be necessary.

A Single Plan versus Gold and Platinum Coverage

Heated debates rage over whether health coverage should be the same for all. In SecureChoice everyone is in the same financing system, and there is a universal pool for the most expensive aspects of medical care.[34] The various coverage options described in Chapters

3–5 offered through the payment intermediaries—the "choice" part of SecureChoice—essentially differ only with respect to co-payment amounts, but not as to which services are covered. The intent is to offer coverage for a broad range of services, leaving it up to the incentives in the system to encourage patients to think twice before asking for care, and to encourage physicians to order such services when appropriate and to decline to order them when they feel they are unnecessary. Two important limitations, however, are built into what is covered. Certain treatments seen as cosmetic and purely discretionary, such as Botox injections to remove wrinkles, are not routinely covered.[35] A second limitation has to do with access to new drugs, devices, and procedures that are still being assessed. Patients can have covered access to such innovations through the appropriate experimental protocols. The controversial question is: Should there be an accommodation for people who do not want to abide by even such limited restrictions?

Internationally the answer to this question varies widely. In Britain, long excoriated by conservatives in the United States for having "socialized medicine," patients can pay physicians "privately" for procedures done in National Health Service hospitals. In Canada, although all physicians are in private practice, they cannot accept private payments if they receive any payments from the public system.[36] The Canadian prohibitions would be politically unacceptable here, but even if they could be implemented, they are an unwise idea, creating hard edges where they are not necessary. SecureChoice coverage is designed to be very broad. It allows wide flexibility in how clinicians choose to use services and purposefully utilizes this variability to assess what works well and what does not. By eliminating sharp boundaries between the services to be included or excluded, it leaves fewer pressure points where special interests can leverage coverage decisions. Instead, innovations will be adopted (or not) as clinicians and patients find them valuable.

A useful analogy can be seen in how drug formularies are applied within an organization such as the Kaiser Permanente HMO. The formulary is developed by Kaiser physicians on the basis of reviews of the evidence concerning when certain drugs are most effective. Depending on one's specific coverage plan, patients have varying co-payments for drugs on the formulary. Kaiser physicians have complete discretion to prescribe FDA-approved drugs that are not on the formulary if they feel their patients require them—and the same co-payments apply. If a patient demands a drug not on the formulary and his or her physician feels that another one would be as beneficial, the patient can get a prescription for the drug but must pay the cost Kaiser incurs for it.

The coverage offered through the UCP is broad enough to be labeled Gold, but some people may want what might be termed Platinum coverage. That is, they may want a plan that pays for *any* service a clinician can legally offer. A drug may be approved by the FDA for use against one type of cancer, but some physicians may want to use it to treat other cancers. There is no legal restriction on their doing so, but many health plans will not cover such "off-label" use, often because there have been no trials of the safety and efficacy of the drug for that use. Platinum coverage can guarantee access to a drug still being evaluated for certain new indications without the patient's having to take a fifty-fifty chance in a trial that the unlabeled pill is the best available treatment in common use rather than the experimental one. In other situations the UCP payment for superior care may be less than what a CDT decides to charge; Platinum coverage will pay the full amount, leaving no balance for the patient. In essence, buying Platinum coverage is like paying for a first-class ticket on a regular jet plane. A first-class seat guarantees certain amenities and a slightly faster exit from the plane, but provides no greater assurance that the plane will not be delayed or baggage lost, or that the passenger will survive a crash. The two-class situation is probably safer for coach passengers because they have the same pilot (and mechanics) as do first-class passengers; if we required all seats to be the same, the wealthy would fly "private" jets and probably hire away the best pilots. Allowing some people to buy (with their own after-tax dollars) Platinum coverage keeps them in the system.[37]

Payment intermediaries have substantial flexibility in designing Platinum coverage packages, generating important evidence on the types of services plausibly discerning people are willing to pay for with their own after-tax money.[38] Because all the claims and quality measures are processed in the same system by the PIs and the UCP, it will be easy to assess whether the additional services used by the Platinum enrollees make any difference in outcomes. SecureChoice should be designed so that the Gold plan will be sufficiently broad to be more than satisfactory to the vast majority of the population. If a certain service—for example, a new implantable device—used only in Platinum plans proves beneficial, in following its mandate to cover superior-quality care the UCP will quickly move to include it in the standard Gold plan. Allowing people the option to "buy up" eliminates debates over whether some bureaucracy is inappropriately limiting access to important innovations. Permitting the rich to purchase Platinum coverage leads to new information allowing better care for all.

The Gold versus Platinum distinction differs in important ways from the distinction between Medicare and Medicare plus supplemental coverage. Medicare supplemental plans offset purposeful co-payment requirements in Medicare; they do not pay for services Medicare determines are not medically necessary. Likewise, supplemental plans do not allow providers to "balance bill" patients if they feel the Medicare rates are insufficient. Supplemental coverage, moreover, increases Medicare's costs because it eliminates the financial incentives for patients that are part of Medicare. These extra costs are not reflected in the premiums for the supplemental plan but are borne by Medicare. Platinum coverage, in contrast, will pay for what might be unnecessary services and possibly "outrageous" fees. The PI offering those Platinum policies, however, receives from the UCP only the age-sex-location-specific amounts associated with

Gold coverage for each enrolled person. Thus the full incremental cost associated with Platinum coverage is passed on in premiums.[39]

Financing: The Bottom Line

SecureChoice is so different from most other proposals under discussion that the standard estimates of cost are not directly applicable. It eschews short-run budget constraints and focuses on creating the incentives to make the system more efficient over time. Almost all analysts agree that the American health care system is not under-resourced in comparison with other systems. Our problems have to do with the mix of medical care resources we use, the amounts we pay certain types of providers, and a system that leaves many without coverage. Even those without coverage usually get the expensive care through hospitals, although they often lack the primary care that could keep them healthier in the first place.

At a minimum, the UCP guarantees payments for the most expensive aspects of care: major acute and chronic illnesses. There is already enough money in the system to do so without requiring any patient co-payments, and the funds left over could cover part of the remaining minor acute care episodes. This could be done with a fully tax-based system if there is sufficient political will. It could also be achieved through relatively simple modifications to the existing employer-based contribution system in conjunction with an individual mandate and income-based subsidies. The current special programs for the poor may already have nearly enough money to cover them through SecureChoice. For the uninsured, new "on-budget" funds will be needed, but these will be partially offset by reductions in cross-subsidies through providers and state and local costs for safety net providers.

The typical individual mandate proposals under discussion envision current insurers competing for enrollees. *That,* however, is a recipe for further increases in marketing, underwriting, and selection costs while amplifying the cacophony of rules and constraints that keep clinicians from developing more efficient practices. Instead, either tax-based financing or the individual mandate proposed for SecureChoice builds on a universal coverage pool that eliminates selection and underwriting problems and has insurers working to help primary care physicians make better clinical and referral choices. The individual mandate option would not necessarily do away with employer-sponsored comprehensive plans. In fact, they could achieve the efficiencies of the bundled payments to CDTs by having the pool manage those costs. Other employer-sponsored plans may choose just to keep their primary care coverage, offloading all the risk for chronic and major events to the UCP. In the long run, however, the UCP and collaborating payment intermediaries will demonstrate convincingly their cost-effectiveness in delivering high-quality care at low administrative cost.

— 7 —

Malpractice, Pharmaceuticals, Medical Education, and Prevention

This book is primarily about changes in how to pay for medical care to achieve better quality more efficiently. Some participants in policy discussions say new approaches to financing would be fine, but the real "culprits" are the malpractice system or profiteering drug companies. Others ask how practitioners will learn to function in a new financing environment and how medical education will be able to continue without access to good "teaching cases." Finally, some argue that the real solution lies in preventing illness, not in curing it more efficiently.

Each of these areas warrants major examination and creation of policy options—efforts that far exceed the scope of this book. These are key areas, however, in which the payment-oriented proposals of SecureChoice would have an impact on, or substantially benefit from coordination with, such policy changes. For example, the transparent collection and availability of quality of care information may raise the anxiety of providers who fear malpractice suits. Giving clinicians economic incentives to assess the value of new drugs, devices, and tests in the context of the overall costs of care will substantially alter the ways in which firms can price innovations and recoup research costs. This chapter does not address all the implications of payment reform on these issues. It does, however, offer ideas that may serve as the basis for future discussions. Key stakeholders not directly affected by the core aspects of SecureChoice may have significant concerns about the indirect effects of the plan. Proactively addressing these concerns may allow them to be seen as opportunities for productive coalitions and even more thoroughgoing changes.

Medical Malpractice: An Ineffective System

The malpractice litigation system is intended to accomplish two major goals: (1) to compensate patients injured by their interactions with the medical care system, and (2) to provide incentives for clinicians and organizations to improve safety and quality. Few argue that the current system achieves those goals in an efficient and effective manner. Most people suffering an injury due to medical care never submit a claim; of those who do file claims, most do not receive compensation.[1] There is little evidence that malpractice litigation brings about improvements in patient safety; anecdotes suggest, in fact, that fear of litigation results in providers' hiding what might otherwise be useful information.[2] The direct cost of operating the malpractice system (for example, attorneys' fees, charges for expert witnesses, and court costs) actually exceeds compensation to patients.[3] More problematic are the enormous indirect costs ranging from the time that providers must spend preparing a defense to the ways in which they practice medicine defensively rather than safely.

A simple "no fault" arrangement could achieve the first goal of a malpractice system by offering compensation to people who have experienced adverse events, but it would do nothing to achieve the second. Medical malpractice litigation, moreover, is rooted in the larger field of tort law. Separating it out for special legislation is fraught with political and legal complications, not the least of which is the fact that it is largely a state rather than a federal issue. Nonetheless, various researchers with extensive expertise in the area have suggested an innovative solution.[4] They recommend the establishment of "health courts" as a viable alternative route for compensation. Patients who have experienced an injury could bring their claim before a health court that uses administrative law procedures to determine if the injury was due to an avoidable compensable event (ACE), and if so, there would be a schedule for compensation. Avoidable compensable events are injuries that (1) are caused by treatment (or the omission of treatment) and (2) should rarely, if ever, occur when care is provided according to best practice.[5] The evidence needed to demonstrate an ACE is substantially less than that required for proof of negligence—the standard required for a conventional malpractice case. While the payments for an ACE would typically be lower, the chance of receiving a reasonable payment would be substantially higher. With less litigation, the administrative costs of the system would be markedly lower. It should also be emotionally easier for a physician to admit to an error that might have been avoidable than potentially be found negligent as a professional. The proposal's authors hope that the health courts will collect information from the cases they deal with to inform safety improvements.

The health court model is a constructive advance in the malpractice debates because it goes beyond caps on awards or procedural changes that simply make litigation less attractive or more difficult. Reducing litigation is attractive to providers but does not achieve better compensation or improved safety. The health court proposal, however, is likely to meet political opposition from the trial attorneys whose role it essentially eliminates. More important, it does little to improve patient safety. Although the data from claims will potentially be available from the health courts, funding pressures on the courts will probably cause them to focus on maintaining case throughput rather than on collecting accurate and valid data about errors. The health court proposal moreover provides only weak incentives for changing the medical processes in ways that hold promise for improving care. Organizations may find it cheaper to compensate injured patients routinely rather than improve safety; so by themselves, health courts may be a step backward with respect to safety. In the current situation, the risk of having to make a very large payout, along with the costs of defense, may provide some incentives for improving safety.

Looking beyond the Health Court

I suggest a modification to the health court proposal that adds a second tier of litigation to create stronger incentives for safety. All settlements and decisions of the health courts would be "semi-public" in that they would be available as privileged information to others (including attorneys not connected with the case) with suitable confidentiality restrictions. Thus providers still need not worry about "being tried in the media" for cases handled in this manner. The settlement information could be used as evidence of a pattern of problems known to a responsible party and not acted upon. Such a pattern could be pursued in a subsequent case alleging corporate negligence.[6] The typical situation in which this would occur is that of a hospital or CDT on notice of a pattern of ACEs for which it has paid a series of claims, with no evidence that it attempted to correct the problems leading to such events.

When errors occur and patients are harmed, they should be compensated fairly and quickly; but the compensation system should provide information and strong incentives to reduce avoidable errors and prevent harm to other patients in the future. The second tier of litigation provides information and incentives for this to happen. Some malpractice attorneys will develop (or hire) the analytic expertise to sift through large volumes of closed health court cases to determine if there are patterns of cases suggesting that a CDT has routinely failed to respond to recurrent avoidable events. Some CDTs will in fact have taken what they thought was appropriate action, but adverse events occurred nonetheless. Those will not be attractive cases to pursue, because the good faith effort would be a solid defense against charges of negligence. Attorneys are likely to pursue cases in which management ignored repeated evidence of problems, especially if they can argue that a larger class of patients was put at risk because of such negligent behavior.

Patients who may come to the health courts (first-tier cases) would be invited to make the details of their case available for possible inclusion in such second-tier litigation. In exchange for sharing their confidential information, they could share in future recoveries from second-tier cases in which their own provided evidence.[7] A set of plaintiffs' attorneys would be involved at the "front end" in helping patients who think they may have been injured by an avoidable compensable event. These attorneys would help patients understand whether an adverse outcome they experienced could have been avoided; if it could not, it will be unlikely to generate any compensation even with the more lenient standards of the avoidable compensable event. If it does appear to be an ACE, the attorney will assist in collecting all the relevant information and presenting the claim, either for direct settlement or to the health court for an administrative review and decision. If the attorney does a good job in collecting information, the case details will be more likely to be valuable to the second-tier attorneys looking for patterns of errors.

With this pattern-oriented model of malpractice litigation few physicians will be at risk, because an individual practitioner is unlikely to generate a detectable pattern of errors that could give rise to a suit for negligence. Physicians will continue to be involved in claims about avoidable compensable events, but these will be perceived as errors to be learned from, while patients will be compensated quickly without needing to prove negligence. Organizations such as group practices, hospitals, and care delivery teams, however, should be alert to patterns of avoidable errors. They may self-insure against the moderately common and low-cost claims that will come to the health courts. Second-tier claims alleging negligence, however, are likely to be substantially larger and require the expert defense and risk spreading that can be offered by a malpractice insurer. Some of these insurers will develop the expertise to help their clients proactively reduce their exposure to such claims. That is, the insurers will also be examining settled and closed first-tier claims for patterns of errors, but their focus will be the opposite of that of the second-tier attorneys. The insurers will look for organizations that have *fewer* than the expected number of avoidable errors and send experts in risk reduction and process improvement to talk with them and understand what they do to avoid such problems.[8] The insurers will then offer advice to their clients on what they can do to improve care, and if they follow through, lower their malpractice premium cost. Their clients will reap a second advantage: by reducing errors they will lower their self-insured payouts for the smaller first-tier claims. If, as some argue, a culture of safety is a key ingredient in quality of care, the benefits of such a culture will redound at both levels.

Involving Physicians

This proposed change to malpractice litigation interdigitates well with SecureChoice's changes in payment for care. Physicians involved in care delivery teams would receive coverage through their CDT for episodes handled by the CDT, aligning the incentives of both the hospital or other facility staff and the physicians. Error reduction will require efforts by all, sometimes involving information systems, care processes, or clinical guideline implementation. The physicians in the CDT may function as a mini–medical staff and choose to restrict the practice of some of its members if they appear too error prone in certain situations. Individual physician errors may no longer be deemed negligent, but a CDT that fails to monitor its members for errors may well be found negligent.

Physicians in ambulatory practice have much lower risk for avoidable compensable events, but they will typically not self-insure for those costs, as might a CDT. Individual ambulatory care physicians will buy malpractice insurance to cover both their potential first-tier costs and the low probability that they might be involved in any second-tier claims. At least in part because of the far lower volume of adverse events per PCP, it will be rare that one could establish a pattern of poor practice.

Group practices will be more subject to potential second-tier claims because they are more responsible for coordinating care among many clinicians. They may be vulnerable if they fail to have reliable information systems to alert their clinicians of drug interactions, if they do not routinely review the quality of care provided by their clinicians, or if they fail to ensure that patients are notified of abnormal test results. Groups may thus find it advantageous to buy group policies for their clinicians, just as CDTs will. They may also reap savings in premiums by enlisting the expertise of malpractice carriers or others in implementing quality improvement efforts. Solo practice physicians may establish informal quality improvement groups analogous to consultation groups often used by psychotherapists to comment on one another's cases. This will allow them to share expertise and error reduction techniques. Malpractice carriers may lower their premiums for physicians involved in such consultation groups that meet certain standards or experience a lower-than-expected level of avoidable events.

With SecureChoice, the detailed utilization and quality data developed as part of the payment system can be linked in a de-identified way with information about adverse events in order to highlight situations that increase or decrease the chances of avoidable errors. These datasets will be available for research to improve safety and quality in much the same way that the authors of the health courts proposal envision. Linking with universal billing data will enormously enhance the value for research because that will create "denominator" information to go along with the "numerator" information derived from the health courts. The incentives provided by the potential for second-tier claims will markedly improve the detail and quality of the data and ensure that they will be collected in a uniform and timely fashion.

Technological Innovation in a Reformed Payment System

Most health economists see technological change as a major driver of rising health care costs; people disagree, however, as to whether such improvements in health are worth their increased cost.[9] The question here is not whether innovation *should* be hastened or slowed but what impact SecureChoice *is likely to have* on the incentives for technology innovation and diffusion. The major focus here is on new drugs and devices; they typically have a very long and expensive development and testing period involving great uncertainty with regard to their market success. This means that firms invest substantial sums in potential new products knowing that many will fail to reach the market. For those that do launch, there is constant uncertainty about when a better product will come on-line and capture the market. These realities seem driven by the nature of the fundamental research, development, and testing processes rather than the behavior of the FDA or the firms.

At the next step, however, certain institutional and other factors become important. The FDA is charged with assessing the safety and efficacy of drugs and devices for the particular purposes proposed by the manufacturer. Clinical trials are then designed to test the drug or device, typically under carefully controlled parameters. It is easier and less expensive to undertake a trial focusing on a narrowly defined patient population with stringent inclusion and exclusion criteria because it will include less statistical "noise" from unmeasured factors. Under pressure to get their innovations to market before the competition, firms will naturally emphasize narrow trials when seeking FDA approval. Once the drug or device is approved, however, there are strong incentives to market it not just for the narrowly defined population on which it had been tested but also for broader populations. Firms are not allowed to encourage the use of drugs for "off-label" indications—conditions for which they have not been tested—but there are instances of this occurring. Physicians have vigorously opposed any regulations restricting their ability to prescribe any approved drug for almost any use. Manufacturers have used direct-to-consumer marketing to encourage patients to ask for certain drugs rather than wait for them to be recommended by their physicians.[10]

Various observers charge that the industry engages in excessive marketing of drugs to physicians and patients, unscrupulous attempts to bias research, aggressive lobbying of Congress, and pressuring of regulators. Although the financial risk associated with each new drug may be enormous, collectively the industry has a very high profit rate; losses experienced by one firm are often offset by the gains of another. The industry argues that high profits are needed to provide the incentives for future high-risk innovation. Indeed, both sides of the story may be true. Although the pharmaceutical industry is not competitive in the classic way, with many small sellers making incremental decisions, there is substantial competition among firms for market share. With huge bets being placed on potential blockbuster drugs, the winners win big; the losers are often subsumed into mergers. The industry as a whole can be profitable while each firm feels it is in a struggle for survival.

New pharmaceuticals targeting specific genetic risk factors, however, will alter the way drugs can be tested and marketed. Such drugs target the precise biological mechanisms that cause disease or symptoms and employ specific ways to intervene in those processes. Many diseases are caused by multiple genetic factors, and the treatment of the disease may require different interventions for each genetic cause. For example, breast cancer is related to several genetic factors as well as other, yet unknown factors. About 25 to 30 percent of women with breast cancer have a gene mutation that overexpresses human epidermal growth factor receptor 2 (HER2).[11] If the tumor has already metastasized, Herceptin has been shown to be effective in women in whom HER2 is overexpressed, but not in other women.[12] This targeted treatment may be highly effective for this subgroup of women, increasing its value to them, but recognizing such targeting limits its potential market. Designing drugs to address specific biological pathways will probably facilitate the development process and possibly lower the cost of testing new drugs. The more narrow populations for which new drugs are relevant, however, will change the ways that drugs will be marketed.

Accelerating Innovation

SecureChoice will accelerate science-based changes, but it can also offer the basis for a new business model. If physicians are given incentives to make more cost-effective choices in the care of patients, they will seek out impartial information as to what works best and at what cost. If a new, high-priced drug is better on average than the existing generics in broad trials but actually beneficial to only a small segment of the relevant population, the best approach may be first to try the generic for each patient rather than the new drug for everyone.[13] Better information will be sought by physicians to identify the best intervention quickly and accurately. Such information is likely to come not from the marketing representatives of the firms but rather from independent groups assessing a broad range of evidence, much of it from newly available observational data. These advice-offering groups could deploy trained educators to visit physicians periodically (as do the drug company representatives), offering information on head-to-head comparisons of the best prescribing strategies in given situations. Physicians may hire these services; alternatively their payment intermediaries could arrange access for them, much as large mutual fund firms offer discounted or free investment planning information.

Drugs targeted to specific population segments, readily available unbiased information on drug costs and effectiveness, and incentives to prescribe wisely pose a threat to a business model that relies on rapid (and possibly excessive) marketing of new products to broad populations to cover the costs of drugs that do not make it to market. If this threat jeopardizes the development of innovative new drugs, it imposes real social costs. Some have proposed public funding and oversight of clinical trials.[14] Although basic research is clearly in the realm of a public good and should be shared widely, public funding may not be well suited to the risk-taking necessary for the translation of research through the development process into new products. There may be an important role, however, for a public, or semipublic, entity to reduce the risks faced by individual firms and thereby maintain innovation side by side with less aggressive marketing.

Reducing the Risks (and Rewards)

From a societal perspective, we need innovative translation of research into effective clinical practice. Public funding of that translational effort is not a first-choice strategy for several reasons. Even apart from the predictable political reaction of the pharmaceutical industry, government agencies are typically not well suited to take the risks required in pursuing new drugs. Given the long time lag needed for research, development, and trials, public agencies would always be asking for money for projects that are not likely to reap rewards until several administrations later, but failures will be much more quickly apparent. Congressional investigations are (perhaps inadvertently) likely to encourage a focus on "sure bets" or, even worse, a preference for drugs to be produced in certain congressional districts. Pricing of drugs for domestic and Third World consumption may be relatively easy, but setting prices for drugs to be sold in other high-income nations will be complex. Before considering public drug development, we should explore simpler ways to reduce the risks that may jeopardize private market solutions.

The value-enhancing incentives created by SecureChoice, in combination with unbiased assessments of drug effectiveness, mean both (1) that innovative new drugs will quickly enter and dominate the market and (2) that the market share of drugs cannot be as easily maintained by aggressive physician- and consumer-based marketing.

The first is a benefit to innovators; the second increases their risk that research and development costs will not be recouped if new and better drugs become available. The simple market response to the latter would be to increase prices and marketing costs to recover investment even sooner, exacerbating the problems we have currently. One way this response to risk can be offset is through reinsurance— essentially paying off the accumulated research and development costs of drugs that "prematurely" lose market share as a result of the unpredictable appearance of better alternatives.

Reinsurance is complex, especially when highly expert and motivated players have the opportunity to purchase coverage selectively. Mandating that all firms buy coverage may be politically impossible; allowing them to reinsure certain drugs selectively would be too risky for the reinsurer (in other words, the government).[15] The challenge is to design a system that builds on the expertise of existing players, maintains a voluntary aspect, and yet does not allow too much adverse selection. Many of these players have significant expertise that should continue to be tapped. For example, venture capitalists have effective nonbureaucratic models of assessing investment opportunities and a portfolio approach to handle their own risk. Manufacturers have enormous expertise in producing and distributing drugs safely and efficiently.

The universal coverage pool will have a substantial interest in continued innovation—if its fruits are appropriately used. From its perspective, innovation brings benefits to patients consistent with its mandate to foster superior care; from a societal perspective, the loss in market share for an older drug is offset by the benefits reaped by the new one. The problem is that the second firm does not compensate the first for its losses. The UCP, moreover, benefits if marketing costs (and hence prices) are reduced and firms do not try to maintain market share artificially when more effective drugs enter the market. The UCP will therefore set aside initial capital to fund an innovation reinsurance pool (IRP) that will eventually be self-supporting. The IRP, in turn, will offer reinsurance against market—but not other—

risks. If a new drug is launched and later suffers a sudden drop in market share because of the appearance of a superior drug, IRP insurance payments will offset part of the lost net revenues. The IRP is not intended to protect firms from the consequences of poor research decisions; it would not cover the costs of drugs that do not make it to market or that are withdrawn owing to health risks that appear after marketing. By not reinsuring such costs, it keeps firms focused on developing the best and safest products. IRP reinsurance, however, allows a firm to set the initial price lower than it otherwise would because its market risk would be covered. The lower price, moreover, may make the drug more attractive to cost-conscious decision makers and lead to more rapid adoption.

The IRP might serve as the reinsurer directly, or it may subcontract that activity to those with more expertise. There would be two approaches to this reinsurance. The first approach is passive, allowing existing firms to buy reinsurance for *all* their new products in the future.[16] Firms will have to assess carefully how this decision to reinsure all their products fits into their long-term business strategy. Current firms, especially the larger ones, may be reluctant to make this commitment in the early years. They may feel that their expertise in marketing to clinicians will make it less likely that they will lose market share to new competitors, and thus reinsurance will be too expensive for the value received.

In the second approach, the IRP can jump-start the use of reinsurance to facilitate risk-taking innovation by working with new health innovation funds, or HIFs. The HIFs would be for-profit organizations begun with a business model and culture designed to operate well in the new SecureChoice market environment. One can think of these HIFs as diversified investors in new drugs, medical technology, and other products to make the system more efficient and effective. HIFs will be independent entities, perhaps receiving some startup funding from the UCP and other investors, especially those that have an interest in holding down the long-term growth in medical costs, such as public employee pension funds.[17] The UCP will initially establish three to five HIFs—companies largely without walls, but owning important products and licenses. HIFs will compete with one another and existing firms in buying or licensing the patents or intellectual property of startups. Not all new ideas will find buyers; others will attract vigorous bidding. Once the HIFs own a potential new product, they will contract with universities or clinical research organizations to undertake trials.

Given their slightly different mission and culture, HIFs will make their research results more transparent than those of conventional firms; the results of successes *and* failures will be in the public domain. For example, they may voluntarily decide that all their trials will be submitted for publication, with the experimental and control arms randomly labeled X and Y; only after acceptance will the reviewers and editors (*and* the HIF) know whether the new drug or the control was superior. Reviewers and readers will then be much more accepting of HIF-sponsored trials as unbiased. Such disclosures and practices will serve as a model for others. For those drugs gaining FDA approval, the HIF will solicit bids from one or more manufacturers for production and distribution. As with commercial firms, HIFs will price their new products so that the profits from their successes cover the losses from their failures, but the HIFs will begin with the expectation that all their products will be reinsured. HIFs will emphasize head-to-head comparisons in their drug tests and seek to purchase the rights to new drugs they expect will do well in such tests. They will therefore be better able to rely on a small sales force because the impartial comparators of drugs will more frequently identify HIF products as "best buys."

The UCP may also raise funding for investment in HIFs by offering to take on the responsibility that large public and private employers have for retiree health benefits. These responsibilities, now carried as liabilities on corporate balance sheets or as public obligations, are increasingly problematic for lenders. In exchange for the actuarial value of the obligation, the UCP will promise to provide coverage in the future for major/acute interventional and chronic care, as well as the appropriate level of minor acute and preventive coverage implicit in the existing plan. In essence, the UCP is betting that it will be able to lower the overall rate of growth in expenditures through its new incentives.[18] In the long run the HIFs should provide reasonable returns not only to their initial investors but also to subsequent purchasers of their shares.

The marketing of new drugs is likely to change over time. Firms probably cannot be prohibited from using their marketing staff to meet with physicians and make presentations, nor can they be kept from advertising directly to consumers.[19] Physicians, however, value their time, and the new payment incentives will encourage their carefully considered use of drugs, imaging, and other medical innovations. Practitioner educators, much like the academic detailers used for years to offer unbiased assessments of drugs, will be popular because they will help answer for the physicians what drugs should be prescribed, when, and for whom. The UCP may undertake some public service ads to help people identify when they should seek treatment for various reasons. Such ads may also describe when *not* to use certain medications, such as antibiotics for viral infections.[20]

Medical Education in a Reformed System

If the drug research and development pipeline is a long one, medical education arguably is even longer: several years of pre-med classes, four years of medical school, and four to six years of residency. During this time the substantial debts incurred probably lead some students to choose specialties with high earnings profiles. These debts make it even more difficult for women (and men) to stretch out their training further to begin a family. Given the high average earnings of physicians in the United States, there has been little public support for federal funding of medical education, as is the case in Europe and Canada.[21]

The structure of graduate medical education (that is, internship and residency), moreover, is not well aligned with the needs of a reformed system. The cost of this training is largely funded through medical centers, in part from supplements to Medicare hospital payments. The medical centers then pay the salaries of physicians in training, requiring long hours (now limited to eighty per week) to offset their low productivity and high supervision needs in the early years. This funding model is biased toward specialties and activities that are "profitable" for the medical center. Primary care is generally not a high priority because it is under-reimbursed and requires extra space.[22]

Even in the current system, changes in medical practice are affecting the way training programs should be structured. Hospital stays are becoming shorter, reducing the available learning time at the bedside. Some medical centers are finding that full-time clinicians serving as hospitalists provide better care more efficiently than relying on the research-oriented faculty to cover inpatient units for a month or two per year. As is obvious to anyone who has tried to navigate the disjointed ambulatory care clinics in most teaching settings, their care is typically organized for the convenience of the faculty rather than the patient.

The new incentives created by SecureChoice will further stress this system of medical education. Payments to care delivery teams are based on efficient and high-quality delivery of care. Teaching hospitals may deliver high-quality care, but few would argue they do so efficiently. With guaranteed universal coverage, patients will not have to agree to be "teaching cases" merely to get their care covered; teaching hospitals will have to compete for patients on the basis of quality *and* cost. Teaching hospitals will also find it difficult to justify charging more than the EDRG payment based on CDTs with superior quality, especially if getting care in their facilities is less convenient and patient centered than in non-teaching settings. The graduate medical education supplements under the Medicare DRG system were intended to offset this efficiency differential, but they will need to be replaced.[23] Because academic institutions are slow to change, and because the new system will require practitioners with somewhat different skills than are now being emphasized, the necessary transitions should be started as soon as possible.

Many nations support higher education with public funds. The U.S. model favors some federal loan support for higher education, and many states offer excellent educational programs in state universities. Special support for (what are seen as highly paid) physicians is unlikely despite their extraordinarily high debt, which is due to both the number of years of costs incurred and the time lag before debt repayment can begin. Some could argue that this is just a private financing problem. It becomes a societal problem, however, if it leads people to choose specialties and practice styles that allow rapid repayment and those physicians then continue to emphasize the same highly paid activities after their loans are repaid.[24]

Changes in the payment system through health reform will create significant transition problems. The mix of specialists who are well supported by a fee-for-service system that rewards interventional work is quite different from the mix that is optimal for a payment system which rewards time spent with patients. SecureChoice allows fees to rise when shortages occur (and fall when there are surpluses) in specialties or in geographic areas, but the long pipelines of training programs and funding need to be made more responsive than they are now. Creative approaches to financing undergraduate (medical school) and graduate (residency) education may address both the problem of overall supply of physicians and the mix of specialties.

Few student loans are differentiated by the type of training or the likelihood the student will be able to repay the loan. The NIH, however, has a program that forgives educational indebtedness for physicians entering research careers, and the National Health Service Corps has a similar program for those who commit to practice in selected underserved areas. The UCP has a clear interest in assuring a continuous flow of new physicians entering practice without overwhelming personal debt.[25] The UCP may therefore establish an educational loan reinsurance pool to guarantee repayment to lenders, thereby lowering the interest rate. Students who choose high-demand specialty areas may also have portions of their loan forgiven with funds from the UCP.[26] Those entering practice in areas of shortage where fees are rising rapidly will have further portions of their loans forgiven. In essence, the UCP will provide selective incentives to trainees to enter those segments of the profession in which the UCP is facing the most rapid fee increases, thereby lowering its costs in the long term.[27]

The financing of graduate medical education is more complex but should also be made much more responsive to workforce needs. The federal government already funds a significant share of graduate medical education through add-ons to Medicare payments. Residents' stipends, however, are well below nurses' salaries, even if we ignore the eighty-hour workweek for the former, leading to a mismatch between skills, tasks, and costs to the organization. In the future, graduate medical education should be funded partly through training grants and partly through tuition, with trainees paid more reasonable salaries for their work. Grant funding to training programs would decouple the training revenue stream from the number of patients seen. Having trainees pay part of their training cost gives them greater incentives to think about the quality of the educational experience. Loan forgiveness incentives for specialty and location choice will also apply to these extra costs. With medical centers and other operating organizations paying trainees reasonable salaries for their *work*, they will more carefully assess whether certain functions should be performed by physicians in training or by other staff. Training grant slots should be adjusted over time to favor those programs which are most successful in attracting trainees and successfully placing them. Programs could focus on physicians heading into clinical care, research, or possibly mixed careers.

Separating the funding flows for training from those for care delivery will give the training programs the leeway to make arrangements with various institutions other than the traditional teaching facilities. Some community-based CDTs may provide excellent sites for well-supervised trainees. Programs will identify ambulatory care settings well suited to training young physicians in delivering patient-centered care; these may not be the traditional specialty-oriented outpatient clinics nestled around the teaching hospital. These new programs may select faculty who can devote a significant fraction of their time to teaching and have career paths that reward such effort. Some academic medical centers may decide that their real mission is research and teach only the next generation of subspecialists, dropping their undergraduate medical school and early year residency programs.

Training programs for physicians heading into CDT-oriented specialties need not be radically different from current models. Their patients are typically in the medical setting for a specific period of time and need focused care during a pre- and postadmission period. Relative to the current training programs, however, more attention should be paid to coordinating care with community physicians. The CDTs will be operating much more as teams than is currently the case, so academic settings may reorient themselves around services rather than disciplines. A training program for cancer specialists should actively involve cancer surgeons, oncologists, radiation oncologists, and other medical specialists, as well as psychologists, social workers, and nutritionists.

Training physicians for effective ambulatory care practice will require additional innovations. Programs may make greater use of hired patient surrogates to give students experience in interacting with patients. Computer-based programs akin to video games may help in learning symptom recognition and decision-making skills. Many patients will be willing to undergo additional physical exams by trainees as part of an extended office visit if they know in advance that this may happen, feel assured that their usual physician is overseeing the trainee, and believe that educating the next generation of physicians will benefit themselves and others. Some community-based settings may even find that having trainees offers a competitive advantage in attracting patients interested in quality, especially if the training program can fully offset the additional costs imposed by the need for extra exam rooms and physician supervision time.

Continuing medical education will also need to undergo major shifts in the new environment with respect to both supply and demand for such programs. Industry sponsorship is already shrinking because of conflicts of interest. Programs for educating clinicians about new drugs, technologies, and treatments will be in high demand, but the new payment incentives will result in those educational programs' emphasizing what works best for which patients and when expensive new technologies need not be used.

Early in the process of reforming the system there will be strong demand for training in how to adapt to new payment systems, identify appropriate new practice styles, work effectively in coordinating care, and be more responsive to patients. Medical schools, perhaps with assistance from business and other schools, should take the lead in developing these programs. This will require research and evaluation of information to be imparted, building on the expertise of health services researchers, social scientists, and others. Professional educators need to be involved in order to develop the training approaches that work best for busy practitioners with substantial real-world expertise, little knowledge about all the implications of the new system, and much anxiety about the future. All of this will require up-front grants to appropriate organizations to develop the new curricula, training programs, and assessment tools.

A Focus on Prevention

Most of the reforms incorporated in SecureChoice are intended to make the medical care system operate more efficiently and achieve a higher quality of care. If they work as anticipated, these reforms will slow the growth in health care expenditures relative to the current trajectory. Even more cost-reducing, however, would be preventing disease rather than just treating it more effectively. Such primary prevention—reducing obesity that can cause diabetes rather than just screening for diabetes—often occurs, or needs to occur, *outside* the medical care system. There are, however, several important ways in which SecureChoice should encourage prevention.

Some preventive care is delivered through the health care system. Those preventive interventions that work well, such as vaccinations, should be fully covered by all payment intermediary plans. The UCP has a financial interest in ensuring that people receive all services that can reasonably be expected to offset future costs. Some of these, such as tetanus shots, will benefit the individual; some benefit the community because they reduce contagion.

Some prevention goals, such as getting patients to give up smoking, may be clear, but the exact methods to achieve those goals are not. This is where SecureChoice should foster creativity and diversity in approaches rather than directly making choices among specific options for coverage. Some of these behaviorally related problems (obesity, substance abuse) are already listed as diagnoses; others (smoking) are not, but are recognized as risk factors.[28] The UCP could offer ongoing chronic illness management payments for such conditions. The base amount might be rather small, say $25 per year for each person with a body mass index (BMI) over a target level of 25, with larger rewards, say $250, for each BMI point a person lost in the preceding year. Rewards per BMI point might be scaled to the expected health benefits, with a smaller reward for an improvement from 26 to 25 than from 30 to 29.[29] Specific procedure codes would be established that reflect the interventions used, such as the type of counseling, exercise program, or even cash incentives for the patient, to help keep track of which seem to be most effective. PIs would seek to understand which approaches work best for their physicians in achieving the desired goals, and which in turn will lower their net premiums by increasing the CIM incentive payments.

Fostering Prevention outside the Health Care System

Primary prevention can and should take place in many venues, including worksites, schools, neighborhoods, communities, and states.

Even if health care were funded entirely by taxes, employers would still have an important stake in the health of their workers. Absenteeism causes staffing problems; "presenteeism" (people coming to work who are nonetheless sick) can cause even greater reductions in productivity. Health conditions that significantly affect employment range from colds and flu to depression and backache. Some employers have banned smoking both indoors and on their property. They have moved parking lots, slowed elevators, and enhanced stairwells to encourage physical activity at the worksite. Cafeteria food has been made healthier, and stress reduction techniques have been implemented. All this is in addition to offering screening programs to detect health conditions and making urgent care centers available on-site to encourage early use. Other employers have offered incentives for employees and their families to join health clubs, exercise regularly, and eat more wisely. What we do not know, however, is how well these efforts really work and what aspects are readily transferable. If appropriately linked, the routinely collected claims data from SecureChoice can be very helpful in this regard. Working within confidentiality protocols, researchers could identify employers that implement certain interventions, and the Funds Clearing House would link those funding sources with the claims of employees and their families who receive some contributions from those employers. Various research designs can be used to assess whether the worksite innovations have an impact on health measures.

Workers' compensation payments are a substantial cost for employers. Universal coverage will subsume many of the medical costs, although not necessarily those associated with minor acute care. Removing much of the incentive to determine which "pocket" is responsible for each cost will create administrative savings and also reduce harm due to delay in treatment. The UCP, however, has an interest in determining whether certain general worksite practices or environments lead to or reduce health problems. It will follow the employment history of workers over time to see if certain types of employers (or, if the data are collected, occupations) are associated with higher probabilities of certain conditions, such as repetitive stress injury, emphysema, or depression. If certain employers have significantly lower rates of such conditions than expected for their workforce and worksite characteristics, further research may help identify specific health-promoting practices.

Neighborhoods, communities, and states can also have important impacts on preventing disease. Communities may support neighborhood gardens, substance abuse programs, or reduced barriers to physical activity. These may be based on funded programs, regulations such as zoning to require sidewalks, no-smoking ordinances, or the creative use of abandoned properties for vest-pocket parks. States can impose taxes on the sugar content in foods or require restaurants to list trans-fats on their menus. Through the use of residential addresses in the Funds Clearing House database, geocoded information on the approximate locations where people live can be linked to claims to assess whether such policy and funding changes affect diagnoses and reported measures of BMI or smoking. Having identified areas with impressive changes in risk factors, researchers can explore what appears to have led to such improvements.

Providing Incentives for Change

Efforts to promote the health of the public should be a core function of government rather than the UCP. This is especially the case when some changes, such as removing the federal subsidy for sugar, are in policy realms far removed from health care. Agencies with research missions, such as the National Institutes of Health and the (much better funded) Agency for Healthcare Research and Quality, should fund the basic research needed. The UCP, however, should set aside a fraction of its overall expenditures for research on topics ranging from new analytic techniques to assessments of health care processes to evaluations of primary prevention initiatives. Independent of federal funding for basic research, the UCP should be able to use its own money to fulfill its mission of improving health in the long term.

Well-designed research and evaluation projects supported by the

UCP will help policymakers decide how to proceed with initiatives that require public funding or legislative changes. In many instances the initial request will simply be for federal waivers to allow states or communities to innovate, with the UCP providing the data and analytic expertise to assess the impact of the changes. Governors and other opinion leaders can then foster evidence-based public policy changes. The UCP will not be in charge of any of these changes, but it may serve as a catalyst for innovation and a tool for monitoring health improvement.

— 8 —

How SecureChoice Would Work
for Patients and Physicians

In this chapter we meet Harvey and Louisa, a middle-aged couple who learn to navigate the newly implemented SecureChoice health care system. They have moved across the country to be close to their grown children, so they face more questions than the typical person who does not need to change providers or think about changing coverage. Harvey and Louisa's story, and that of their children, employers, and providers, illustrates how the new system works "on the ground." Taken together, their experiences reflect a range of issues, preferences, and concerns that are likely to be raised about how SecureChoice will work.

Choosing Coverage

Let us assume that SecureChoice has been passed after substantial political discussion and compromise. The result is universal coverage of major acute and chronic illness care by means of an individual mandate with extensive income-based subsidies. Although retaining the traditional employer-based system was more complex than shifting to a fully tax-based approach, it was more politically viable and provided the votes needed for a tax increase directed at enhancing equity.

Harvey's employer is a national firm that had tailored its overall compensation package and health insurance to attract and retain workers, offering excellent health benefits regardless of employee location. While SecureChoice was still new, though growing in popularity, Harvey's employer decided to keep its standard self-insured health coverage for all its employees (even in the most rural of areas), while allowing those employees to opt into SecureChoice coverage where it was available. This was in response to the requests of those who wanted to be able to combine employer contributions from several family members or jobs into a single package. Harvey reviewed his employer's conventional coverage and SecureChoice, recognizing that under the new law both he and Louisa were required to demonstrate coverage for at least major acute care episodes and chronic illness care.

The firm's conventional plan was a popular preferred provider organization, or PPO, plan. It offered a relatively wide network of physicians and hospitals. If Harvey and Louisa saw providers within the network, the PPO would pay 80 percent of the negotiated fees, after a $500 deductible was met. If they saw non-network providers, the plan paid 60 percent of the set PPO fee, leaving them responsible for the difference between that amount and the provider's charges. Each of them had a $2,500 yearly out-of-pocket maximum based on covered charges. The benefit package appeared broad but excluded coverage for any services the PPO deemed to be experimental or medically unnecessary. Harvey could not find out how these coverage decisions were made and could not get information on the likely costs for treating common problems. Although the PPO's Web site showed the fees charged by its providers for various tests and services, this information was not presented in a way that Harvey and Louisa found useful.

Harvey's employer pays most of the cost for his coverage and part of the cost for his spouse's coverage. Louisa's new employer is willing to offer a partial contribution for her own health benefits, but it cannot be combined with Harvey's under his employer's conventional PPO package. Using SecureChoice offers them additional flexibility:

Harvey's employer is indifferent as to whether he chooses the conventional PPO or SecureChoice. If Harvey picks the latter, his employer simply transfers the actuarial equivalent that it would provide toward his and Louisa's PPO coverage to the Funds Clearing House account that he designates.[1]

Louisa's employer contributes its funds on a tax-exempt basis to the same account. In addition, Harvey and Louisa can add their own after-tax dollars, so they can afford a wide range of coverage options. This arrangement is new for Louisa's employer. Before the SecureChoice legislation it struggled with offering coverage, eventually dropping it. As a small firm with twenty-five employees, it found that its premium costs were constantly rising, and some workers could not afford to participate. After one enrollee's child had a major illness, the carrier refused to renew coverage without an exorbitant increase in premiums. Now, with SecureChoice, Louisa's employer simply offers a salary reduction plan in which workers reduce their hourly wage by an amount that is transferred to the Funds Clearing House. That amount is treated as if it were an employer contribution for health insurance and is not subject to payroll and income taxes.

If Harvey and Louisa chose the conventional PPO option, their choices would be limited by the plan selected by Harvey's employer. Although offering a wide range of physicians and hospitals, it allows no choice of financial incentives because of the PPO carrier's concerns about selection. Deductibles and co-payments have their greatest impact on frequently occurring low-cost events (in other words, minor acute care). Enrollees' decisions about such incentives reflect both their preferences for such relatively low-cost care and unmeasured risks of major, costly events that have a much greater impact on overall premiums. With the UCP covering most of the risks associated with major acute episodes and chronic illness management, the payment intermediaries can allow such selection based on patient preferences and simply have it reflected in the premiums quoted.[2]

Harvey decides he wants a coverage plan similar to the one offered by his employer's PPO, providing the same coverage if he decides to see any physician or go to any hospital regardless of what his primary care physician may recommend. In general, Harvey likes deciding whether "things are worth it": asking the price of the specials at restaurants, personally managing his stock portfolio, and shopping for the best airline deals. As the SecureChoice coverage is complete for all major and chronic illness care, he likes having choices on how to structure his coverage for minor acute care, optional preventive services, and supplemental costs if the provider he uses charges more than the UCP pays the CDT. The expected out-of-pocket and premium costs of all these coverage options appear quite manageable. Whereas people in his age range (sixty to sixty-four) use roughly $4,300 in medical care each year (with a great deal of variability in use across individuals), once chronic illness care and major acute episodes are removed, the average cost is less than a quarter of that (and the variability is also much reduced).[3] Harvey is comfortable bearing the financial risk associated with large co-payments per visit and a substantial deductible, except for mandated preventive services—all of which reduce his monthly premium. He wants to make sure, however, that his plan will cover any extra charges that might be billed by care delivery teams or specialists he may use, and this increases his premium.

Louisa's preferences are quite different. She likes to build rapport with her primary care physician and then rely on his or her recommendations. When their children were young, she and Harvey would argue over whether it was worth the office visit fee to have them seen by their pediatrician when they began to show what might be symptoms of an illness, or what might also just have been a spell of crankiness. Louisa decides that she wants coverage with no deductible for minor acute or preventive services, a $25 co-payment for office visits, and no co-payment for telephone and e-mail consultations. She is, however, willing to accept higher co-payments for services received from providers who are not part of her primary care physician's referral network because she feels it is unlikely that she would seek such care.

Harvey and Louisa initially thought about these coverage differences in a generic way because they had not chosen primary care providers and did not know the payment intermediaries associated with the local providers and the exact coverage options and prices they offered. At first this process felt a bit strange, but Harvey pointed out that it was analogous to the choices they'd had to make when they were transferring their 401(k) retirement funds. Although he hadn't decided yet which firm (such as Vanguard, Fidelity, or Schwab) he would choose, he knew that each offered roughly the same mix of mutual funds, so they could achieve whatever balance of investments they wanted irrespective of which firm administered the account. Likewise, all the payment intermediaries offer similar coverage options; differences in premiums across PIs for a given kind of coverage are nearly all determined by the practice styles and fees of the physicians chosen by the patient.[4]

PIs and independent consumer organizations offer free-access Web sites that allow potential enrollees to assess the costs associated with coverage differences. When Harvey and Louisa enter their age and sex information as well as their chronic illnesses, they can then examine a wide range of co-payment and other options to see the implications for monthly net premiums, expected out-of-pocket costs, and the chances that out-of-pocket costs will exceed a certain amount. Some Web sites allow people to work though video game–type scenarios involving acute and chronic illnesses to see how they would feel about hypothetical sets of co-payments or limited networks.

Selecting a Medical Home

Harvey and Louisa had never before thought about having a "medical home." Their prior relationships with their physicians had begun long before the health reform efforts that resulted in the Secure-Choice plan, which requires everyone to identify a medical home, usually a primary care physician, nurse practitioner, or physician assistant.[5] Sometimes a medical clinic or occasionally a subspecialist serves as the medical home for a person. From a clinical perspective, the medical home serves as a source of guidance and referrals as well as a provider of many ambulatory care services. The medical home is also responsible for keeping track of the patient, assuring that certain screening tests and other preventive services are undertaken, and properly managing chronic illnesses such as diabetes and hypertension. All this requires at least a minimum of record keeping. Some clinicians are involved in large group practices and have their own electronic health record systems. Others use record systems built on the claims data processed by the PIs and electronically supplied lab results supplemented with limited information they input after each visit.

The medical home is the organizing concept for determining provider-based premiums. The UCP carries the risk of occurrence of major acute and chronic illnesses and pays the amount needed by providers who offer superior-quality care, adjusting for geographic differences in wages. What is left reflects (1) the costs of minor acute and some preventive care for the average person in a given age-sex category, and (2) the differential costs associated with that particular physician's more or less conservative use of services and higher- or lower-than-average fees.[6] By processing the claims associated with all the care obtained by all the patients with a given medical home, the PI can determine relatively easily the impact these "practice style" factors will have on the overall cost for patients in a given age-sex category. Patient preferences for styles of care and co-payment options also affect the total cost, as well as how it is split between premiums and out-of-pocket expenses.

Harvey and Louisa take different approaches to finding a primary care physician in their new community. Harvey goes on-line to one of several "doctor-finder" Web sites. All allow him to enter information on his location and preferred coverage options and show the premiums and expected out-of-pocket costs for all providers in his area who are willing to serve as a medical home. Some Web sites have also drawn information from publicly available databases to include objective information on where practitioners trained and their areas of clinical focus. Sites may also include indicators of the style of care offered by the primary care practitioners and specialists used by the patients of those PCPs. Some of these data are derived from billing information: the mix of face-to-face and e-mail or telephone visits, and the proportion of visits for certain common problems that result in referrals for tests or to specialists. Quality scores on various standardized measures are also aggregated and presented. Some Web sites have solicited "scenario" information from the practitioners in which they provide brief descriptions as to how they would handle patients presenting with certain signs and symptoms, having certain types of chronic illnesses, or facing decisions regarding end-of-life care. Such scenarios do not have "right" or "wrong" answers but rather reflect differences in approach or philosophy that may be important to both clinician and patient. Some Web sites solicit information from patients about the care they received from various clinicians and facilities. Although these reports are no more objective than Zagat ratings of restaurants, some people find them useful.

Louisa relies on a low-tech approach that has worked for people for years—asking friends and neighbors. She asks for recommendations about doctors, engaging friends and family in conversations about the type of physician with whom she would feel most comfortable. (Having moved, she retains ninety days' coverage under her former PI's plan for out-of-area services, just as she had when traveling.) With SecureChoice, physicians need not worry that their patients may be forced to change doctors because an employer switches health plans. Instead they can pay attention to ensuring a good match between their own style and the preferences of prospective patients. Many offer "get to know you" visits at nominal or no cost to discuss how they practice.[7] After ruling out one whose premium seemed well above the others' and whose recommendations were not markedly better, Louisa met with three physicians and a nurse practitioner who collaborates with a physician. She chose one of the physicians who seemed to be a good match, knowing that if the match turned out not to be to her liking, she could change to another provider within ninety days.

Providers adjust their fees shortly before the end of the year, so PIs can quote new premiums for the coming year that are based on existing practice patterns and new fee levels. Each year a small number of people change their medical home because they are unhappy with the care they receive or with the projected costs of coverage and out-of-pocket expenses. Prior to such changes, if the enrollee has chosen a plan with very comprehensive coverage, PIs usually point out to them how accepting some additional out-of-pocket expenses may reduce their premiums. If the higher costs appear to be due to fee increases that are out of line with most in the area, PIs alert their providers to this and warn them that these new fees may cause some patients to leave for other practices.

Harvey decides to see Dr. Steven Killy, a young internist well trained in the use of cutting-edge diagnostic tests, who appears to rely heavily on consultations with subspecialist colleagues. He makes extensive use of e-mail to connect with his patients, follows evidence-based guidelines, and has a busy practice. Most of his patients are like Harvey in that they do a fair amount of self-management and self-referral to specialists, while preferring to have some of their own financial "skin in the game." Louisa chooses Dr. Mac Wilby, an older family physician. On the one hand, he seems happy to spend as much time with her during office visits as she wants, billing the PI for his time in ten-minute increments. He also charges for telephone consults if they exceed five minutes. On the other hand, he tends to be very conservative in his use of tests and believes that by building a relationship with his patients, listening carefully to their descriptions of symptoms, and suggesting what often appear to be home remedies, he is able to provide similarly high-quality care as his colleague Dr. Killy.

Although both are happy with their choice of physician, Harvey decides to test out how the Web sites characterize the premiums for Dr. Killy and Dr. Wilby. He inputs his own background information into the PI Web site linked to Dr. Killy using first his own coverage preferences, then Louisa's.[8] He then does the same exercise on the site linked to Louisa's physician's PI. Not surprisingly, if he were to apply Louisa's preferences for full coverage with no deductible and only nominal co-payments, but with a provider network reflecting Dr. Killy's usual referral patterns, the premium would be substantially higher. This is due to the impact of co-payments and deductibles on patient demand for care, and the fact that Dr. Killy's patients tend to see a wide range of providers, many of whom charge more than the average. If Louisa were to ask for Harvey's choice of coverage, with high deductibles but supplemental costs from CDTs extensively covered, her premium would be lower but her out-of-pocket costs substantially higher. Both Harvey and Louisa are thus able to confirm that the coverage options they have independently chosen match both their preferences and their preferred physician practice style.

The experiences of their three children provide other examples of how the system works. Susan, their twenty-five-year-old daughter, had been getting her care though a large group practice HMO. She liked that plan, with its built-in referral system and integration of primary and other care. The HMO owns its own hospitals and feels that because its physicians' practice style markedly reduces the need for hospitalization, its patients who are hospitalized are more complex to treat than those with the same diagnoses normally seen by CDTs. The HMO asked the UCP to let it take on full risk for its enrollees and is allowed to do so because very few of its enrollees switch back to the UCP.[9] The HMO reallocates some of its savings resulting from its lower hospitalization rates to further subsidize primary care. Unlike other SecureChoice options, it offers a limited range of co-payment schemes and abjures using deductibles because of its preferred practice style. Susan's employer contributes the age-sex-based amount that it offers for all its employees.

Joseph, their eldest, appreciates the risk pooling inherent in the new plan. Joseph and his wife, Meighan's, first child, Alana, was born with a rare congenital heart defect requiring frequent monitoring, ongoing medication, and the prospect of several surgical repairs as she grows. Joseph's first employer had good health benefits that covered most of the costs of Alana's care. Although he felt that a job change would best suit his career, he was concerned that other employers would not offer such good coverage, or that if they knew about Alana's health condition (which had been reported in the town newspaper), they might not even hire him. With SecureChoice, the cost of covering Alana is based merely on her age and sex; the UCP directly covers her hospitalizations and provides monthly CIM payments on her behalf to offset the costs of her chronic illness. There are only a few children in her community with her condition, so much of her care is obtained at the tertiary referral center an hour or so away, and when she needs corrective surgery, it may well have to be at a highly specialized center several states away. All of this care is covered by the UCP.

Harvey and Louisa's youngest son, Sam, has suffered recurrent episodes of severe depression. He lives independently, but his depressive episodes have made it difficult for him to finish college and retain steady employment. He had been on and off Medicaid and often found that he had to interrupt his care with therapists because many would not accept the low fees Medicaid offered. SecureChoice addresses this problem with income-based subsidies behind the scenes: the fees paid to clinicians are the same regardless of whether a patient is being subsidized. The UCP covers the costs of managing Sam's chronic illness; the monthly costs of coverage for minor acute care are billed to his account at the Funds Clearing House.[10] The FCH receives payments from Sam's employers when he is working and from the Federal Health Equity Agency on a quarterly basis as his earnings fall into the subsidy range. These payments cover the subsidized share of his premiums and co-payments; remaining costs are billed to Sam's credit card. If need be, Harvey and Louisa can also transfer funds into his account. His coverage—and access to various providers—remains the same as his subsidy status fluctuates.[11]

Navigating the Medical Care System

Harvey developed a lingering cough and began by taking the usual home remedies. When it got progressively worse after several weeks, he went to see Dr. Killy, who ordered a chest CT. Finding evidence of pneumonia, he prescribed a new antibiotic reputed to be effective against unusual strains of bacteria. The imaging center and radiologist submitted their usual fees through their own payment intermediary, GreenCo. GreenCo passed these through the automated claims clearing house to Dr. Killy's payment intermediary, OrangeCo, which paid the imaging fees and the price it had negotiated for the antibiotic with the manufacturer. Harvey's plan included substantial co-payments, which he paid when billed.[12]

A few months later Harvey experienced chest discomfort at 3 AM and went to the emergency department at the local hospital. The staff did a thorough workup and ruled out a heart attack. The coverage Harvey had chosen from OrangeCo requires a significant co-payment for emergency visits that do not result in a hospitalization; had he needed to be admitted, the EDRG payment from the UCP would have covered the preadmission costs. While waiting for his final lab results before being discharged, Harvey queried the physician as to why he didn't admit everyone with chest pain so the patients could avoid having to make any co-payments. The response was that "automatic" admission would represent poor-quality care: hospitals are dangerous places with the potential for infections and other iatrogenic illnesses. The emergency department fees, which are quickly paid by the plans, are such that the staff has no reason to admit patients unnecessarily. The UCP, moreover, reviews the rates of admissions for "rule-outs," highlighting those rates that are either too high or too low and providing feedback to emergency room physicians on their practices relative to those of high-quality centers. The emergency physician also told Harvey that he could have called Dr. Killy or been seen in an urgent care site; either might have first asked about the pepperoni pizza and beer Harvey had had while watching the Super Bowl and decided that a full ER visit was probably not warranted.

The next incident was not directly associated with overindulgence; several weeks later Harvey experienced major chest pain. The emergency department to which he was taken by ambulance quickly determined that he had had a mild heart attack and admitted him for treatment. The care delivery team found several coronary arteries with significant blockages and recommended bypass surgery. The UCP covered the full cost of his emergency visit, his admission, and also the subsequent bypass surgery. Harvey, however, preferred to have his procedure done at The Heart Institute (THI), a facility specializing in cardiovascular procedures. The care delivery team at THI was one of the first to make the transition to the expanded DRG payment system because the physicians already owned the specialized cardiac surgical facility. They accepted referrals from a wide area and were recognized for their quality. Although their experience and cost patterns were in the upper half of the outcomes distribution used by the UCP to set its rates, the THI-based CDT set its fees substantially above those offered by the UCP for cardiovascular EDRGs. Harvey's Platinum PI plan paid 80 percent of the extra fee.

Dr. Wilby manages Louisa's diabetes along with her minor acute and preventive care. Dr. Wilby's payment intermediary, BlueCo, receives a relatively small monthly payment from the UCP because Louisa's diabetes is comparatively mild and well controlled. In general, the UCP payment for mild stages of chronic conditions is slightly above their average cost of treatment. Payments for more severe stages of chronic conditions, though larger because the care is more complex, are priced at the average cost for cases of such severity. This gives PIs, and hence the physicians, incentives to diagnose early and keep their patients as healthy as possible.

The coverage option Louisa chose has no deductible and low maximum out-of-pocket costs. BlueCo prices its coverage knowing that Dr. Wilby spends a good deal of time with his patients and charges in ten-minute increments. Louisa selected an office visit co-payment of $20 for a basic fifteen-minute visit plus an additional co-payment of $10 for each ten-minute increment. Her typical visit may last forty to fifty minutes, and she feels it is well worth the cost. Dr. Wilby encourages his patients to call if they have concerns about symptoms or other issues. He finds that this "easy access" approach allows him to engage his patients in their care, making it easier for those with diabetes to keep their blood sugar under control. BlueCo has observed Dr. Wilby's outstanding results for such conditions and has asked him to share his approach at local medical meetings.

During one visit Dr. Wilby notices that Louisa has some troubling new symptoms and refers her to various specialists for assessment. Some are in his usual referral network; with them Louisa incurs a nominal co-payment. Others are outside the narrow network she had chosen, but because her primary care physician made the referral, BlueCo waives the extra charges for out-of-network use. After several workups Louisa is confirmed as having late-onset multiple sclerosis (MS). The UCP begins making additional monthly payments to BlueCo to offset the costs of the additional chronic condition.[13] After a while it becomes clear that Louisa's MS will be dominating her medical encounters and that careful management of various minor acute problems may interact with her ongoing MS treatment. She has developed a trusting relationship with Dr. Sara Frank, a neurologist who happens not to be in Dr. Wilby's usual referral network. After discussing various options with both physicians, she changes her medical home in the middle of the year to Dr. Frank.[14] As a subspecialist, Dr. Frank does not usually manage primary care problems, but she has a payment intermediary that has designed plans for physicians who take on responsibility for managing complex cases and collaborate with primary care physicians such as

Dr. Wilby for routine problems. With the enhanced monthly CIM payments from the UCP, Louisa's net costs change very little from what they were previously.

Seeing SecureChoice from the Physician's Perspective

Primary care physicians such as Drs. Wilby and Killy are generally satisfied with the new arrangements. Rather than having to deal with complex and apparently arbitrary rules from dozens or hundreds of different insurance carriers, they find payment intermediaries competing for *their* business. The PIs' fees are closer to the 2–3 percent charged by credit card companies than the 15–20 percent retained by current insurance carriers for administrative costs and profits. To a large extent these savings arise from much lower marketing and underwriting costs, much less need for claims adjudication, and much-reduced insurance risk. The PIs compete with one another not just on administrative costs but by offering innovative software and decision support tools to help the physicians improve their practices. They facilitate access to other vendors to assist physicians in the electronic transfer of information on lab results, specialists' reports, and the like.

Physicians have much more autonomy in the way they operate their practices. Drs. Wilby and Killy clearly have different practice styles and approaches and can adjust both their fee patterns (for example, Dr. Wilby's long visits and phone consultations) and fee levels as they see fit. They can individually design their implicit referral networks, which the PIs can implement much as if they were a physician-specific preferred provider organization. They can emphasize generic drugs, complementary and alternative medicine, or the latest and most expensive new drugs and imaging techniques. With this autonomy, however, comes far more financial responsibility. Traditional insurers insulated providers by setting premiums on the basis of average costs across all physicians but used external constraints on fees and practice patterns to manage overall costs. In contrast, the PIs simply pass on the cost implications of each physician's practice style and fees to his or her patients.[15]

Some patients may feel that the extra costs of the more expensive physicians are worth it, because of either the higher perceived quality of care or the level of information and service they receive. Some physicians, however, seek to learn how they can lower their patients' costs without necessarily reducing their income. Dr. Killy, for example, may ask his PI to provide information on how his practice style differs from those of other physicians with similar patients who achieve high quality scores. The PI provides such information in a user-friendly format, often including access to seminars by the physicians with the best practices. For example, instead of immediately prescribing one of the new antibiotics for patients with pneumonia, like Harvey, many of his colleagues find that older antibiotics are just as effective in most instances. Some have established protocols whereby an office assistant calls the patient within a week to see if the drug seems to be working, and if not, they use a second-line antibiotic. Dr. Killy also learns that some of his colleagues have identified radiologists who routinely offer (and bill for) telephone consultations to advise primary care physicians when expensive imaging studies are immediately warranted, or when a simple X ray or a week of watchful waiting is appropriate.

Subspecialists are somewhat more mixed in their responses to the new system. Those focused on inpatient care generally join the newly developing care delivery teams. Some effort is often required to develop the governance structure and rebuild trust between physicians and hospitals. Once that is done, however, the practice of medicine seems more harmonious. It is now easier to share coverage and learn techniques from colleagues. Hospitals are more open to making changes in nurse staffing and other decisions to improve workflow. Likewise, physicians more readily compromise on formularies and sets of orthopedic devices and other equipment that were previously seen as "the hospital's costs." The CDTs monitor when there are slack resources, such as operating room time on weekends, and offer surgeons bonuses for scheduling elective procedures at such times. Many of the observations on how to improve processes come from the nurses who are active participants in the operational and compensation plans of some of the CDTs.

The UCP focuses its quality scores on patient outcomes after adjusting for risk factors. These risk adjustment techniques undergo constant improvement as CDTs collect more data and the science of outcomes assessment and risk adjustment improves. CDTs demand more detailed information, both on other measures of quality and, more important, on the processes used by those CDTs that score high on quality measures *and* low on resource use. Various firms have become quite successful in identifying the practices that seem to work best. While these practices undergo rigorous trials, some CDTs attempt to implement the changes, thereby generating additional information on what works and why.

The main problem from the perspective of the subspecialists is that there seems to be somewhat less work to go around than before. This likely reflects both an oversupply of specialists as well as the adoption of somewhat more conservative practice styles and recommendations by primary care physicians and their patients. Some specialists decide to retire earlier than they had planned rather than joining the new CDTs. Others serve as consultants to the CDTs on a fee-for-service basis or fill in when members of the CDT are on vacation. Hospitalists are in much-increased demand, however, and some internists refresh their skills in order to focus their practice in that area. The more structured coverage schedules of the CDTs facilitate part-time practice, making it easier for physicians to balance career and family.

Specialists who focus primarily on ambulatory care also vary in their responses to SecureChoice. Many of those who primarily manage chronic illnesses view the system as freeing. The chronic illness management payments from the UCP are not tied to specific treatments or services, allowing substantial flexibility in how care is delivered. The payment intermediaries develop information on what works best and pass this information on to clinicians. New approaches develop in the way care is organized and paid for, such as using nurses and other staff to do home visits, encourage behavior change, and comfort people as their health declines.

Although patients choose a single medical home on which premiums are based, this does not mean that all ambulatory care is directly provided or managed by these medical homes. Sam's depression needs a mixture of ongoing therapy and psychopharmacology, areas in which primary care physicians are frequently not expert. Sam's family physician has referred him to a clinical psychologist who primarily manages his mental health care. The clinical psychologist spends significant time conferring with the psychiatrist with whom she collaborates in managing Sam's medications, and each is paid for such time. Ongoing assessments of the quality of care, such as the length of time Sam is able to go between depressive episodes and hold a job, as well as his own evaluations of his mood state over time provide valuable information. This helps inform his mental health professionals and others as to what approaches seem most promising.

Outpatient-focused specialists develop strong, continuing relationships with the medical homes of their patients. The two-way flow of information aids each in managing relevant aspects of patient care. Sometimes the information is simply transmitted by phone, but practices are increasingly being connected electronically in various ways, even without sharing comprehensive electronic health records. The PIs facilitate this process by making available the claims-based information for each shared patient, automatically linking in other information, such as lab results, to separately submitted billing claims.

Some specialists had developed practices relying on significant capital investment, such as radiologists who have invested in their own CT and MRI equipment. In the "old world," in which imaging tests were highly reimbursed, this was an excellent business decision; in the "new world" of SecureChoice this may or may not be the case. The new emphasis on payment is for clinician expertise and time. Radiologists may make more money charging for consultations—explaining when a test should be used and collecting information that can help in the interpretation of findings—than simply by charging for the test. Whether there will be more or less need for radiologists is unclear, but there will likely be fewer tests. Those who are best able to target the use of their expertise are likely to be the busiest. In many instances, radiologists find it more efficient to use the equipment in hospitals than to have their own.[16]

Reforming the System: A Moving Target

This scenario of how Harvey, Louisa, and others fare in the new system represents how the U.S. health care might operate a few years after the reforms outlined in this book take hold. It is a snapshot, however, of a system designed to be adaptive and dynamic rather than static. Various players, in particular physicians, CDTs, and malpractice attorneys, have incentives to assess performance and enhance quality, efficiency, and safety constantly. Others, in particular the payment intermediaries and malpractice carriers, have incentives to collect data, process it into usable information, and help physicians and others utilize that information to improve practice.

Patients and clinicians have much more freedom and ability to meet their own needs in this new system, but they also bear more responsibility for the decisions they make. The UCP absorbs the major and uncontrollable risks, but the patient- and physician-based plans require patients to bear (to the extent their income allows) the incremental costs of the decisions they and their clinicians make with respect to practice style and fees. Payment intermediaries no longer intrude in either the clinical or fee-setting aspects of medical practice, but they also no longer protect physicians and patients from the implications of their choices. Many would agree that this is a more desirable situation than what we have now; the scenario suggests that Harvey and Louisa would certainly agree. Chapter 9 addresses how this may come about and how we can manage the transition to such a plan.

— 9 —

Getting There:
Policy Choices, Implementation,
and Transition

Numerous policy and political decisions must be made in order to craft and implement a plan as far-reaching as SecureChoice. This book provides only a sketch of what must be considered; its goal is to present new ideas for discussion, modification, and compromise within the political process. The range of issues is broad, but having more issues in play simultaneously may allow new coalitions to develop strategies for implementation. What may be necessary is a national Health Care Compact in which the various parties commit to the outlines of an overall approach to health care reform.

This final chapter outlines key questions that must be addressed in such a Compact. It also highlights new roles for existing (and sometimes new) players in the health care system, setting the stage for the bargaining processes that will underlie the politics of policy. A final section addresses transition issues in implementing the new plan.

A Health Care Compact

SecureChoice will affect all Americans and the business and professional interests of all health care providers. It touches upon fundamental values involving personal choice, social equity, and the public-private sector balance. Achieving SecureChoice will require visionary leadership which makes people willing to trust that the uncertain outcomes of major change are better than the certain failures of our current system and of incrementalism. The breadth of SecureChoice may be its greatest disadvantage, since there is something for almost everyone to fear, *and* its greatest advantage, since there are benefits for almost everyone, as well as the potential to enlist allies not normally involved in health care. For example, if we do not rein in long-term growth in health expenditures, the impact on the federal budget will have serious consequences for capital markets.

For far too long, discussions about expanding coverage to the uninsured have foundered on the insistence by fiscal conservatives that costs need to be controlled in order to afford expansions in coverage. The cost containment efforts, however, have usually focused on administrative controls and fee constraints—anathema to providers. Patients have often seen the cost containment efforts of managed care as limiting *their* choices while saving money for *others*, not themselves. The result has been decades of political stalemate. SecureChoice provides a new solution: restructured incentives for patients and providers, enhancing both choice and responsibility. It has few arbitrary constraints, relying instead on market incentives for greater efficiency and higher quality. The reliance on markets and minimal government intervention may be attractive to the right, but the right may not like the increased taxes needed to assure fair and adequate income-based subsidies. Universal coverage and protection of the poor may be attractive to the left, but the left may be uneasy about the long-term vulnerability of income-based subsidies and the continued reliance on tax incentives for employment-based contributions.

A Health Care Compact to formalize and protect the necessary compromise may be the best way to achieve the legislative consensus needed to move forward. It not only will bring together the president and both parties in Congress, but also must have the active and open support of the major interest groups. The Compact should generate the same political security as Medicare's "third rail" status. It should incorporate a clear vision for health and health care, building on a long-term societal commitment to equity and improvement combined with flexibility and choice. It should put people, not costs, first. The commitment should be to cover whatever it takes to achieve high-quality care.

The incentives of the system will be relied on to bring down the rate of growth in health care costs. The nation faces—but so far Congress has refused to address—an impending crisis on the issue of how to fund the implicit Medicare obligations to the baby boomers. If carried on the books and then converted to an investment trust, as General Motors had to do with its retiree obligations when it transferred them to the United Auto Workers, the amounts would be staggering. The UCP will be implicitly assuming that obligation on behalf of the nation. It will need as much creativity and support as possible in undertaking that task. The Health Care Compact would provide a vehicle to do that.

The challenge in achieving the necessary consensus in a comprehensive long-run proposal that requires compromise among opposing players is the fear that if one gives up something now in exchange for future promises, the promises will not be kept. A Health Care Compact is needed to allay those fears. It should be carefully designed to preclude partisan tampering in the future but to allow well-vetted policy changes in keeping with the original intent. There are some key policy choices, however, that need to be addressed explicitly. These include the appropriate role of government and governance structures, how SecureChoice will be financed, and how value-laden health care issues will be addressed.

Key Issues to Address

One of the underlying controversies in health reform has been between those who see health care as a right, best protected through a universal entitlement analogous to Social Security, perhaps with a government-run system, and those who do not see health care as something to be guaranteed by the public and prefer to keep govern-

ment's role to a minimum. Although I believe that a just and equitable society should guarantee the availability and accessibility of
health care to its members, I find the arguments for government provision or control of health care delivery far less compelling. This con-
viction led to the design of SecureChoice, with features to facilitate
dynamic flexibility and efficiency, but with both strong market and
equity characteristics. The opportunity for compromise is here; the
question is whether it can be achieved and maintained.

Although various special interests may lose some advantages with
the market-driven processes of SecureChoice, once it is in place, individual organizations will succeed or fail depending on how they
adapt to the new rules. This will create new special interests that will
maintain these new rules of the game, enhance the stability of the
system, and reinforce the Compact. The equity- and value-based aspects of SecureChoice, however, will be more vulnerable because
they will not have the same political constituency.

Public versus Private Financing of Coverage

A core feature of the Compact will be determined by the political decision on the mode of financing. At one extreme, the system can
be fully publicly financed, probably with a broad-based tax such
as increased payroll or income taxes or a new value-added tax. Various taxes have slightly different incentive and equity implications as
well as ideological advantages and disadvantages. The largely payroll-
based Medicare tax maintains the notion that everyone (or at least
all workers) pays the same percentage of his or her earnings and
thus should be eligible for identical benefits. At the other extreme,
the income tax is paid only by people with incomes above a certain
amount, and the rates increase somewhat as income increases. This
progressiveness is attractive to those who value equity, but it supports the idea advanced by some that the better-off are being taxed to
subsidize those whom they may see as the "unworthy poor." Somewhere in the middle is the value-added tax. Used in most other in-

dustrialized nations, it is essentially a tax on consumption. While it is apparently regressive because its percentage does not rise with income, this problem can be offset with increased income tax credits for those with low incomes—or, given the purpose here, with income-based subsidies for health insurance.

A completely tax-based system would incorporate the ideal of universality in coverage. The question is whether tax funding for *everyone* would extend to *everything*. Most "universal" coverage proposals featuring tax financing focus on a basic benefit package and incorporate the potential for people to add coverage beyond the basic package. SecureChoice follows this approach, but in an unusual way: it covers everything involved in treating major acute and chronic illnesses, along with selected preventive services. It envisions that at least some co-payments of various forms would be retained for minor acute care. Tax-based funding, moreover, will still be needed to offset the co-payment costs of those whose incomes are low.

The SecureChoice design offers several options with respect to the extent of tax-based financing. At one extreme, public funding can be used to cover the major acute and chronic illness care provided through the UCP *and* most of the premiums associated with the remaining coverage. What is left to the consumer would be only the co-payments and differential costs associated with providers whose practice styles and fees are above the "norm," as well as the costs of "Platinum coverage." Those with very low incomes would still need subsidies to offset at least part of those residual costs. At the other extreme, coverage through the UCP (directly or indirectly) would be required by an individual mandate; extension of the current employer-based tax subsidy would facilitate voluntary contributions. Coverage for minor acute and less critical preventive services could be tax subsidized through the same mechanism. Much more substantial income-based subsidies would be needed to make these mandates and coverage for minor acute care affordable for people with low incomes. A middle option would use taxes to cover the costs of UCP coverage but leave the remainder of care to the individual, again with subsidies for those with low incomes. In each instance I am assuming sufficient tax revenue to cover the subsidies needed (or direct coverage) to ensure that everyone is covered. The question, then, relates to the appropriate role for government funding *beyond* that needed to achieve the desired level of equity.

To avoid risk selection and free-rider problems, everyone needs to have coverage for services that address major acute and chronic illness; hence the creation of a universal pool. There is a certain logic to funding the UCP through taxes, and this can be done in such a way that everyone feels engaged in the process, much as is the case with the Medicare program. More important is the control issue: fully tax-paid financing of the UCP may require direct government oversight and involvement that could restrict flexibility and give too much power to special interests.[1] The greater the degree of tax funding, the greater the need for careful protections—both structural and political—built into the Compact to keep special interests from hijacking SecureChoice.

The question of public versus private funding for minor acute episodes is even more complex. People may make different decisions with respect to the care they want for these relatively low-cost events, and some may feel that their coverage is not worth the taxes they would pay. A fully tax-funded approach will almost certainly increase the pressures to use standardized benefits, such as is now the case with Medicare. This requires that a government agency decide exactly which services belong in the benefit package and which ones do not, how deductibles and co-payments are set, and what fees are allowable. This level of micromanagement is vulnerable to political pressures. More important, it lacks the flexibility and mass customization designed into the patient- and provider-based premium approach. Embedding enough protections in the Compact to maintain this flexibility with respect to both minor acute care and preventive care will be particularly challenging because of the wide range of issues and constantly changing medical possibilities.

Whether the current tax exemption for health insurance should be extended to voluntary coverage for minor acute care (the middle option) is both a technical and a political question. People should have maximum flexibility in the design of their coverage and the trade-offs between monthly premiums and co-payments or deductibles; it would not be reasonable to offer tax subsidies for premiums but not for co-payments. The current tax system, however, does not differentiate between coverage for major acute and chronic episodes and for minor acute care, so there may be resistance to eliminating all the tax benefits for the latter. Yet there is less rationale for extending tax exemption for *all* the net premiums and co-payments charged by the payment intermediaries (PIs), especially the costs associated with fees (or practice styles) that are substantially above the average. A compromise would be for the Compact to require the UCP to specify what would be considered "Gold coverage," not just for major acute and chronic care but for everything else as well, and allow this to be tax exempt. The additional premiums for Platinum coverage, or the costs of care not included in the Gold package, however, would not be tax favored.

All versions of the mandate model will require subsidies to make the premiums and out-of-pocket costs affordable for everyone, preferably through income-based subsidies. As discussed in Chapter 6, this is technically feasible and not overly complex, but it relies on Congress to appropriate and the president to spend the necessary money to fund the subsidies. Guaranteeing this support will be important in getting the compromise needed to pass SecureChoice with mandates.

An important feature of the Compact is that it moves to a unitary system from the perspective of providers; that is, each has to deal with only one payment intermediary. Although patients may choose a variety of co-payment and deductible options, the services covered and referral patterns used do not depend on who is contributing the money for the patient's coverage—whether her employer, her family, or the Federal Health Equity Agency. From the perspective of the physician, each patient should be equally welcome, and the focus of treatment should be on the patient's disease and preferences, not on the subsidy. Keeping "the system" together will enlist provider support in political efforts to make sure that the subsidies are adequately funded.

The Compact would largely supplant the funds currently channeled through Medicaid, SCHIP, and certain other programs for the poor. It makes sense for the income-based subsidy to be funded—or at least administered—at the federal level. It may also be politically wise to keep some of the income-based subsidy as a state responsibility with the supplemental funds channeled though the Funds Clearing House. The need for subsidy dollars will be countercyclical, because during recessions, employment-based contributions will fall, as will incomes, and the subsidy will therefore have to increase. As states are typically precluded from borrowing to meet their obligations, they will pressure Congress to increase its share, much as happened with Medicaid during the 2001 recession.

A third component of the Compact might be to include an "autopilot" aspect to the funding, much as increases in Social Security benefits are tied by formula to the consumer price index. The subsidy amount could be tied to various factors, such as maintaining a constant ratio in the proportion of disposable income spent on health care between those who are subsidized and those in a certain range above the subsidy line. In periods of extreme fiscal crisis, even entitlements can be changed, but requiring purposeful and visible action to reduce the subsidy is quite different from requiring action to increase or maintain it.

Similarly, some would argue that the unlimited exemption of employer-paid health insurance premiums from income and payroll taxes is a historical accident that should be reversed rather than reified. It has been in place for so long and is so embedded in expectations, compensation packages, and pension plans, however, that changing it may be overly disruptive. On a more subtle level, as a tax expenditure, it does not come up for annual review; as expenditures on health insurance increase, the cost to government rises automatically. This lack of control can be seen as problematic, or it can be an advantage if cost containment is to be handled by the incentives of the plan. A Compact is needed to assure providers and patients that the government share will not be arbitrarily cut.

Value-Laden Choices

The Compact will need to address—or perhaps agree *not* to address—certain value-laden issues that are sometimes stumbling blocks in health care discussions. Some groups feel strongly that specific services, such as abortion and contraception, must be included in benefit packages, and others feel as strongly that they must be excluded. Other decisions will also be necessary, such as how many trials of assisted reproductive technologies should be covered, or whether the UCP should pay for extreme or extended life support measures or for care in cases that doctors deem futile. In the first category are services about which there is usually little dispute as to clinical effectiveness, but about which some people have strong ethical or religious-based feelings. There should be no compulsion on providers to offer any services that they feel are either clinically inappropriate or morally unacceptable; a pluralistic society with increasingly diverse religious and ethical beliefs, however, should not use its health plans to impose the will of one group on others.

Decisions about coverage for life support or futile treatment are more complex. At times the arguments are based on religious values, as in the Terri Schiavo case, but often what is debated is who should make decisions on behalf of an individual. Because a significant fraction of medical care costs are incurred in the last year of life, some believe that cost containment will have to address the use of resources in such cases. Before we struggle as a society to resolve the difficult question of whether the UCP should set guidelines as to when to "pull the plug," we need to do better at eliciting patient preferences for palliative care. Enough people may decide that they do not want to pursue aggressive end-of-life care that the cost-based arguments for setting limits become moot.

A third set of decisions is already partially addressed by some conventional insurance coverage. Many plans limit benefits for cosmetic procedures, infertility treatment, or ongoing psychotherapy. The common themes here are that the interventions are discretionary, typically designed to improve quality of life, and usually provided by specialists who are enthusiastic about their benefits. Current approaches to coverage restrictions are problematic because whenever treatment can be postponed, people may select into specific health plans in order to obtain the benefit. The UCP eliminates this adverse selection problem but also raises public policy questions about whether some of these decisions, such as going through six or more rounds of expensive assisted reproductive interventions, should be borne collectively.

In general, the Compact should set the expectation that Secure-Choice will cover everything that would medically benefit the patient, leaving decisions on specific services for specific individuals to the providers and patients. The UCP should be willing to pay enough to cover the same services as those needed by providers who achieve superior outcomes. Difficult choices, however, will sometimes need to be made by the UCP; it should establish a broad-based panel to set guidelines for handling these complex ethical and economic issues. Among the categories that warrant consideration are (1) high-cost interventions that may result in the short-term postponement of death, such as certain cancer treatments; (2) high-cost interventions with a low probability of major success, such as in vitro fertilization; (3) very-high-cost services with a high probability of success for a few people, such as those with Gaucher disease (over $100,000 per year per patient); (4) moderate-cost services with quality of life benefits for many people, such as cosmetic surgery; and (5) low-cost but low-benefit interventions with wide applicability, such as routine bone density scans for low-risk patients.

The UCP may decide that some of these services are no longer experimental (and therefore no longer eligible for coverage through a trial) yet would "break the bank" if they become the standard of care without better assessment or incentives. One approach would be for the payment intermediaries to offer riders (an aspect of Platinum coverage) for a comprehensive package of such benefits, thereby mitigating the adverse selection problem. Thus if the UCP decides that its bundled payment for assisted reproductive interventions will cover three attempts, the rider might pay for an additional three trials. Ideally the income-based subsidy would also be applied to the purchase of such riders.[2]

Governance Considerations

The governance of various components of the new system will be of enormous interest to some players; one can easily imagine arguments over exactly how many seats should be on each oversight body and how many would be filled by the House, the Senate, and the president, and what their terms might be. Such details must be postponed until a real legislative proposal is drafted. Well before such time, however, consideration should be given to certain underlying features and issues. Indeed, governance decisions may be critical to the Compact because they will structure how easy or difficult it will be to make significant changes in SecureChoice and who will be able to influence such decisions.

The universal coverage pool should focus largely on macro, or big picture, issues. It should operate with the goal of balancing revenues and payouts in the long run; recognizing that there will be some fluctuations in this balance over time, it may therefore build up reserves. Whenever possible the UCP should set broad guidelines and allow the detailed implementation of those guidelines to be handled in a formulaic manner. Thus the policy may be that EDRG rates are set at the locality-adjusted cost of high-quality care. The determination of "locality" should be done in a manner that is formula driven and not, as is the case now, subject to congressional pressure to include a specific hospital in a different locality in order to increase its Medicare payments.

This argues for a relatively autonomous entity, similar to the Federal Reserve, to oversee the UCP. It should make periodic reports to Congress on how SecureChoice is operating with respect to both cost and quality. Appointments to this oversight board should be for long terms, as with the Federal Reserve Board, and the expectation is that they should be as apolitical as possible. The arguments for such an independent structure are stronger if some of the funding for the UCP comes from coverage purchased by individuals or through reinsurance purchased by employer-sponsored plans.

The UCP oversees only part—albeit a very large part—of the funding of the health care system. The long-term performance of the system will also be affected by investments in new health care technology and in the health care workforce. States may require federal funding for new health promotion activities. Federal and state legislation in areas ranging from farm subsidies to transportation policy affects both health and the need for medical care. Even with a well-funded, income-based subsidy program, separate funding will be needed for special programs and safety net providers to help those for whom simply providing coverage is not enough. Congress is unlikely to cede long-term authority over such decisions to the UCP—nor would that necessarily be a wise thing to do, even if politically possible in the moment. The UCP board of governors or a similarly independent group, however, could play a valuable role by incorporating into its annual report assessments and suggestions as to policy and funding changes that would further improve the health of Americans.

New Roles for Existing Players

The restructured health system will involve new roles for many of the current players. Their assessments of how such roles fit will partially determine political reactions to the proposal. Even where a group has a diminished role, individual firms within that group may do very well. Organizations and individuals will succeed through meeting the demands of patients directly or indirectly by assisting the providers who are most responsive to patients. There will be less opportunity for interest groups to exercise power via political processes—either in Congress or in agency decisions. While threatening to some, this may be freeing to others.

Physicians will return to center stage, but the parts to be played by various specialties will change. Primary care physicians will be paid for establishing medical homes for their patients and will have more flexibility in their practice with far less administrative burden. They will be able to spend as much—or as little—time with their patients as they wish and set their fees as they desire. The payment intermediary they choose to manage the claims of their patients will help them in this process, providing various analytic and decision-making tools based on their own data and those of other practitioners. The PIs will also help these primary care physicians understand that the financial implications of their practice style and fees, as well as those of the practitioners to whom they refer, are reflected in the premiums and co-payments borne by their patients. Gaining this increased flexibility and freedom is offset to some extent by losing the ability to have their own decisions averaged across all physicians in an area. The results reported back by the PI may not always be welcome, but physicians will be able to seek analyses from other groups that are not in the PI business, or to select an alternative PI that may be more helpful.

Specialists, to switch to a football metaphor, will essentially become either quarterbacks or special team members. Quarterbacking specialists will coordinate and provide complex diagnostic and management services. Their expertise will sometimes be sought by primary care physicians to reach a diagnosis in a complex case, carefully titrate medications, or offer selective referrals for complex interventions. Occasionally they will take primary responsibility for the ongoing management of a patient with a chronic condition, as in the example of Louisa at the end of Chapter 8. When in the latter role, they will provide the medical home for that patient and face the same incentives as PCPs. Primary care physicians and these quarterback specialists will develop even closer relationships than they may have now. Unconstrained by health plans, limits on the amount of time they can bill for advising patients, and arbitrary networks of "preferred providers," quarterback specialists and PCPs will be able to choose among all the available specialists for referrals. They will recognize the differing inclinations some may have, and when several have comparable technical expertise, PCPs will occasionally choose one over another for a particular patient in order to achieve the best match between the patient's preferences and the specialist's interpersonal and clinical style.

Specialists may educate PCPs about how to improve their management of certain patients with chronic illness or when to refer patients for diagnostic workups. Even though all are paid on what appears to be a fee-for-service basis, the emphasis will be on fee for "time and expertise." A specialist who can listen carefully and teach the PCP what to look for, thereby reducing the need for expensive tests and procedures, will be in demand—and will be rewarded for that ability.

The "special team" roles will be filled primarily by interventionists and by the providers of diagnostic information, such as radiologists and pathologists. They will usually be brought in by a PCP or "quarterback" specialist to do something for which they have special expertise. They may be part of a care delivery team (CDT) or may work separately with their own equipment and facilities. Those who are part of a CDT will coordinate far more with their colleagues and hospital partners than is the case currently. Though giving up some of the autonomy they now have, they will be far more protected from intrusive oversight by payers.

This new model builds on changes that are already occurring in medical care delivery with a growing split between physicians who practice in hospitals and those who do only ambulatory care. Comprehensive coverage of inpatient and expensive interventional care by the UCP requires clearer boundaries between physicians who decide whether to refer a patient for admission or intervention and those who profit by the services being delivered. The current anti-kickback or "Stark laws" that try to address this problem would be modified to allow financial arrangements among the various parties inside the CDT but limit them between the CDT and those outside it.

Hospitals will find fewer changes in their roles, except for the development of direct working relationships with physicians through CDTs. They will be attentive to clinicians in doing so because specialists who are not happy with the hospital and its CDT can shift to other CDTs and take their patients with them. Within the CDTs, physicians and hospitals that engage more productively with each other will achieve operating efficiencies and quality improvements benefiting the whole. Developing the governance structures and internal incentive arrangements to facilitate such engagement, however, may be an initial challenge. Although nurse practitioners and other clinicians may become CDT participants, as front-line members of the care delivery process staff nurses are likely to have an important role on behalf of the hospital in improving workflow and enhancing safety and quality. Hospital administrators may need to adopt some of the "shop floor empowerment" techniques pioneered by Toyota so that all presumed power is not vested in the physicians.

Not all care currently offered by hospitals will be delivered through the CDTs. Hospitals may partner with independent radiologists to provide imaging services for outpatient care. Hospitals also may support separate urgent care facilities—distinct from true emergency or trauma care—either on-site or at satellite locations to provide off-hours coverage for primary care physicians. Providing such services in a newly competitive market will challenge many hospitals to be more efficient, more careful in how they allocate overhead, and more thoughtful in their patient service and coordination.

Not-for-profit hospitals will need to reconsider how they will continue to warrant their tax-exempt status. With the advent of universal coverage for inpatient care and most other expensive services, offering free care will no longer be a way of demonstrating "community benefit." Among the roles that may be fruitfully explored, however, is community-based health promotion—ranging from improving the availability of healthful foods in local stores, to reducing violence in the streets, to working with schools to promote healthy lifestyles. Some hospitals will build on existing outreach programs for populations with special needs, such as language translation services or cultural awareness. Others will become deeply engaged in the training of new health professionals or in facilitating research that enters the public domain.

Health insurance carriers will experience a substantial change in certain aspects of their role. Those that become payment intermediaries will continue to pay claims, but the nature of that business will have changed substantially. With cost- and service-sensitive physicians, rather than employers, as their primary clients, the PIs will focus on rapid, low-cost claims processing. Rather than attempting to deny every claim that might be questioned, the PIs will find it more effective to examine patterns of claims to detect potential fraud; the occasional error will not be worth pursuing.

The actuarial and analytic expertise of the current carriers will help them design co-payment plans that provide appropriate incentives for patients in managing their minor acute care. This expertise will be even more valuable as specialists seek out new ways to arrange payments across multiple providers and services for chronic illnesses such as psychiatric problems and cancer care. Some carriers will build on their own in-house expertise; others will contract with firms that specialize in analyzing data. Yet an additional opportunity—and challenge—will be for carriers to shift from marketing coverage to employers to becoming information and service providers to physicians.

PIs will compete for physicians' business through the administrative services they offer rather than the premiums quoted for the "coverage" of their patients. They are thus less likely to confront the traditional underwriting cycle in which firms get into price wars by setting premiums below expected health costs to increase their market share and then have to catch up in subsequent years. The increased stability and predictability in earnings may be attractive to investors. Carriers, however, will be pressured to innovate continually, because firms with payment expertise outside of health, such as credit card firms, may enter the market by partnering with others that can offer specific analytic expertise.

Highly integrated medical groups are likely to experience relatively little change in their day-to-day operations. Those currently not taking on risk as HMOs may experiment in doing so if they perceive efficiencies to be gained in staffing, information coordination, or practice styles. Alternatively, they may purchase reinsurance from the UCP to cover hospitalizations and partner with a PI to cover out-of-area benefits. Some prepaid group practices may now benefit from favorable selection, while others may suffer from the obverse; as these differentials will be largely obviated, they will need to compete more on the basis of true performance.

Independent insurance brokers may perceive a threat from the creation of SecureChoice but may find an even more important role to play in this new setting. Most brokers now earn commissions on the coverage they obtain for their clients. These are typically small employers or individuals, but the vast majority of people currently have coverage selected by their employers and have few choices. Under SecureChoice the patient's physician chooses the PI, but every patient has a wide range of choices with respect to the specific coverage options offered. Some coverage options, especially those that rely on a high deductible for minor acute care, may be integrated with savings accounts of various forms. Brokers may offer advice about health insurance coverage in combination with automobile, home, life, and long-term care insurance, as well as overall financial planning and portfolio management, perhaps even linking this to tax preparation. Some employers may cover the cost of such services as part of a benefit package, helping their employees make the most of their overall compensation. With PIs constantly improving their coverage options, people will have greater need to seek out the advice of impartial experts; the demand for such information will come from all patients, not just the few currently buying individual coverage.

The employers' role will change substantially, although this will depend somewhat on whether SecureChoice is fully tax supported or continues to rely on employment-based contributions. Even if the latter occurs, unless an employer decides to keep its current plan, it will no longer need to worry about the specifics of the coverage provided. Some employers may shift to a salary reduction plan, allowing all workers to direct part of their wages in a tax-preferred manner to their health coverage account. Employers with long-term obligations for retiree health insurance may pay the UCP to take over that liability, thereby reducing their long-term financial risk and improving the attractiveness of their stock.

Some employers that now use their benefits to build worker loyalty may continue to do so by paying for benefits counseling and helping their employees take a long-term perspective on compensation. SecureChoice, moreover, will encourage employers to focus more attention on employee *health*. Medical costs associated with occupation-related injuries and illnesses will be covered by the plan rather than separately through workers' compensation benefits. The disability benefits of workers' compensation will remain, however, and the comprehensive data collected by the pool will make it easier to identify industries or firms with above-average injury rates and costs. The UCP may seek reimbursement of those costs or, more likely, first pressure firms to address the causes of the injuries. Carriers of workers' compensation, moreover, are likely to mine these data to identify firms with lower-than-average injury rates in order to identify best practices. Employers may also shift their attention to health promotion, both at the worksite and at home or in the community, to enhance productivity through reduced work loss.

Government roles will also change. If Medicare is rolled into the plan, the federal government will have a much-reduced direct role in most aspects of medical care delivery. Unlike Medicare, which is deeply involved in decisions about covering specific new services and adjusting fees and hospital payments, the UCP is committed to paying whatever it takes to provide superior care, leaving clinical choices and cost containment to the built in incentives of the system. The primary federal role will be funding the Federal Health Equity Agency to provide income-based subsidies for premiums and co-payments. The administration of this, however, is far simpler than the current federal-state Medicaid program, relying on a small set of programmatic rules and direct linkages to the Internal Revenue Service. Certain federal health care programs will continue; special programs addressing the needs of select populations with limited health care resources or highly intertwined social and health problems, such as inner city residents and Native Americans living on reservations, should be continued and enhanced.

Focusing more on the pure public good aspects of federal involvement, the Food and Drug Administration should continue to assess and regulate the safety and effectiveness of new drugs and devices. SecureChoice, however, will facilitate far more effective post-marketing surveillance of new drugs as well as enrollment of people in clinical trials for Phase III assessments. This will speed the approval of new drugs and devices while making it easier for physicians or the FDA to limit the use of less beneficial or frankly harmful innovations. Federal funding of fundamental research spanning the spectrum from the biomedical research portfolios of the National Institutes of Health and the National Science Foundation to the health services research portfolios of the Agency for Healthcare Research and Quality should be expanded, with much greater proportionate growth in the latter. Just as pharmaceutical and biotech firms support the translation of basic research into applications, the UCP may support applied research that will help in assessing health care delivery, analytical tools, and innovations in care. The federal government should continue and expand its funding loans for the education of health professionals. This may be done either directly or by transferring resources to the UCP, which will be closer to the information identifying specialty and geographic areas of special need.

The UCP will have a long-term perspective on the health care system and health in general. By implicitly assuming responsibility for health care costs decades from now—and in some instances explicitly offloading such responsibility from employers and labor unions in exchange for up-front funds—the UCP has a clear interest in lowering the rate of growth in health care costs.[3] The incentives built into SecureChoice are designed to facilitate that goal, but they focus more on health care providers than on the fundamental determinants of health. The UCP's data systems, however, will help monitor changes in factors such as obesity, violence, and accidents. The UCP may also advocate for federal funding of demonstration projects, call for policy changes in realms as diverse as education or agriculture, and even press for formal health impact assessments analogous to environmental impact assessments.

State roles in health care are varied and complex. The income-based subsidy will largely replace existing Medicaid, SCHIP, and similar state-based programs. States may increase the range or depth of the subsidy for their residents. States have primary responsibility for regulating insurance plans and HMOs; they may extend these rules to payment intermediaries. Physicians, however, are likely to hear complaints from their patients much more rapidly and may implicitly police the behavior of PIs by being able to switch at will to more responsible and responsive ones. State licensing of professionals and health facilities provides some important protections for patients but often simply supports the economic positions of specific interest groups. CDTs, in particular, may press for more flexible scope-of-practice rules as they take on greater financial and malpractice risk.

One can hope that all of the current players find their new roles more appealing than under the status quo, but change—even a positive change—often meets resistance. Moreover, it would be dishonest to imply that there will be no losers. Achieving a more efficient allo-cation of resources will involve some disruption. The "administrative waste" in underwriting and claims processing, or the heavy mar-keting of new drugs to physicians and consumers, represents income for some people. Far simpler enrollment and claims processing will mean fewer sales representatives and claims processors. In some cases the generic roles may change and even improve, but there will be ac-tive parts for fewer players. Procedures, images, and lab tests will still be used in patient care, but probably in smaller numbers than cur-rently projected. Physicians in those specialties may thrive by apply-ing their skills and expertise—sometimes by explaining when a pro-cedure or test need *not* be done, probably reducing employment opportunities for some of their staff. A smaller role for government will lead to fewer jobs in certain agencies.

Even where jobs may be cut or profits reduced, however, some people and firms will do very well. In this market-oriented ap-proach it is difficult to predict precisely where the rewards will be. SecureChoice is demand driven, requiring physicians, CDTs, and PIs to respond to patient preferences. Manufacturers and others—even academic training programs—will, in turn, need to be more respon-sive. Those who are able to respond creatively will be well rewarded.

Transition Issues

Though largely built on existing organizations, SecureChoice involves many new relationships and processes that need time to be tested and brought to scale. Furthermore it is designed to maximize vol-untary behavior and change, which also takes time. Employers and employees who are comfortable with their current comprehensive health plans will be able to keep them and meet the mandate. Like-wise, physicians and other providers should be able to phase them-selves into the new system. It may be important, however, to harness and lock in the political momentum for change with a Health Care

Compact and begin immediately certain activities with long lead times. This will probably require some incremental expenditure as the old and new systems operate in parallel.

Bringing New Systems On-Line

An important starting place—and one with potential for relatively quick benefits—is the establishment of care delivery teams in select clinical areas. To some extent physicians and hospitals already work together, but the relationship is often fraught with conflict, and current anti-kickback laws prohibit gainsharing. The priority of new legislation should be to allow the formation of CDTs, with appropriate safeguards to preclude undue financial benefits to physicians and others who refer patients to the CDT yet allow reasonable compensation for consultations by the patient's usual physician. The Medicare program may then invite the formation of CDTs to participate in a new expanded DRG (EDRG) payment system that bundles the traditional Medicare payments for hospitalization with payment for those physician services that usually occur during such episodes. The new CDTs would have to develop governance models and ways to allocate funding internally, as well as provide assurances that they will abide by the new anti-kickback regulations and make data on the services they actually use available to Medicare and the newly formed UCP. Medicare, in exchange, should set the EDRG rates on the basis of components of care that reflect current practice, but should promise (1) not to lower payments if the CDT achieves savings and there is no evidence of worsening quality, (2) to exempt the EDRG payment amounts from future across-the-board cuts in Medicare payments, but (3) to allow compensation to rise with across-the-board increases. CDTs may choose to address all Medicare services or just certain service lines, such as oncology care or orthopedics. In preparation for this, the UCP, in conjunction with Medicare, will identify what preadmission and postdischarge services should be included in the bundled payment as well as the level of risk reinsurance that is needed for outlier cases. Whereas traditional Medicare demonstrations are typically required to be budget neutral from Medicare's perspective, the UCP should use some of its initial funding to offset the costs and risks that may be incurred by either Medicare or the new CDTs in establishing this new model of care.

Simultaneously, significant resources should be invested in developing and assessing measures of outcome-based quality and resource use—key components of the information the UCP will need to determine payments to CDTs. SecureChoice can be implemented with payments based on average quality, but it will be far better to have outcome measures for at least some important categories of inpatient care to set the expectations of payment on the basis of what it takes to achieve superior outcomes. Data already in hand or reasonably available allow the calculation of risk-adjusted death rates for heart attack, pneumonia, and coronary artery bypass surgery patients and readmission rates within certain periods for conditions such as congestive heart failure. Measures of resource use may be approximated with nurse staffing information and the procedure and other information normally included in Medicare claims.

Developing the patient- and provider-based premiums for ambulatory care will be a greater challenge, but the task is not insurmountable. Transitional aspects of the SecureChoice legislation will allow potential payment intermediaries and clearing houses to gear up. For example, one current barrier is that, with a few exceptions, no entity has access to all the claims associated with the patients of sets of physicians.[4] Most insurance carriers closely guard their own claims files or see them as belonging to the large employers for whom they process claims. The UCP may invite carriers to participate in start-up efforts. Those that make available to the UCP all their claims files (de-identified with respect to patient but not provider) will gain access to data pooled from all the other participating carriers, but without dollar amounts for charges and payments.[5]

With such data in hand, the UCP would solicit multiple proposals from organizations wishing to serve as clearing houses for the claims processing. These new claims clearing houses (CCHs) will develop the electronic "pipelines" to move claims quickly and efficiently from providers to the PI responsible for the patient and feed back information to the providers about their practices as well as to transfer the payments directly into their bank accounts.[6] The CCHs would develop simple bill submission software that meets SecureChoice standards to pre-process claims for normal electronic submission to Medicare, Medicaid, and conventional carriers. Thus, physicians' offices that sign up with the CCH will immediately simplify their billing under the current system while easing their transition into the new system. The UCP will require that the CCH interfaces be compatible, preventing the "first mover" from locking in clients.[7]

The CCH efforts will be available on-line, providing an immediate incentive to physicians to modify their billing workflow in exchange for simpler and faster claims submission. Much of the other work will be off-line, as carriers and other potential entrants to the PI market develop the information and experience necessary to design and price coverage. The pooled claims information collected by the UCP will be freely available to entities gearing up to become PIs (and providing their own data) but will not initially include the information needed to identify specific providers. All PIs in the same area will have access to the same claims data, but they will be able to access the fees only of the physicians with whom they have relationships. PIs, however, can invite physicians to release to the PI their encrypted identifiers along with their fees.[8] The PI could combine this information to estimate what premiums it will quote for a particular physician under various co-payment options. The PIs will also compete in offering M.D.-friendly software to help physicians assess the impact on their premiums of different fees and practice patterns.

PIs with access to patients having conventional coverage could offer as a transition to SecureChoice optional "individualized preferred provider networks."[9] Physicians with relatively higher-cost practices may be less likely to participate during this transitional period—or at all. Once SecureChoice is implemented fully, they may see their patient base slowly shrink over time unless they can convince their patients that their services are worth the extra cost.

It is difficult to specify with certainty how long the transition will take, but the changes I have outlined should be possible to achieve within a five-year period. SecureChoice does not require universal implementation of complex new electronic health records or the development and testing of sophisticated new risk adjustment techniques. Such innovations will greatly enhance the long-run performance of the system, but they can be added incrementally. The early stages of the transition are purposefully intended to be voluntary; even in the end, some employers may choose to design their own health plans, and some providers may choose to stay outside the system. Most, however, will find the new arrangements far simpler than present procedures as well as economically rewarding.

The time frame for thoroughgoing changes in medical education is substantially longer. Academic institutions change very slowly, and the educational pipeline is very long. Even if a new curriculum were implemented next year, the first physicians fully trained in that new model would enter practice roughly eight years later. If they were responding to the relative attractiveness of specialties today, or even in the early transition phases, they might well be misled. Early funding is needed for debt repayment programs to help steer students toward the careers that will be most needed in the future. Chapter 7 outlined some approaches for better aligning training and demand. Change in academic institutions can be jump-started with grants for periods of three to five years during the transition period to retool their curriculum for medical students and to develop new continuing education programs for physicians already in practice. This training will focus on evidence-based work for both clinical interventions and organizational change; it may be as important for physicians to learn how to develop and function in a new CDT as it will be to learn a new prescribing pattern.

Drug development also has a long pipeline, and the transition period will likewise be critical. The flow of new research findings into products that can improve health may be jeopardized by financial market jitters about how firms will fare under the new system. The transition period by itself will be helpful because, since most new drugs have an effective patent life of about seven years, many that are currently on the market will be off-patent and relatively untouched by the time the new incentives are implemented. Offering reinsurance to manufacturers for effective new drugs that lose market share to better later entrants should calm the financial markets somewhat. Health innovation funds may buy the rights to earlier-stage innovations that might otherwise not receive venture capital funding; competition among the HIFs, however, will ensure that these are fair prices.

The transition period should give physicians and hospitals time to develop CDTs that meet their needs. PIs will grow the data and expertise to price and administer patient- and provider-based policies. New organizations will arise to analyze and process data, convert it to useful information, and meet the needs of clinicians who want to learn how to provide better care more efficiently. If the system works even partially as well as intended, it will quickly attract physicians who prefer the new balance of empowerment and responsibility. Employers will find that they can continue their previous contribution policies while simplifying their compensation packages and better meeting the needs of their employees. Many of the working uninsured, once they are able to buy new age-rated policies, will do so even before an individual mandate is implemented. The mandate, of course, must go hand in hand with the income-based subsidy. How that and other national programs are addressed is a deeply political question beyond the purview of this book. A few observations, however, can be offered.

Leading the Transition with Existing Programs

Medicare and Medicaid are not just the two largest domestic programs but two of the potentially greatest beneficiaries of improved cost containment and quality. Medicare can take the lead in conjunction with the UCP in bundling payments to CDTs. Relatively simple legislation could allow Medicare beneficiaries to apply the actuarial value of their coverage to buy into the combination of the UCP and plans with patient- and provider-based premiums. Those who want to stay in their current plans would be allowed to do so.

Such an approach has advantages beyond being voluntary and legislatively unthreatening to Medicare. Medicare already has the most comprehensive claims dataset, so it could greatly facilitate building the administrative infrastructure required by the CDTs and PIs. The high cost associated with the elderly means that a relatively small number of patients would need to switch to the new model to make the business case for changing clinical and business practices. Patients would not have to switch physicians under the new plan to obtain the flexibility and (probably) lower premiums that it would offer. Medicare, however, faces a risk in this voluntary approach: those likely to switch to the new option are apt to be seeing physicians with relatively conservative practice styles. This will leave Medicare with patients increasingly concentrated among the physicians who use the most resources. Though not the same as classic risk selection—the sicker patients may be the ones attracted to SecureChoice, with its better coverage—this will present Medicare and Congress with a dilemma. They could continue to feed that more expensive practice style with increasing appropriations or apply across-the-board fee reductions, as in the past, to manage the Medicare budget. The first is not likely to be a politically viable solution as the UCP gains enrollment and visibility. The second will simply speed the process of transition, especially if physicians who refuse to participate in Medicare because of falling fees can continue to see their patients if they enroll in SecureChoice. The latter is also not a bad outcome in terms of transition to the new plan.

Making the transition is more complex for Medicaid. Most state programs have minimal co-payment requirements but often also have limited benefit packages, stringent eligibility rules, and low fees that limit provider participation. Medicaid expenditures are even more concentrated among the very sick than is the case for other payers, largely because some people, especially the disabled, become eligible *on account of* their illnesses. A voluntary transition approach is impossible because of their low incomes. Medicaid recipients would not be able to buy into the SecureChoice program even at age-sex rates without massive subsidies. A transition approach that could work, however, would be for state Medicaid programs to contract with the UCP for its expanded DRG payment model (at UCP rates) for inpatient care. This may be actually more expensive for some states than Medicaid payments, but it would be a step toward an integrated system.[10] A second step would be for Medicaid programs to contract with the UCP system to manage chronic illness care—a significant fraction of current Medicaid costs apart from long-term care. Full transition, however, will require complete implementation of income-based subsidies.

Toward a More Effective and Responsive Health Care System

Fundamental reform to achieve greater efficiency, more quality, and enhanced responsiveness *is* possible. Models tried in other countries will not work here because of our history, politics, and values. They also fail to build on the innovation and diversity that characterize the United States. Simply expanding the kind of coverage we now have, moreover, will not solve the other problems we face in our health care system. Indeed, simply expanding reimbursement-based plans will merely worsen the cost pressures.

We *can* do much better. The good news is that our health care system has plenty of resources to care for our population. We do not really need more money; we need better-designed incentives. Looking at the current system makes it clear that patients, providers, insurers, and others respond to existing incentives in predictable and understandable ways. To achieve a far more responsive and cost-effective system, we have to think differently. The changes, however, are not all that complex once we step back from what exists and carefully plan what we would like to have in its place.

SecureChoice is a proposal for fundamental reform. It has the potential to improve care markedly and slow the rate of growth in health care expenditures. It is not just an exercise in economics but takes into consideration the political realities of change. Secure-Choice should set the standard for the realistic assessment of alternatives. Slogans are not blueprints; architectural concepts without solid engineering will not stand. A carefully constructed new design for health care, however, can well serve both future generations and ourselves.

Notes

1. Build on What You've Got

1. Constrained fees can limit access, however, as demonstrated in a study of scheduling waits to see dermatologists for (hypothetical) Medicare patients with worrisome moles in contrast to patients willing to pay cash for Botox injections. Jack S. Resneck Jr. et al., "Short Wait Times for Patients Seeking Cosmetic Botulinum Toxin Appointments with Dermatologists," *Journal of the American Academy of Dermatology* 57 (2007): 985–989.

2. Peter D. Jacobson et al., "Litigating the Science of Breast Cancer Treatment," *Journal of Health Politics Policy and Law* 32 (2007): 785–818.

3. For example, the California Supreme Court has held (and the U.S. Supreme Court declined to overturn) that Catholic Charities is not exempt from a California law mandating coverage by employers for contraceptives on the same basis as other prescription drugs. "High Court Declines Religious Dispute over Contraceptives; Catholic Charities Challenged Law on Drug Coverage," *San Francisco Chronicle,* October 5, 2004.

4. James Trussell et al., "The Impact of Restricting Medicaid Financing for Abortion," *Family Planning Perspectives* 12 (1980): 120–130.

5. Carmen DeNavas-Walt et al., "Income, Poverty, and Health Insurance Coverage in the United States: 2006" (Washington, D.C.: U.S. Government Printing Office, U.S. Census Bureau, 2007).

6. "Wal-Mart Memo Suggests Ways to Cut Employee Benefit Costs," *New York Times,* October 26, 2005, www.nytimes.com (accessed February 5, 2008).

7. DeNavas-Walt et al., "Income, Poverty, and Health Insurance Coverage."

8. "Carmakers in for a Long Haul in Paying Retiree Health Care," *New York Times*, September 15, 2004, www.nytimes.com (accessed February 5, 2008). The fall 2007 negotiations between the automakers and the United Auto Workers essentially shifted this responsibility to the union in exchange for tens of billions of dollars in funding. "UAW and GM: Deal or No Deal?" *Business Week*, September 18, 2007, www.business week.com (accessed February 7, 2008).

9. The California legislature established (and renewed) the California Health Benefits Review Program to provide unbiased assessments of the medical effectiveness, cost, and public health implications of proposed new mandates. See www.chbrp.org.

10. Vishal Agrawal et al., "Consumer-Directed Health Plan Report—Early Evidence Is Promising: Insights from Primary Consumer Research" (Pittsburgh: McKinsey & Co., 2005), www.mckinsey.com (accessed November 2, 2005); and Stephen T. Parente et al., "Evaluation of the Effect of a Consumer-Driven Health Plan on Medical Care Expenditures and Utilization," *Health Services Research* 39, no. 4, pt. 2 (2004): 1189–1209.

11. Melinda B. Buntin et al., "'Consumer-Directed' Health Plans: Implications for Health Care Quality and Cost" (Oakland: California Health-Care Foundation/RAND, 2005), http://www.chcf.org (accessed November 1, 2005).

12. Leslie J. Conwell and Joel W. Cohen, "Characteristics of Persons with High Medical Expenditures in the U.S. Civilian Noninstitutionalized Population, 2002" (Rockville, Md.: Agency for Healthcare Research and Quality, 2005), www.meps.ahrq.gov (accessed November 27, 2005).

13. Kenneth Arrow, "Uncertainty and the Welfare Economics of Medical Care," *American Economic Review* 53 (1963): 941–973.

14. The terminology in this arena is sometimes contentious. I typically use "consumer" when referring to a person outside a treatment setting and "patient" when referring to someone getting care. I use "provider" to refer to clinicians and organizations that offer care, reserving "clinician" or "practitioner" to include a range of health professionals such as physicians, nurse practitioners, psychologists, and clinical social workers who may independently treat patients.

15. In the Kaiser system the physicians treat only Kaiser patients, and Kaiser patients get nearly all their care from Kaiser clinicians. Because people need to find new physicians if they leave Kaiser, this reduces their inclination to leave the plan relative to people in HMOs where one can change plans and keep the same physician. The greater "connection" means Kaiser sees its enrollees as potentially lifetime members.

16. Elliott S. Fisher et al., "The Implications of Regional Variations in Medicare Spending. Part 1: Health Outcomes and Satisfaction with Care," *Annals of Internal Medicine* 138 (2003): 273–287; Elliott S. Fisher et al., "The Implications of Regional Variations in Medicare Spending. Part 2: The Content, Quality, and Accessibility of Care," *Annals of Internal Medicine* 138 (2003): 288–298.

17. John E. Wennberg, "Unwarranted Variations in Healthcare Delivery: Implications for Academic Medical Centers," *BMJ* 325 (2002): 961–964; John E. Wennberg, "Dealing with Medical Variations: A Proposal for Action," *Health Affairs* 3 (1984): 6–32.

18. Michael D. Cabana M.D. et al., "Why Don't Physicians Follow Clinical Practice Guidelines? A Framework for Improvement," *Journal of the American Medical Association* 282 (1999): 1458–65.

19. Gerard F. Anderson, "Medicare and Chronic Conditions," *New England Journal of Medicine* 353 (2005): 305–309.

20. Peter Q. Eichacker et al., "Surviving Sepsis: Practice Guidelines, Marketing Campaigns, and Eli Lilly," *New England Journal of Medicine* 355 (2006): 1640–42.

21. Linda T. Kohn et al., *To Err Is Human: Building a Safer Health System* (Washington, D.C.: National Academy Press, 2000).

22. A. R. Localio et al., "Relation between Malpractice Claims and Adverse Events Due to Negligence: Results of the Harvard Medical Practice Study III," *New England Journal of Medicine* 325, no. 4 (1991): 377–384; T. A. Brennan et al., "Relation between Negligent Adverse Events and the Outcomes of Medical-Malpractice Litigation," *New England Journal of Medicine* 335 (1996): 1963–67; Troyen A. Brennan and Michelle M. Mello, "Patient Safety and Medical Malpractice: A Case Study," *Annals of Internal Medicine* 139 (2003): 267–273.

23. Discussions of malpractice often address bad outcomes (death, or injury) in the legal definition of malpractice but not mistakes or errors.

For example, medical malpractice is defined as "failure of one rendering professional services to exercise that degree of skill and learning commonly applied under all the circumstances in the community by the average prudent reputable member of the profession with the result of injury, loss or damage to the recipient of those services or to those entitled to rely upon them." Bryan A. Garner, ed., *Black's Law Dictionary*, 6th ed. (St. Paul: West Group, 1990), 959, as cited in "Limiting Tort Liability for Medical Malpractice" (Washington, D.C.: Congressional Budget Office, 2004), 3.

24. B. A. Liang, "A System of Medical Error Disclosure," *Quality and Safety in Health Care* 11, no. 1 (2002): 64–68.

25. There are three sociological definitions of professionalism. The first, traditional definition distinguishes professions from other occupations in terms of the work itself. Professionals possess an intellectual technique that requires special training. The second, revisionist definition holds that one cannot distinguish professions by the nature of the work or training. What is distinct about professionals is not the nature of the work but that it is socially constructed by the status that comes with a profession. This definition holds to "labeling theory," or the power of society to create reality by categorizing the world in a certain way. The third, critical definition agrees with the second definition that professionalism is socially created but emphasizes that this social construction is not a random or evolutionary process but rather an intentional process in power seeking. Professionalism requires having political control over one's own work. This definition takes into account how professions restrict access to training and certification that provides membership. See, for example, Magali S. Larson, *The Rise of Professionalism: A Sociological Analysis* (Berkeley: University of California Press, 1977).

26. Victor R. Fuchs, "Economics, Values, and Health Care Reform," *American Economic Review* 86 (1996): 1–24.

27. David M. Cutler, "Making Sense of Medical Technology," *Health Affairs* 25 (2006): 11–29; J. D. Kleinke, "The Price of Progress: Prescription Drugs in the Health Care Market," *Health Affairs* 20 (2001): 43–60.

28. This is in sharp contrast to the situation in most parliamentary systems, in which the ruling party has near-complete control of the policy process.

2. Overview of a Restructured Health Care System

1. The care that has been shown to prevent or make it markedly easier to treat major acute and chronic illnesses is included in the first category. The rest of preventive care is in the second.

2. Concepts and acronyms such as UCP are summarized in the glossary at the end of the book.

3. See discussion in Chapter 3.

4. Economists often focus on decisions "at the margin," for example, not the first test needed to determine the diagnosis, but the sixth one to make absolutely sure. In many cases a patient may enter a hospital needing to pay 100 percent of the costs for the first $500 of care, then 20 percent of costs for the next $10,000 of the bill, and then nothing further because the maximum out-of-pocket amount has been reached. For such patients, if the cost of hospitalization is likely to exceed $10,500— as is often the case—this essentially implies a $2,500 fixed cost, with additional services rendered "free" at the margin. In that scenario the patient has no financial incentive to decline additional tests and treatments as long as they offer some benefits above their inherent risks.

5. This description of inpatient versus outpatient care is an oversimplification of how SecureChoice is designed. There is a good bit of detail in Chapter 4 on the "difficult to categorize" episodes.

6. It probably does not matter much whether the physicians, hospitals, and health plan are part of the same entity or linked by exclusive contracts. Various state laws, for example, often require the physicians to be a separate medical group, but this does not seem to matter except for legal expenses.

7. For incentive reasons it is best that not everything be fully tax funded even if this were politically possible. Given the general American resistance to taxes, I do not spend much time on a fully tax-financed option.

8. This obviously ignores the ways in which co-payments and deductibles affect patient demand for care. Capitation plans usually rely much less on such patient incentives, while FFS plans use them as a primary tool for cost containment.

9. Provider-based interventions probably have a small role in disease prevention relative to lifestyle changes that may be influenced by the media,

tax incentives, and legislation. Such societal interventions are addressed in Chapter 7.

10. "The Advanced Medical Home: The Patient-Centered, Physician-Guided Model of Health Care" (Washington, D.C.: American College of Physicians, 2006), www.hhs.gov/healthit/ahic/materials/meeting03/cc/ACP_initiative.pdf (accessed June 9, 2008).

11. Leslie J. Conwell and Joel W. Cohen, "Characteristics of Persons with High Medical Expenditures in the U.S. Civilian Noninstitutionalized Population, 2002" (Rockville, Md.: Agency for Healthcare Research and Quality, 2005), www.meps.ahrq.gov (accessed November 27, 2005).

12. R. Adams Dudley et al., "The Best of Both Worlds? Potential of Hybrid Prospective/Concurrent Risk Adjustment," *Medical Care* 41 (2003): 56–69.

13. This is a generic model of SecureChoice which assumes that it is not all tax funded and includes some employer contributions to the UCP and enrollee premiums for minor acute and preventive care. Other funding options for SecureChoice are discussed in Chapter 6.

14. Rudolf Klein, "The Troubled Transformation of Britain's National Health Service," *New England Journal of Medicine* 355 (2006): 409–415.

15. Clifton Gaus, "An Insider's Perspective on the Near-Death Experience of AHCPR," *Health Affairs* W3 (2003): 311–313. "Medical Guesswork," *Business Week,* May 29, 2006, www.businessweek.com (accessed February 8, 2008).

16. For thoughtful discussions of the clinicians' perspective, see Atul Gawande, *Complications: A Surgeon's Notes on an Imperfect Science* (New York: Henry Holt and Company, 2002); Jerome Groopman, *How Doctors Think* (Boston: Houghton Mifflin, 2007).

17. Amos Tversky and Daniel Kahneman, "Rational Choice and the Framing of Decision," in *Rational Choice: The Contrast between Economics and Psychology,* ed. Robin M. Hogarth and Melvin W. Reder (Chicago: University of Chicago Press, 1986), 67–94.

18. None of this is well described by rational choice models often used by economists. This is not to argue that economic approaches to understanding how the health care system works are flawed. Rather they are more applicable in some situations in which economic variables such as price dominate than in other aspects of clinical decision making. Furthermore, as discussed elsewhere in this book, the economic variables

are often rendered moot; for example, when an out-of-pocket maximum on patient expenditures is reached, coinsurance becomes irrelevant. A knee-jerk reaction bringing economic incentives back full force, however, is inappropriate. Instead we need to assess when economic assumptions and incentives are most applicable and useful.

19. Although the circumstances are quite different, the recent example of Canada illustrates my point here. The Canadian health care system, in place for decades, has federal funding but is actually implemented at the provincial level, and each province has precluded the sale of private insurance to cover services paid for by the provincial plans. This single-payer aspect was struck down in 2005 by the Canadian Supreme Court on the basis of its interpretation of the Quebec (but not the Canadian) charter terms relating to individual rights. The constitutional issues in the United States would be different, but the case demonstrates how even a generally well accepted system can be upended by a narrowly designed challenge.

20. Peter R. Orszag et al., "Addressing Rising Health Care Costs: A View from the Congressional Budget Office," *New England Journal of Medicine* 357 (2007): 1885–87.

21. Not everyone agrees with this perspective. Some prefer a system in which legislation can be used to preclude certain behaviors thought by some to be reprehensible or immoral. Arguments about contraception, abortion, and physician-assisted suicide come to mind.

22. Fifty thousand dollars is a rough breakpoint for QALY used in the NICE evaluations in Great Britain.

23. This hypothetical case is an example of the type of flexibility that, if used effectively, may convince the public that the system is fair and humane, and thereby prevent the emotional reaction to "difficult calls." A real case is that of a seventeen-year-old who died before an HMO would reverse its decision that a liver transplant in her case would be experimental and thus not covered. "Cigna Stands by Its Decision on Transplant," *Los Angeles Times,* December 25, 2007, www.latimes.com (accessed January 5, 2008). As shown in later chapters, physicians will be able to make such decisions for their patients as individuals, knowing that the cost implications will be borne by their patients collectively. An occasional "yes" will have little impact on overall premiums.

24. Historically there have been some notable exceptions, such as the Manhattan Project's development of the atomic bomb. The mid-twentieth century, however, was also a period when government service was more highly valued than it is today.

25. The history of anti-tobacco regulation is instructive in this regard. In many attempts, advocates repeatedly found themselves outmaneuvered by the industry at the federal level. They discovered instead that numerous simultaneous grass-roots actions with respect to indoor air rules stretched the usually generous resources of industry and that occasional victories could be built upon. See, for example, Michael Givel and Stanton Glantz, "Tobacco Industry Political Power and Influence in Florida from 1979 to 1999," Center for Tobacco Control Research and Education, University of California, San Francisco, 2003.

26. The Congressional Budget Office "scores" proposals in terms of their impact on federal expenditures over a five-year horizon. While difficult for even small changes, this is essentially impossible to do in an objective manner for proposals such as this one that fundamentally change the way the health care system operates. Various assumptions can be made, however, to come up with estimates that could appropriately inform the discussion.

3. Covering the Cost of Care

1. This discussion derives from a classic work on insurance markets. Michael Rothschild and Joseph E. Stiglitz, "Equilibrium in Competitive Insurance Markets: An Essay on the Economics of Imperfect Information," *Quarterly Journal of Economics* 90, no. 4 (November 1976): 629–649.

2. "Huntington's Disease: Hope through Research," National Institution of Neurological Disorders and Stroke, www.ninds.nih.gov (accessed February 8, 2008).

3. This is not precisely true, but it is difficult to determine exactly what the trade-off from an employer's perspective is. All the employer's expenditures for labor costs are charged against its bottom line. Some of these are direct wages and health insurance premiums. Some are the employer's share of payroll taxes, which are levied on wages (sometimes up to a fixed amount per year) but are not applied to benefits. Managing

the health benefits, however, costs the employer money through the need for extra positions in the human resources department, mailings during open enrollment periods, and the like. As will be discussed in Chapters 6 and 9, many employers have structured their overall compensation packages around a preferred mix of benefits and wages. Whether a total "cash out" of health benefits into wages would be exactly compensation neutral is unclear, but economists agree that the employer share is a "contribution" in name only.

4. Paul Starr, *The Social Transformation of American Medicine* (New York: Basic Books, 1982); Patricia A. Butler, *ERISA and State Health Care Access Initiatives: Opportunities and Obstacles* (New York: Commonwealth Fund, 2000).

5. This sample is based on people with employment-based coverage provided by a number of national health plans that submitted their data to Ingenix for use in risk adjustment. This subsample of 311,673 people had twenty-four months of continuous coverage.

6. Included in the "hospitalized" category are episodes of care that involve major procedures and anesthesia even though the patient may be treated on an outpatient basis or be in the facility for less than twenty-four hours.

7. Preventive care episodes can involve a hospitalization, but this usually occurs when there is a complication, such as a perforation during a colonoscopy, or for procedures defined as preventive (for example, prophylactic mastectomy) that are unusual. Owing to their small number, they are included in the "acute hospitalization only" category.

8. Most studies of the concentration of expenditure look at similar data in a different fashion, merely presenting the proportion of expenditure accounted for by the top 5 percent or 20 percent of "spenders." With the exception of the bottom group—those with no claims—the categorization in Figure 3.1 is based on the nature of the episode experienced by people, not the magnitude of their expenditures. There are some people with MA/I episodes who spent relatively little (5 percent of people with MA/I episodes due to chronic illness had expenditures below $3,179; 1 percent had expenditures below $1,542). Some people with only minor acute or preventive care had substantial expenditures (for 5 percent they were over $2,230, and for 1 percent they were over $4,285).

9. With insurance data one typically observes what is called "regression to the mean"; that is, people with unusually high expenditures in one year will typically have lower expenditures in the next year. This would certainly be true if all health care needs were due to random occurrences. Some problems, however, if observed in one year are predictive of continuing use in subsequent years. These include the classic chronic conditions such as diabetes and congestive heart failure. Some problems may actually be negatively associated with subsequent use: for example, a kidney transplant eliminates the need for ongoing dialysis, and childbirth in one year is negatively associated with pregnancy the next. The data in Figure 3.2, moreover, take into account regression to the mean by comparing 2004 expenditures on the basis of a categorization of 2003 health problems. Regression to the mean explains why those with no costs in 2003 do not also have zero costs in 2004. The important message is that an insurer of those people can be rather certain its average costs will be substantially lower than that of the overall pool.

10. If one were to assume that there is no social argument for spreading the risk of chronic illness, in theory voluntary insurance could be priced to cover the truly unpredictable major acute events, such as a hip fracture or first heart attack; most people with adequate incomes would probably buy such coverage voluntarily at a fair price. If we move from theory to the real world, however, such an approach would result in interminable haggling over whether an admission, such as for stroke, was due to a chronic illness or was "truly" unpredictable.

11. This assessment is based on the type of care they had and the reasons assigned for that care, not the dollar cost of their episodes. A woman with cancer undergoing expensive outpatient chemotherapy who is briefly hospitalized for an auto accident would be included in the major acute hospitalization category even though her chronic illness management costs may have exceeded her hospital costs.

12. This proposal to have a universal pool cover the costs associated with the high-cost areas of inpatient care and chronic illness bears some superficial similarities to proposals for reinsurance pools. See Katherine Swartz, *Reinsuring Health: Why More Middle-Class People Are Uninsured and What Government Can Do* (New York: Russell Sage Foundation, 2006). Reinsurance is simpler because it requires only that insurers keep

track of claims for each person, and when they exceed a certain amount, the reinsurance pool reimburses the carrier for part or all the extra cost. This allows carriers to set premiums in a less "discriminatory" manner because the costs of very high use enrollees will be reimbursed by the pool. The universal pool described here for all major and chronic illness costs, however, is purposefully designed to address two problems that remain with simple reinsurance: residual incentives for selection and appropriate incentives for providers. With reinsurance, carriers are still fully at risk for claims costs up to the threshold and for part of the costs above the threshold, leading them still to want to avoid people likely to have high expenditures. Once the threshold is reached, however, they will have much less incentive to attempt to manage costs either directly or by engaging with providers. Making the pool *fully* responsible for most episodes likely to be expensive gives the pool reasons to design incentives for providers to seek better ways of caring for those patients.

13. These data are from employer-based plans and do not include Medicare expenditures. The vast majority of people over the age of sixty-five included in these data are eligible for Medicare, but if they are working, their employer's plan is the primary payer.

14. Such policies could be similar to some of the current high-deductible health plans, many of which are paired with health spending accounts to maintain tax subsidies. The key difference is that the plans currently marketed focus on all health care; here they would be applied only to minor acute and preventive care. The implications of this distinction for selection and incentives in seeking clinically appropriate care are enormous.

15. As is the case throughout this chapter, I am ignoring the equity issues in mandating coverage without assuring that low-income people can afford it. Chapter 6 addresses these issues.

16. A recent study demonstrates this by examining the images presented in advertisements by health plans. In more competitive markets, plans were much less likely to show images or text that would be attractive to people who were sick (for instance, a person in a wheelchair) and much more likely to include images attractive to those who are healthy (for example, a couple playing tennis). Ateev Mehrotra, Sonya Grier, and R. Adams Dudley, "The Relationship between Health Plan Advertising and

Market Incentives: Evidence of Risk-Selective Behavior," *Health Affairs* 25 (2006): 759–765.

17. There is an extensive literature on the difficulties in achieving adequate risk adjustment. See, for example, L. I. Iezzoni, "The Risks of Risk Adjustment," *Journal of the American Medical Association* 278, no. 19 (1997): 1600–1607; Richard Kronick and Tony Dreyfus, *The Challenge of Risk Adjustment for People with Disabilities Health-Based Payment for Medicaid Programs: A Guide for State Medicaid Programs, Providers, and Consumers for the Center for Health Care Strategies, Inc.* (Princeton: Center for Health Care Strategies, 1997); Joseph P. Newhouse, Melinda Beeuwkes Buntin, and John D. Chapman, *Risk Adjustment and Medicare* (New York: Commonwealth Fund, 1999); Wynand P. M. M. van de Ven and Randall Ellis, "Risk Adjustment in Competitive Health Plan Markets," in *Handbook of Health Economics,* ed. A. J. Culyer and J. P. Newhouse (Amsterdam: Elsevier Science, 2000). The problem is largely the difficulty in predicting costs for next year on the basis of diagnostic and other data from this year. The solution offered here is not to add more and more detailed (and expensive-to-collect) data, but to shift from attempting to predict future medical needs and instead pay for them after the fact. The payment should not be simple reimbursement, however, but fixed amounts based on categories of patients. Medicare has done this in paying hospitals since 1983. This Prospective Payment System is prospective in the sense that the amounts per type of case are set in advance; the mix of cases for which the hospital is paid is determined retrospectively. R. A. Dudley et al., "The Best of Both Worlds? Potential of Hybrid Prospective/Concurrent Risk Adjustment," *Medical Care* 41 (2003): 56–69; H. S. Luft and R. A. Dudley, "Assessing Risk-Adjustment Approaches under Non-random Selection," *Inquiry* 41 (2004): 203–217.

18. Even for people with "comprehensive" benefits, multiple carriers may be involved because various types of coverage have been "carved out." For example, one carrier may deal with mental illness, another with pharmacy, and a third with other medical costs. If the problem is potentially work related, still other carriers may become involved.

19. As indicated earlier, all preventive care episodes account for less than 5 percent of total expenditures. They could be rolled into the UCP at relatively low cost, but this would create strong incentives for manufacturers

to develop new technologies that are "preventive" yet may offer few benefits and even create harm. Thus SecureChoice should cover only those preventive services shown to be cost-effective, allowing other preventive services to be included in "voluntary coverage" and assessing when they should enter the mandated package.

20. Such software, in this case the Symmetry system from Ingenix, was used to process the data underlying the results in Figure 3.1 and Table 3.1. Several other vendors have comparable products, and various products are being considered for use by Medicare.

21. This approach works well if there is professional triage to direct an anxious patient to the urgent care provider rather than the emergency department, and if all co-payments are waived for those who go to the emergency department (ED) and are then subsequently admitted or determined to have needed the higher level of care the ED can offer. J. Hsu et al., "Cost-Sharing: Patient Knowledge and Effects on Seeking Emergency Department Care," *Medical Care* 42 (2004): 290–296; M. Reed et al., "Care-Seeking Behavior in Response to Emergency Department Copayments," *Medical Care* 43, no. 8 (2005): 810–816.

22. Michael E. Chernew et al., "Impact of Decreasing Copayments on Medication Adherence within a Disease Management Environment," *Health Affairs* 27 (2008): 103–112; A. M. Fendrick et al., "A Benefit-Based Copay for Prescription Drugs: Patient Contribution Based on Total Benefits, Not Drug Acquisition Cost," *American Journal of Managed Care* 7 (2001): 861–867; A. Mark Fendrick and Michael E. Chernew, "Value-Based Insurance Design: A 'Clinically Sensitive' Approach to Preserve Quality of Care and Contain Costs," *American Journal of Managed Care* 12 (2006): 18–20; A. Mark Fendrick and Michael E. Chernew, "Value-Based Insurance Design: A 'Clinically Sensitive, Fiscally Responsible' Approach to Mitigate the Adverse Clinical Effects of High-Deductible Consumer-Directed Health Plans," *Journal of General Internal Medicine* 22 (2007): 890–891; A. Mark Fendrick and Michael E. Chernew, "Value-Based Insurance Design: Aligning Incentives to Bridge the Divide between Quality Improvement and Cost Containment," *American Journal of Managed Care* 12 (2006): 5–10.

23. Studies of variations in practice have been under way for decades, largely by researchers at Dartmouth Medical School. Over the years they

have demonstrated wide variations in resource use across geographic areas and physicians associated with various hospitals. Not surprisingly, because people are not randomly assigned to such groups, some have argued that such variations do not conclusively show that those receiving more care do not receive better quality. The weight of evidence is actually in the opposite direction: those in lower-use areas seem to have no worse, and sometimes better, measures of quality. See, for example, Elliott S. Fisher et al., "The Implications of Regional Variations in Medicare Spending. Part 1: The Content, Quality, and Accessibility of Care," *Annals of Internal Medicine* 138 (2003): 273–287; Elliott S. Fisher et al., "The Implications of Regional Variations in Medicare Spending. Part 2: Health Outcomes and Satisfaction with Care," *Annals of Internal Medicine* 138 (2003): 288–298. Even if objective outcomes were precisely the same, aggressive testing might result in more reassurance than watchful waiting. Whether the extra reassurance benefits the patient or the physician is another question. Aggressive testing can also result in more "false positive" results, creating anxiety when there is actually no cause for concern.

24. In this context I am using the term "practice pattern" to characterize all the resources used or ordered not just by the patient's PCP but also by other providers seen by the patient. Overall cost will reflect both practice patterns and the fees charged for those services. These issues are discussed in much more detail in the next chapter.

25. Repeated minor acute episodes can accumulate and may cause a significant demand for safety net services if such coverage is totally voluntary. There are also public health and other reasons for requiring that everyone choose a PCP as a medical home to keep track of immunization and other medical records. It would be reasonable for SecureChoice to require that everyone have at least a high-deductible provider-based plan though a PCP. For those who have not enrolled in advance, enrollment would occur either at the time of the first visit to a PCP or within thirty days of the visit.

26. J. J. Fenton et al., "Influence of Computer-Aided Detection on Performance of Screening Mammography," *New England Journal of Medicine* 356 (2007): 1399–1409.

27. This is analogous to some pharmaceutical benefits with low co-payments

for generics, higher co-payments for selected (preferred) brand-name drugs, and still higher co-payments for drugs not on the formulary. Nearly all such plans allow for second-tier coverage of non-formulary drugs if the preferred drug does not work for the patient.

4. Organizing Care and Paying Providers

1. Recent studies have indicated, for example, that more erythropoietin is actually worse for patients. James R. Wright et al., "Randomized, Double-Blind, Placebo-Controlled Trial of Erythropoietin in Non-Small-Cell Lung Cancer with Disease-Related Anemia," *Journal of Clinical Oncology* 25 (2007): 1027–32. Likewise, some of the newer, more expensive drug-eluting stents for patients with clogged arteries seem worse than the bare metal ones. Demosthenes G. Katritsis, Evangelia Karvouni, and John P. A. Ioannidis, "Meta-Analysis Comparing Drug-Eluting Stents with Bare Metal Stents," *American Journal of Cardiology* 95 (2005): 640–643.

2. "When Trust in an Expert Is Unwise," *New York Times*, November 7, 2007, www.nytimes.com (accessed December 1, 2007).

3. In the early days of Medicare it was proposed that DRG payments include the professional services provided by hospital-based radiologists, anesthesiologists, and pathologists. These professions mounted an effective campaign to be excluded from the payment to the hospital. The CDT model proposed here would include all physicians providing care in the facility, with payment going to the CDT rather than the hospital.

4. It would probably facilitate care to have a single CDT in each hospital, along the lines of Elliott Fisher's medical staff model. See Elliott S. Fisher et al., "Creating Accountable Care Organizations: The Extended Hospital Medical Staff," *Health Affairs* 26 (2007): 44–57. Allowing multiple CDTs in the same hospital, however, will level the playing field in the initial negotiations as hospitals and the physicians on their medical staffs come together to share financial responsibility. In particular, it will reduce the ability of a small number of holdouts to prevent the development of a CDT for those willing to form one.

5. In part this is a "numbers" problem. Even with one CDT handling all the patients in a certain category in a hospital, it may be difficult to detect

differences in quality. Splitting the patients across CDTs both lowers the number of cases in each and, more important, demands much finer quality-focused risk-adjustment measures. The "one CDT per hospital for each type of episode" rule need not be rigid. A multi-campus hospital could easily track patients and outcomes in each unit. Likewise, some major teaching hospitals have established separate "teams" for patient care management and outcomes assessment. Most hospitals, however, are not large enough to be realistically expected to support such approaches.

6. The development of CDTs is likely to be contentious; hospitals and physicians have not always had good relationships with each other. Allowing physicians to be members of competing CDTs may encourage individual physicians to feel that they have more bargaining power vis-à-vis the hospital, and that their individual interests will not be sacrificed for the good of their colleagues. In small or rural communities in which one hospital may be the "only game in town," the negotiations may be more fraught, but the symbiotic relationship among the players is more obvious.

7. "Admission" in this context includes episodes that may require a significant intervention and use of a facility and may thus be eligible for a major acute/interventional episode payment. This separation mirrors the distinction between occurrence and production risk. For the same reasons that gainsharing rules are designed to prohibit unnecessary surgery, the UCP can be a relatively passive payer for MA/I care only if its new gainsharing rules ensure that MA/I episodes are not being manipulated by the clinicians who will be paid by the episode. If that distinction is maintained, the UCP can be far less intrusive in its monitoring of the necessity for each admission than are current insurers and Medicare.

8. In practice there are adjustments based on local wage costs, as well as hospital-specific capital costs and teaching subsidies. The key point, however, is that unless a specific case is very expensive and is considered an "outlier," the hospital is essentially facing a fixed price once the nature of the case is determined. One current problem with DRGs that EDRGs will attempt to correct is that the former often give "credit" for additional diagnoses that may be complications attributable to poor care rather than comorbidities that were present at admission.

9. One may argue that the UCP should pay only for superior-quality care, or at least impose financial penalties on providers who fail to achieve superior-quality care. Although this is an attractive concept, its implementation is problematic. Independent of any political considerations, identifying the quality measures that will be used to determine who gets paid (or who gets paid how much) will be extraordinarily complex. Even when objective measures can be determined, there will often be multiple measures and much argument as to the cases in which it is most appropriate to apply them. Furthermore, quality differences between providers just above and just below the "cut line" will almost always be very small, and hence distinct classifications will be difficult to justify. Paying even low-quality providers what it takes to achieve superior care may amount to a bonanza for them, but only until their patients move to other, higher-quality providers. It is worth noting that now there are few incentives for quality, so this proposal is certainly better than the status quo.

10. For example, while in 2002 the national average for outlier payments was 5 percent of Medicare payments, they accounted for 17 percent of Tenet Hospitals' Medicare payments. "A Scandal-Ridden Tenet Stands by Its Man," *Business Week,* November 25, 2002, www.businessnessweek.com (accessed October 5, 2007).

11. Reinsurance usually describes the situation in which an insurance company offsets part of its risk by purchasing coverage from other insurers. The primary insurer typically carries much of the risk; the reinsurance policy comes into play only if expenditures are very large. Thus an insurer may write fire insurance policies for individual homes but buy reinsurance against the possibility that a whole neighborhood goes up in flames, causing it to pay off on many policies at once. With Secure-Choice, the UCP bears the occurrence risk and passes the production risk on to the CDT. The CDT in turn would usually cover most of its costs with the EDRG payments, but may buy reinsurance against the risk associated with the occasional unusually long hospitalization. Reinsurance is a fairly specialized business, typically with a small number of customers and infrequent claims of large magnitudes. This allows detailed examination of each claim, facilitating exploration of why the case was unusually expensive.

12. As will be discussed in Chapter 5, transparency in the underlying information is an important part of this overall proposal. If reinsurers simply dealt with CDTs on a case-by-case basis, there would be little opportunity for learning. With all the underlying data available, researchers and coalitions of CDTs (probably referral centers in this case) will identify subsets of EDRGs that have a high likelihood of being very expensive, regardless of where they are treated. The UCP would periodically split EDRGs into subgroups to better match the underlying risk.

13. The successful management of patients with cystic fibrosis is a classic example of this type of innovation and its identification. Atul Gawande, *Better: A Surgeon's Notes on Performance,* 1st ed. (New York: Metropolitan, 2007).

14. Here (and elsewhere) I describe how people and organizations will work with the new incentives of SecureChoice to perform better and more effectively. Not everything and everybody, however, will work so well; inadvertent problems and bad behavior will occur. Default mechanisms will be needed to make sure, for example, that coverage is guaranteed to those who fail to enroll and just appear at a hospital needing admission. Likewise there will be a few CDTs that find ways to "game" the system. Instead of just positing regulatory mechanisms to root out questionable behavior, SecureChoice includes various incentives for parties involved in transactions to monitor value. Sanctions may still be needed to deal with egregious cases, however.

15. Dani Hackner et al., "The Value of a Hospitalist Service: Efficient Care for the Aging Population?" *Chest* 119 (2001): 580–589; Robert M. Wachter, "An Introduction to the Hospitalist Model," *Annals of Internal Medicine* 130 (1999): 338–342; Robert M. Wachter and Lee Goldman, "The Hospitalist Movement Five Years Later," *Journal of the American Medical Association* 287 (2002): 487–494; Robert M. Wachter and Steven Z. Pantilat, "The 'Continuity Visit' and the Hospitalist Model of Care," *American Journal of Medicine* 111 (2001): 40–42.

16. Lawrence P. Casalino, Kelly J. Devers, and Linda R. Brewster, "Focused Factories? Physician-Owned Specialty Facilities," *Health Affairs* 22 (2003): 56–67; Anthony N. DeMaria, "Heart Hospitals: For Better or Worse," *Journal of the American College of Cardiology* 43 (2004): 1923–24; K. J. Devers, L. R. Brewster, and P. B. Ginsburg, "Specialty Hospitals:

Focused Factories or Cream Skimmers?" *Issue Brief: Center for Studying Health System Change* (2003): 1–4; Leslie Greenwald et al., "Specialty versus Community Hospitals: Referrals, Quality, and Community Benefits," *Health Affairs* 25 (2006): 106–118; Stuart Guterman, "Specialty Hospitals: A Problem or a Symptom?" *Health Affairs* 25 (2006): 95–105; John K. Iglehart, "The Emergence of Physician-Owned Specialty Hospitals," *New England Journal of Medicine* 352 (2005): 78–84.

17. This issue is present for all CDTs. It may be more problematic for specialized facilities because they may be starting with practice patterns that assume a less complex, more homogeneous mix of patients *within* an EDRG. The fact that many were organized around a more entrepreneurial model than most voluntary hospitals suggests they may be more opportunistic in responding to the SecureChoice model, especially in the early years, when payment and other issues are not fully worked out.

18. A major concern is likely to be raised about the need for such "unnecessary" tests to protect against potential malpractice claims. Chapter 7 outlines an alternative to the current malpractice system to eliminate this concern.

19. Thomas R. Konrad et al., "Physician, Practice, and Patient Characteristics Related to Primary Care Physician Physical and Mental Health: Results from the Physician Worklife Study," *Health Services Research* 37 (2002): 119–141.

20. There is far too little empirical experience with different organizational sizes and arrangements to know whether there is an optimal size or structure for ambulatory care delivery. The discussion here focuses on how a new payment model could work in an extremely fragmented system in which nearly all the "signals" and incentives have to be economic. In more formal organizations other rewards, such as prestige, and other tools, such as leadership, can be used.

21. As with long-term care, which should be addressed separately, services for the combined educational and medical needs of the severely developmentally disabled or those with severe mental illness requiring extended hospitalization should be addressed through specially designed and funded programs.

22. Credit card companies provide an excellent example. They are financially responsible for fraudulent bills but typically do not carefully ex-

amine every charge. When charges fall outside a pattern—say, a rug purchased in Morocco appears for a cardholder whose charges usually come from California vendors—the request will be denied because it may be due to identify theft. If the charge is preceded by numerous small restaurant charges in Morocco, the company will assume that the cardholder is on vacation. The concept of an "acceptable degree of error," however, does not work well in public systems. Such errors are typically uncovered by the opposing political party and are classified as "fraud and abuse," resulting in pressures to root out every error regardless of the administrative and other costs involved in doing so.

23. David J. Brenner and Eric J. Hall, "Computed Tomography: An Increasing Source of Radiation Exposure," *New England Journal of Medicine* 357 (2007): 2277–84.

24. State law and family expectations will determine at what age a child's medical information may be withheld from the parents.

25. The FCH is designed merely to transfer payments among accounts and should not have to bear the risk that a family won't pay. Otherwise it will need to perform credit checks and other costly maneuvers. Income-based subsidies will eliminate most of the payment problems; the rest can be addressed by having shortfalls added to the family's federal tax bill.

26. The next chapter addresses how SecureChoice will risk-adjust payment *within* chronic conditions.

27. The concepts underlying this process are sensitivity and specificity, combined with underlying population prevalence. T. W. Loong, "Understanding Sensitivity and Specificity with the Right Side of the Brain," *BMJ* 327 (2003): 716–719.

28. For example, the UCP may mandate that every coverage package offered by PIs must include the cost of yearly mammography for women over the age of forty as well as the cost of the expected number of CT and other diagnostic tests appropriate for women of that age. Thus, on average, the "right" number of tests have been paid for, and the challenge is for the clinicians to decide for whom they should be done.

29. Alain C. Enthoven and Laura A. Tollen, "Competition in Health Care: It Takes Systems to Pursue Quality and Efficiency," *Health Affairs* (2005): 420; Alain C. Enthoven and Laura A. Tollen, *Toward a 21st Century*

Health System: The Contributions and Promise of Prepaid Group Practice,
1st ed. (San Francisco: Jossey-Bass, 2004).

30. Lyndia Flanagan, "Nurse Practitioners: Growing Competition for Family Physicians?" *Family Practice Management* 5 (1998), www.aafp.org (accessed February 8, 2008).

5. Choices

1. In practice, data would be organized in relational databases so they can be accessed in various ways. These three key variables will allow various important analyses described in this chapter. Because each person is linked to a medical home or primary care provider, the term "principal provider" is used here in a generic fashion to identify the person or entity most responsible for the episode. For an MA/I episode, this would be the care delivery team; if a PCP delegated chronic illness management to a subspecialist, the latter would be the principal provider for that CIM episode.

2. Alain C. Enthoven, "Consumer-Choice Health Plan (Second of Two Parts): A National-Health-Insurance Proposal Based on Regulated Competition in the Private Sector," *New England Journal of Medicine* 298 (1978): 709–720; Alain C. Enthoven and Richard Kronick, "A Consumer-Choice Health Plan for the 1990s: Universal Health Insurance in a System Designed to Promote Quality and Economy (1)," *New England Journal of Medicine* 320 (1989): 29–37; *Harnessing Openness to Transform American Health Care* (Washington, D.C.: Committee for Economic Development, 2008), www.ced.org (accessed February 8, 2008).

3. Greg D'Angelo, "Health Care Tax Credits: The Best Way to Advance Affordability, Choice, and Coverage," *Heritage Foundation WebMemo,* November 28, 2007, www.heritage.org (accessed December 8, 2007).

4. This research began even before the landmark Rand Health Insurance Experiment and continues. Joseph P. Newhouse, *Free for All? Lessons from the Rand Health Insurance Experiment* (Cambridge, Mass.: Harvard University Press, 1993). For the purposes of this discussion, unless otherwise qualified, the term "co-payment" is used to refer to a fixed charge per visit or episode and "coinsurance" to represent situations in which a

patient is responsible for a fixed percentage of the costs incurred after a deductible.

5. "Bargaining Down That CT Scan Is Suddenly Possible," *New York Times,* February 27, 2007, www.nytimes.com (accessed December 5, 2008).

6. The UCP covers the cost of chronic illness management by transferring funds to the PIs. Chronic illness and acute care, however, may interact. For instance, a patient choosing to use telephone consults for minor acute problems will be less frequently in the office, and therefore will have fewer "chance" opportunities to have her blood sugar checked for her diabetes.

7. The simulation techniques to produce such estimates are available and are not difficult to implement. H. S. Luft and R. A. Dudley, "Assessing Risk-Adjustment Approaches under Non-random Selection," *Inquiry* 41 (2004): 203–217.

8. Not everyone uses computers or is Web literate. Chapter 9 describes how independent insurance brokers can help fill this need for guidance. In practice, what are described as two separate Web sites here would probably be seamlessly integrated from the user's perspective. The first, however, uses national data with simple adjustments for local prices; the second reflects the choices available locally. The local site would probably incorporate the information from the national site in its own format. It is important to note that there is no reason for any site to have a monopoly on the information, so separate sites are likely to develop, for example, catering to certain language groups.

9. All PIs will be required to offer at least the same basic sets of co-payments, maximum out-of-pocket (MOOP) options, and so on to allow rough comparison in costs across providers. An implicit assumption here is that differences across providers will be relatively large in comparison to PI-specific differences in coverage options. The requirement that PIs price (and offer) certain standard sets of coverage will not force them to offer packages for which they have no takers for that type of coverage. For example, a PI working for PCPs with primarily low-income patients may find few takers for a very high deductible coverage and might not be able to price that appropriately. Requiring that the PIs actually offer the standard packages that serve as the basis for their customized versions will prevent them from quoting low premiums for

plans that are not really available and charging higher ones for those actually being offered. To return to the car analogy, the second-level comparison is when the customer decides to get the deluxe version of the sedan rather than the stripped-down version. The third level is the decision to add the top-of-the line stereo and cargo net in the trunk.

10. Over time, CIM payments may include various physiological measures, such as CD4 count for HIV or FEV_1 for asthma, but patients may not know these values or report them accurately.

11. When our daughter developed asthma, we were shocked when her pediatric allergist offered to drop off the equipment she needed. She explained that she always did so because it allowed her to do a quick scan for potential allergens in the home. Unfortunately for her, this was not a "billable" visit.

12. Current PPO networks are often imposed on providers and patients. In SecureChoice the network can be customized by the PCP to include providers with whom the PCP is most comfortable. Consumers would have a choice of narrow or broad networks with premium differentials reflecting patients' preferences rather than illnesses.

13. Much as one would like to rate airlines by their on-time arrival rates, no one would want to fly on a punctual airline whose planes crash. Episode outcome measures should focus more on the reason for the treatment than on the occasional complication. People have a hip replacement to improve their functional status, but some unfortunately experience a severe infection, occasionally resulting in death. The goal should be to make the surgery always so safe that no one gets an infection. Until care becomes as safe as flying, the panel would need to decide on an infection rate above which care should not be considered to be superior even if the functional status (of survivors) is high.

14. J. M. Bentley and D. B. Nash, "How Pennsylvania Hospitals Have Responded to Publicly Released Reports on Coronary Artery Bypass Graft Surgery," *Joint Commission Journal on Quality Improvement* 24 (1998): 40–49; E. L. Hannan et al., "Improving the Outcomes of Coronary Artery Bypass Surgery in New York State," *Journal of the American Medical Association* 271 (1994): 761–766. See also www.calhospitalcompare.org (accessed February 10, 2008).

15. With the underlying data readily available and with various professional

and advocacy groups encouraging better measurement, the risk adjustment will improve over time. The key point is that for the primary purposes of the UCP, there is no need for it to wait for the "perfect" risk adjustment model.

16. The outcome measures need not be frozen forever, but should be much
more stable than the risk adjustment measures and models. Even if a
"perfect" model were available at the outset, improvements in medical
care require reestimation of the risk models each year. Experience with
various risk-adjusted "report cards" suggests that continued enhancement of the models, including adding new variables, is well accepted by
clinicians and hospitals and welcomed because it represents continuous
improvement.

17. These cases will be excluded from both numerator and denominator in
the reports. If the risk models are appropriately calibrated, this will not
affect the results. The risk model panels and staff, however, will have access to both included and excluded cases. If CDTs are able to identify patients prospectively whose true (ex post) rate of bad outcomes is greater
than that predicted by the model, analysts should be able to learn what
additional factors need to be measured and include those factors in subsequent years. CDTs, however, may well find that although the patients
they chose to exclude from assessment often had poor outcomes, they
actually had predicted rates of bad outcomes that would have more than
compensated for that. Technical issues in the estimation of risk models
using logistic functions result in giving a little extra "credit" for the
highest-risk patients; if this results in greater acceptance, correcting for
such errors may be unwise.

18. Some clinicians express a concern that the mere publication of measures
will open them to malpractice suits. There is little evidence of this,
largely because most suits begin with an identified patient rather than
an attorney following up on an outcome rate reported in the newspaper.
Chapter 7, however, offers a different perspective on malpractice that
uses statistical measures to improve quality more effectively while reducing the concern of individual physicians about suits.

19. "Aetna Agrees to Change in Physician Ranking Methods," *California
Healthline,* November 14, 2007, www.californiahealthline.org (accessed
February 8, 2008); Valerie Baumen, "Accord with Empire Blue Cross

Blue Shield to Rank Doctors," November 14, 2007, www.newsday.com (accessed December 8, 2007); Martin N. Marshall, Patrick S. Romano, and Huw T. O. Davies, "How Do We Maximize the Impact of the Public Reporting of Quality of Care?" *International Journal of Quality in Health Care* 16 (2004): 157–163; Patrick S. Romano et al., "A National Profile of Patient Safety in U.S. Hospitals," *Health Affairs* 22 (2003): 154–166; Eric C. Schneider and Arnold M. Epstein, "Use of Public Performance Reports: A Survey of Patients Undergoing Cardiac Surgery," *Journal of the American Medical Association* 279 (1998): 1638–42. Physician concerns about harm occasioned by public reports are likely to be mitigated as more reports are produced, since they will no longer be "news." This does not, however, necessarily reduce their potential to influence self-improvement behavior.

20. Such observational studies, even those using sophisticated statistical methods, complement rather than replace what can be learned from well-controlled randomized trials. The latter, however, are far more expensive and typically lag behind practice. By the time they are published, clinicians often argue that the treatment approaches being compared have already been supplanted.

21. It is not clear whether legislation would be necessary to identify those who refuse to cooperate. It may be sufficient for the groups attempting to assess quality to share the information about which clinicians and CDTs refused to cooperate when they had been identified as having high-quality, low-cost care. While clinicians may not want their local competitors to know exactly how they achieve their results, they should be less circumspect. Occasional refusal is certainly understandable because cooperation may be disruptive to workflow. Consistent refusal, however, may call for a public explanation, at least if requested by journalists.

22. Few patients will search out detailed information about the quality of care offered by various specialists, although some do so even now. More likely, primary care physicians will use such information in responding to patient requests for appropriate referrals. The presence of a wide range of measures is important in helping patients understand that quality *does* vary across providers and settings and that they can choose, or ask their PCP to help them choose.

23. Some Web sites will offer pre-weighted measures that fit well for a set of stereotypical patients, much as investment sites may first assess a potential client's tolerance for risk, time horizon, and other factors before suggesting a mix of investments. Other sites may offer people the ability to set rather complicated criteria, such as requiring at least some CDTs within ten miles to have high-quality scores for emergency admissions, but a willingness to go thirty miles for CDTs with high scores for schedulable admissions.

24. "WellPoint Doctors to Get Zagat Ratings," *USA Today*, October 21, 2007, www.usatoday.com (accessed November 24, 2007).

25. Cathy Charles, Amiram Gafni, and Tim Whelan, "Shared Decision-Making in the Medical Encounter: What Does It Mean? (or It Takes at Least Two to Tango)," *Social Science and Medicine* 44 (1997): 681–692; Dominick L. Frosch and Robert M. Kaplan, "Shared Decision Making in Clinical Medicine: Past Research and Future Directions," *American Journal of Preventive Medicine* 17 (1999): 285–294; Robert A. McNutt, "Shared Medical Decision Making: Problems, Process, Progress," *Journal of the American Medical Association* 292 (2004): 2516–18. See also www.fimdm.org (accessed February 9, 2008).

26. There is a large and complex literature on social and individual preference. Aside from the wide variability across individuals, social preferences can take into account future generations as well as interactions among individuals. Most of this chapter focuses on improving information for individuals. Chapters 6 and 7 address issues that are more relevant at the societal level.

27. Michael Pine et al., "Enhancement of Claims Data to Improve Risk Adjustment of Hospital Mortality," *Journal of the American Medical Association* 297 (2007): 71–76.

28. In practice, CIM payments will be made to the PI on the basis of the patients associated with each PCP. As the PCPs will have access to information showing exactly how much is included for such data reporting, they could ask for it simply to be passed on to them. Uncooperative PIs will soon find themselves replaced by other PIs. Alternatively, PIs may develop (or purchase) software and other tools for their PCPs to make such data collection easier and more efficient.

29. PCPs selected as a medical home may require that their patients allow

the PI to notify them of any bills submitted by other clinicians. It would then be up to the PCP to request (with the patient's implicit or explicit permission) that relevant clinical information be incorporated in an overall medical record. Electronic transfer of such information would obviously be ideal but not necessary.

30. Even more problematic is the risk faced by a plan that developed a reputation for very high quality, especially for complex and expensive conditions, since this would make it particularly attractive to the sickest patients. Its good performance would result in adverse selection and financial ruin.

31. A good example of this collective action is the Integrated Healthcare Association in California, which brings together large payers, health plans, medical groups, and others. It has successfully implemented a pay-for-performance program. See, for example, "Pay for Performance," California Health Care Foundation, January 2006, www.chcf.org (accessed February 8, 2008), and www.iha.org (accessed February 8, 2008).

32. These restrictions stem from federal legislation referred to as the Health Insurance Portability and Accountability Act of 1996, Public Law 104–191, enacted August 21, 1996, also referred to as HIPAA. Parts of HIPAA were intended to facilitate uniform data collection and transmission while enhancing and protecting the confidentiality of patient information. Its implementation has been controversial among researchers because it has made access to data far more complicated. In large part this is because HIPAA focuses on the current holders and users of patient data—providers and payers—with significant penalties for misuse of data by themselves or anyone with whom they share data. Because restrictions and penalties are not directly applied to subsequent users, current holders have been especially skittish about sharing data. This problem has been exacerbated by the lack of clear guidelines to providers and review boards. Roberta B. Ness and Societies of Epidemiology for the Joint Policy Committee, "Influence of the HIPAA Privacy Rule on Health Research," *Journal of the American Medical Association* 298 (2007): 2164–70.

33. Premium information, of course, is publicly available, but providers have the ability to set their own fees. If they could "see" the fees charged

by their compatriots, it would be easier for them to act collectively in setting fees, contrary to antitrust laws.

34. HIPAA makes an important distinction between de-identified information which has so many variables removed that individual records cannot be linked back to a person, and "limited dataset" information, which excludes easily identifiable information, such as name and address, but may include information such as birth date that might allow someone with expertise and other data to trace the record back to a patient. Researchers may seek a "waiver of authorization" from the relevant review boards (often several) to use such information without the express approval of each person in the dataset. In exchange, the researcher typically promises to use the data only for a specific project and to keep it in a secure environment. HIPAA, however, does not extend any penalties to breaches by researchers who inappropriately use such data. The proposed modifications to HIPAA focusing on the use of data for research will make it easier to use the data appropriately while adding security protection for patients. Ness and Societies of Epidemiology, "Influence of the HIPAA Privacy Rule on Health Research."

35. Academic researchers are typically driven to develop new ways of doing things and then publish the early findings. Several steps may then be needed to adapt those findings to user-friendly formats, but these often provide little academic reward. Licensing gives the researcher incentives to develop products far enough so that the market can appreciate their potential application and respond with an offer to take the next steps. Nonexclusive licensing allows the researcher to make sure the tools are not purchased and hidden, for example, by a firm with a similar product already on the market.

36. This 5 percent coverage notion was first used by the Rand Health Insurance Experiment to capture use by people experimentally assigned to the high-deductible plans. Chapter 6 discusses how this arrangement would work.

37. The key problem is with either the occurrence of very rare side effects or the higher-frequency occurrence of side effects that are naturally common. To detect differences in such rates requires very large sample sizes; to design clinical trials to assess such effects would further delay the potential benefits of drugs and devices that are ultimately shown to be

beneficial. The trade-offs in the appropriate testing and marketing of drugs and devices are discussed in Chapter 7.

38. Rather than placing the UCP in the position of having to respond to congressional pressures to "reassign" certain rural hospitals to distant metropolitan areas or having some facilities suffer in compensation because they are just over a county line, local wage adjustments can be based on average wage rates across those zip codes from which a facility draws its workforce.

6. Financing SecureChoice

1. For a more complete discussion of these incentive issues, see Harold S. Luft, "Insurance and Payment for Care," *FRESH-Thinking: Focused Research on Efficient, Secure Healthcare* (2007), www.fresh-thinking.org/docs/workshops_070301/Paper_H-Luft_accepted.pdf (accessed February 9, 2008).

2. Steven R. Machlin and Marc W. Zodet, *Out-of-Pocket Health Care Expenses by Age and Insurance Coverage, 2003,* Statistical Brief 126 (Rockville, Md.: Agency for Healthcare Research and Quality, 2006), www.meps.ahrq.gov (accessed February 9, 2008).

3. More information on these estimates is in the report cited in note 1. In brief, it is based on a sample of nearly eight million people with commercial coverage in 2003 from a variety of national carriers that submitted their data to Ingenix, Inc. The overall data exclude dental and long-term care costs; for the purposes of this discussion I also exclude drug coverage because that is often provided by separate plans with separate co-payment arrangements. Covered charges included in these data averaged $1,398 per individual. The Medical Expenditure Panel Survey reported a national average cost for commercially enrolled people of $2,206, of which 27.3 percent was for dental and drug costs. David Kashihara and Kelly Carper, *National Health Care Expenses in the U.S. Civilian Non-institutionalized Population, 2003,* Statistical Brief 103 (Rockville, Md.: Agency for Healthcare Research and Quality, 2005), www.meps.ahrq.gov (accessed February 9, 2008). The $1,398 is roughly comparable to the $1,603 implied by MEPS.

4. This is not to suggest either that such care is at the appropriate standard

or that many providers do not attempt to get the uninsured to pay for their care, sometimes to the extent that the patients have to declare bankruptcy.

5. Contrast this situation with the example of higher education. Many students do not go to college because of its cost; their grades are not good enough to make them eligible for the elite schools that are willing to offer need-based scholarships. If one were to ensure that every student able to do the coursework could go to college at no cost, there would be an enormous increase in demand for places, and significant new resources would have to be devoted to building classrooms and hiring faculty. A comparable increase in demand would not occur with appropriately designed universal coverage for major health care needs.

6. A wide variety of tax-based approaches can raise comparable amounts of money. The classic argument is that the income tax is more equitable because it is progressive, with higher percentage rates paid by those with more income and no taxes being paid by those with very low incomes. A payroll tax is levied only on wages and not on other sources of income such as dividends and capital gains that are far more prevalent among the wealthy. Various tax breaks and deductions, however, often reduce the effective income tax rate (relative to all income, not just taxable income) paid by the wealthy. A consumption-based or value-added tax, common in Europe, does not have the apparent progressiveness of the income tax but may be at least as progressive in effect, especially if a refundable income tax credit offsets some of the incremental taxes on low-income people. If such taxes are used to fund coverage for the poor, the net progressive effect is even greater. Payroll, sales, or value-added taxes are implicitly imposed on everyone, creating a stronger rationale for a unitary, solidarity-based approach than an income tax model, which explicitly transfers money from rich to poor.

7. This is the $209 billion in forgone taxes that results in $589 billion in employer and employee premiums. Thomas M. Selden and Bradley M. Gray, "Tax Subsidies for Employment-Related Health Insurance: Estimates for 2006," *Health Affairs* 25 (2006): 1568–79.

8. One could argue that it should not matter if, say, $589 billion in employer-paid health insurance is replaced by $589 billion in payroll taxes offering the same or better coverage. Most economists see the mix

of wages and benefits as part of an overall compensation package; some recognize that employers differ markedly in how they structure benefits. For example, to recruit comparable faculty, the University of California and Stanford need to offer comparable levels of total compensation. UC has a more generous health and pension package and, not surprisingly, lower salaries. If a universal coverage plan were tax financed, it would disrupt that balance—probably leading UC wages to rise relative to Stanford's. UC pensions, however, are tied to wages, making such an adjustment far more complex to implement. This is an example of how important the real-world considerations are when one is applying theoretically superior solutions.

9. The Hyde Amendment was passed by Congress in 1976, barring the use of federal funds to pay for abortions, largely in response to the 1973 U.S. Supreme Court's decision in *Roe v. Wade.* Medicaid cannot use federal funds to pay for abortions, except in the case of rape, incest, or endangering the life of the woman. (As of 2007, however, seventeen states independently provided funding for abortions.) Federal government employees pay for abortions out of pocket, as do U.S. military personnel and their families, federal prisoners, Peace Corps volunteers, and patients of the Indian Health Service.

10. George J. Annas, "'Culture of Life' Politics at the Bedside: The Case of Terri Schiavo," *New England Journal of Medicine* 352 (2005): 1710–15.

11. Both the MA/I and CIM types of episodes lend themselves to ongoing monitoring of conditions and payment approaches that can reduce gaming. If everything deemed "preventive" is automatically covered, however, this essentially brings back a fully insured FFS model for those services. This is not problematic for services that are valuable. Recent evidence suggests, however, that not all preventive services are even helpful (for example, computer-assisted assessment of mammograms), let alone cost-effective. This question is addressed in more depth in Chapter 7.

12. SecureChoice uses the naturally occurring variability in geographic practice patterns to learn what it takes to achieve better outcomes, adjusting for patient risk factors. The UCP uses local wage information to adjust for differential costs of inputs but does not adjust for higher use of resources that does not result in better outcomes.

13. Even in the fully tax-funded model, there is little reason for the UCP

to handle direct enrollment. Technologies for enrollment are likely to change over time. Customer service and responsiveness as people move and desire to change providers are important, and the UCP will have few advantages in this regard. Because ambulatory care is paid and monitored through the PIs, they should be the entry point for enrollment, merely sending the UCP information on who is covered. If a mandate model is used, the Funds Clearing House described elsewhere allows coordination across family members and sources of payment.

14. Over time, some categories of physicians (for instance, certain surgical specialties and hospitalists) may have all their activity paid through CDTs, leading to a loss of independent fee data. Much as is the case with current Medicare reporting by hospitals, the UCP would require all CDTs to submit annual reports on their costs and disbursements. Economists have developed various ways to approximate the "returns" (wages and shares of profits) to various types of labor and other inputs in enterprises with a mix of outputs, such as patients in various EDRGs.

15. This flexibility is implicit if SecureChoice is not completely tax funded. If public financing is used to cover the costs of care, as part of the political process providers will demand ironclad commitments that the Congress will not decide arbitrarily to reduce the funding of the UCP, for example, because defense spending is rising and a tax increase is politically infeasible. Chapter 9 addresses some of these political issues, which also arise in the context of maintaining commitments to income-based subsidies if the system is *not* tax financed.

16. This assumes, as is likely, that most people will include in their plan supplemental coverage for costs charged by CDTs that exceed what is paid by the UCP. There is little to be gained in terms of incentives to shift the incremental costs of higher fees to the patient in the midst of care rather than when the consumer is considering a referral. Negotiations over whether the higher fees are warranted by better quality are probably best done by the PCP or by the PI on the PCP's behalf.

17. Hospitals incur costs simply in negotiating contracts with insurers, and the billing operations required to deal with individual insurers are substantial. They would probably much prefer to get paid through a CDT. Especially as an increasing fraction of patients are covered through

CDTs, hospitals are likely to increase their charges to insurers continuing to pay on a fee-for-service basis.

18. This option could be seen as a plausible "work-around" for ERISA exemptions if that legislation cannot be changed and employers do not wish to "cash out" their contributions. In essence, the employer-sponsored plan would continue to be the "face" seen by the enrollee, but it would function like a standard payment intermediary behind the scenes. (This is the opposite of current ERISA plans, in which enrollees think they are insured by Blue Cross or Aetna, but in fact those carriers are merely processing claims on behalf of the employer.) A more substantive reason for the MA/I + CIM reinsurance option is if an employer has designed an ambulatory care benefit package that includes certain health promotion characteristics, such as stress reduction classes, and perhaps is even coordinated with worksite efforts. The PIs chosen by the PCPs of the patients covered by that employer may not offer those specific packages; this option allows the employer to offer them the benefit enhancements without having to ask each PI to create a new coverage package. Practitioners will still deal only with their own PI, which will then pass on the charges and premiums to the employer's plan. Employers will not be able to offer effectively less generous benefits or lower fees through this mechanism because practitioners will not accept discounted fees, and employees will be better off taking the contribution amount and opting for individual coverage through a PI (see discussion later in this chapter).

19. Although I use the term "reinsurance" here, it differs markedly from conventional reinsurance, which simply reimburses a primary insurer for costs exceeding a given amount. Such conventional reinsurance offers few incentives or mechanisms for appropriate care management. Chapter 5 outlined how a restructured payment system would create such incentives. The reinsurance described here transfers to the UCP a class of risks that conventional plans cannot manage well. By consolidating risks and payments, the UCP is able to offer providers incentives that encourage high-quality care.

20. Suppose a plan has a way of attracting low-risk (or avoiding high-risk) enrollees. If it reinsures them with the UCP, it pays the average cost per "risk cell," and any gains are averaged by the UCP. Contrariwise, a plan

attracting high-risk people will pass them on to the UCP, which absorbs their extra costs. The plan cannot, however, easily charge them more than the average because another plan will be able to undercut that price by offloading the risk to the UCP. The UCP spreads the risks of high- and low-cost enrollees across its total pool.

21. Gender is a much less important actuarial factor, and legislators will have to address whether gender-linked premium differences are to be allowed.

22. The UCP will offer a tool for these calculations based on its actuarial experience. Some very large employers may have sufficient data and expertise to do their own, perhaps more sophisticated, adjustments, accounting for how benefit design in the coverage they offer differentially affects the implicit contribution by demographic cell.

23. Long-term care insurance, possibly integrated with life, disability, and other coverage, may be an attractive new benefit.

24. Many employees who decline coverage now obtain it through their spouse but forgo the potential contribution. Any type of "cash out" of employer contributions will be particularly problematic for those employers offering more for employees choosing family rather than single coverage. It is legal for employers to offer more for employees who cover their families, but the economic rationale for this is weak.

25. The coinsurance and deductibles in the Medicare benefit are designed to reduce patient use. When these co-payments are covered by a supplemental plan, however, use goes up, and most of the additional cost is borne by Medicare, not the supplemental plan.

26. Payments to plans under Medicare Advantage are risk-adjusted to a far greater extent, largely because of the perception that they attract enrollees who present lower-than-average risk. Risk adjustment could be used in a similar manner for those who choose SecureChoice. Legislation would have to address the fact that the benefit package under SecureChoice may not be the same as the Medicare package.

27. Children, parents, and pregnant women make up three-quarters of the Medicaid population but account for 30 percent of Medicaid spending. *Medicaid: A Primer* (Washington, D.C.: Kaiser Family Foundation, 2007), www.kff.org/medicaid/upload/Medicaid-A-Primer-pdf.pdf (accessed February 9, 2008).

28. Broad-coverage direct-service programs, such as Veterans Administration Health and Indian Health, are more problematic because the federal government actually employs the providers who deliver care to people with special entitlements. People could be offered a "cash out" option to convert to SecureChoice, but this might decimate the programs and leave them unable to care effectively for those who do not switch. This may be particularly problematic for geographically isolated patients and providers (especially in the Indian Health Service) or for special programs such as spinal cord injuries in which the VA excels. One option might be to allow individual opt-out *and also* let the federal providers deliver services under SecureChoice to all patients.

29. The FCH can be quite flexible in this regard, but as I discuss later in this chapter, in determining income for the purpose of subsidies, the relevant "family" members and incomes may be defined differently.

30. Most people will know they are not eligible for a subsidy and will not request the FCH even to contact the FHEA. The complications here largely have to do with decisions regarding whose income should be counted for the purposes of subsidy. In the example of the father taking partial responsibility for the child no longer living with him, it is not clear whether all of his income would be included in the equity calculations, and if so, how that would affect calculations for potential subsidies for his new primary family. These decisions may also be affected by state law regarding responsibilities of divorced parents. While too complex for this discussion, they are far simpler than Medicaid eligibility rules.

31. In an ideal world, federal subsidies would be so high that this would not be an issue. More realistically, the federal dollars going into the FHEA will be a political compromise, and some states will choose to add subsidies for their residents. This would be done through the FHEA, eliminating extra bureaucracy. Comparisons across states of medical use and outcomes will allow assessments of the benefits of additional subsidies.

32. There is a reasonable concern about income-based subsidies creating a high marginal tax rate for low-income people. This gets into complex issues of taxes and labor force incentives. Substantial work is needed to see how problematic this issue will be once premiums are based on age-sex cells. If most of the work disincentive effect is at the very low end of the

income scale, the income-based subsidy could begin its phaseout above that point. The effect on premiums (especially among the young) of the high costs of a small number of disabled people unlikely to work anyway may be reduced by covering their costs in the UCP directly through taxes rather than having them spread over all enrollees in those age cells.

33. "Individual Taxpayer Identification Number (ITIN)," www.irs.gov (accessed February 9, 2008).

34. As described earlier, conventional plans would not be outlawed, but most will eventually buy into the UCP, and those that do not will need to meet its coverage standards.

35. There would probably not be a blanket exclusion for cosmetic surgery because some procedures following an injury or to repair a medical problem would certainly be covered. These judgments are notoriously elastic; many rhinoplasties are currently covered because they are described as correcting a deviated septum. Because part of these costs would be reflected in the premiums attributed to each medical home, incentives would be generated for primary care physicians to seek out specialists who use reasonable indications. Similar judgment would be applied to selective referrals to fertility specialists who follow reasonable protocols.

36. This prohibition has been struck down by the Canadian Supreme Court with respect to its application in Quebec. It is under challenge in other provinces.

37. If some CDTs were able to fill their schedules completely with patients having Platinum coverage, this could lead to a two-class system, with those CDTs able to hire the very best practitioners. This is unlikely to occur, but if it does, the UCP (and independent analysts) will be able to see if there is any difference in outcomes.

38. Classic insurance principles assume that people would have to buy Platinum coverage in advance of needing care. If Platinum simply offers what most people think of as frills, there is no reason why a carrier could not develop a policy that would cover the "extras" and price it with the expectation that it *will* be used, that is, that it can be purchased after a diagnosis.

39. Two policy issues would eventually need to be addressed with respect to Platinum coverage. In theory, tax-favored employer contributions could

be high enough to cover even the cost of incremental Platinum premiums. It is not clear that this will be a real problem, especially because other tax-favored uses of such contributions are likely to offer greater value to the very small number of people who would be eligible for them. If the plan works as one would hope, Gold coverage would be so attractive that very few people would buy Platinum coverage. Few people flying in first class are actually using their own after-tax dollars to purchase those tickets. The second policy choice focuses on the other end of the spectrum. Platinum coverage should ideally be not just for the rich but for all people who value health care much more highly than other expenditures. A truly equitable society would offer income-related subsidies to allow even the poor to make choices at the margin between using their limited income for, say, better housing or for Platinum coverage. Getting everyone into Gold coverage with appropriate income-related subsidies, however, is a sufficiently daunting political challenge.

7. Malpractice, Pharmaceuticals, Medical Education, and Prevention

1. T. A. Brennan, C. M. Sox, and H. R. Burstin, "Relation between Negligent Adverse Events and the Outcomes of Medical-Malpractice Litigation," *New England Journal of Medicine* 335 (1996): 1963–67; Elizabeth Graddy, "Juries and Unpredictability in Products Liability Damage Awards," *Law and Policy* 23 (2001): 29–45; A. R. Localio et al., "Relation between Malpractice Claims and Adverse Events Due to Negligence: Results of the Harvard Medical Practice Study III," *New England Journal of Medicine* 325 (1991): 245–251; D. M. Studdert et al., "Negligent Care and Malpractice Claiming Behavior in Utah and Colorado," *Medical Care* 38 (2000): 250–260.

2. An important exception is that of anesthesiology, which had extraordinarily high malpractice costs in the 1960s and 1970s. The profession instituted a process to learn from errors and then made changes in how care was delivered in the operating room to reduce the chances of error. K. B. Domino et al., "Awareness during Anesthesia: A Closed Claims Analysis," *Anesthesiology* 90 (1999): 1053–61; D. M. Gaba, "Anaesthe-

siology as a Model for Patient Safety in Health Care," *BMJ* 320 (2000): 785–788.

3. T. A. Brennan and M. M. Mello, "Patient Safety and Medical Malpractice: A Case Study," *Annals of Internal Medicine* 139 (2003): 267; D. M. Studdert et al., "Claims, Errors, and Compensation Payments in Medical Malpractice Litigation," *New England Journal of Medicine* 354 (2006): 2024.

4. Michelle M. Mello et al., "'Health Courts' and Accountability for Patient Safety," *Milbank Quarterly* 84 (2006): 459–492.

5. This differs from both negligence (in which only events caused by fault are compensable) and standards of strict liability (in which all injuries caused by treatment are compensable). Ibid.; L. R. Tancredi and R. R. Bovbjerg, "Advancing the Epidemiology of Injury and Methods of Quality Control: ACEs as an Outcomes-Based System for Quality Improvement," *QRB Quality Review Bulletin* 18 (1992): 201–209.

6. Corporate negligence liability in health law is well established, reflecting the responsibility on the part of an organization such as a health plan or hospital to ensure quality care. "What Is Corporate Negligence Liability," American Bar Association, www.abanet.org (accessed February 10, 2008). One of the current limitations to wide application of this doctrine is the separation between the hospital and medical staff, whereby the hospital can claim it has no control over the procedures the medical staff uses to police quality among its physicians. Establishing CDTs as entities responsible for the continuum of care would probably make this issue moot. The CDTs would need to bear the risk of suits and combine efforts to accept responsibility for quality. In the absence of CDTs, the second-tier litigation option would have to rest on firm contractual agreements between the hospital and members of its medical staff. In this scenario, physicians could expect an easier defense against suits (via an ACE settlement) if they waived the defense of separation of functions so that the medical staff effectively partners with the hospital in implementing changes that will make corporate negligence liability a reasonable course of action.

7. Defendants would be precluded from making settlements in health court cases conditional on plaintiffs' agreeing to keep the details of the case confidential.

8. The basic approach to the data analysis will be similar for the second-tier attorneys and the malpractice insurers: careful assessment of the data for unusual patterns followed by detailed analysis of the specifics of the case. The malpractice carriers and second-tier attorneys will probably contract with firms having the necessary statistical, clinical, and organizational expertise to undertake this work.

9. Victor R. Fuchs, "Economics, Values, and Health Care Reform," *American Economic Review* 86 (1996): 1–24. David Cutler has estimated the benefits and costs of various new technologies for addressing certain clinical problems. See D. M. Cutler and Mark B. McClellan, "Is Technological Change in Medicine Worth It?" *Health Affairs* 20 (2001): 11–29.

10. Richard L. Kravitz et al., "Influence of Patients' Requests for Direct-to-Consumer Advertised Antidepressants: A Randomized Controlled Trial," *Journal of the American Medical Association* 293 (2005): 1995–2002.

11. Dennis J. Slamon et al., "Studies of the HER-2/Neu Proto-Oncogene in Human Breast and Ovarian Cancer," *Science* 244 (1989): 707–712; Dennis J. Slamon et al., "Use of Chemotherapy Plus a Monoclonal Antibody against HER2 for Metastatic Breast Cancer That Overexpresses HER2," *New England Journal of Medicine* 344 (2001): 783–792.

12. Gottfried E. Konecny et al., "Therapeutic Advantage of Chemotherapy Drugs in Combination with Herceptin against Human Breast Cancer Cells with HER-2/Neu Overexpression," *Breast Cancer Research and Treatment* 57 (1999): 114.

13. Such a decision obviously depends on the clinical situation. It is much more feasible when one can try drugs sequentially and there is little risk in delaying the use of the possibly more effective, but certainly more expensive, drug. When either time or physiological factors make such sequential trials impossible, there will be market pressures to develop effective tests (such as identifying which women have overexpression of HER2) to determine the best strategy in advance.

14. Tracey R. Lewis, J. H. Reichman, and A. D. So, "The Case for Public Funding and Public Oversight of Clinical Trials," *The Economists' Voice* 4 (2007): 3.

15. If firms can selectively purchase reinsurance, it is likely that they will do so for those products they feel are most risky, keeping the best ones to

themselves. If the industry were to be "forced" to buy reinsurance from the government, there would be interminable discussions about the appropriate "price," especially as many feel the industry is already overly profitable.

16. As discussed earlier, it will be impossible for a reinsurer to accept risk for only some products of a firm.

17. The HIFs allow such entities to hedge their investment risk while helping them contain their long-term obligations for employee medical costs. Other pension funds may choose to shift some of their investments from traditional pharmaceutical companies with riskier business models into the HIFs, with their greater likelihood of long-term stable returns.

18. The public entities (or their unions) may be appropriately concerned about the guarantee of the UCP in this regard. A "doomsday scenario" requiring backup by the federal government may be part of the political deal needed to bring forth SecureChoice (discussed in Chapter 9).

19. "Cannot" is used advisedly here. For decades the FDA prohibited direct-to-consumer advertising. It is not clear whether legal interpretations prohibiting constraints on "commercial speech" would apply in this regard. Rather than dealing with the time delay and uncertainty in judicial decisions, however, we can circumvent the issue.

20. The added independence the UCP will have by *not* being directly part of the government will aid in its ability to undertake such ads.

21. Henry R. Desmarais and M. M. Hash, "Financing Graduate Medical Education: The Search for New Sources of Support," *Health Affairs* 16 (1997): 48–63.

22. The number of medical students choosing primary care residencies has been falling for the last several years, probably because primary care incomes are well below those in the procedure-oriented specialties. Many medical educators have decried this trend, but residency stipends are typically the same across training programs. Stipends for residents at the Mayo Clinic, for example, are $45,344 in the first year, rising to $57,624 by the seventh year. (These are figures for 2007; www.mayo.edu/msgme/benefits.html.) A potentially simple solution even without complete health reform would be to raise stipends for primary care residents, thereby attracting more students into those training programs.

23. Medicare's approach to supplemental payment for teaching is not well designed to encourage a shift toward primary care trainees.

24. A purely market-driven policy would argue that if physician payment levels and patient incentives are appropriate, such errors in career choice will become known, and the system will self-correct. In the long run this is probably true, but two concerns need to be raised. Specialists in the affected fields will probably seek to exercise political influence to protect their earnings. More important, if wise policies can prevent these career choice errors from occurring, there is a substantial savings in human capital.

25. Educational debt is an important factor for other health professionals, and programs may be designed that will work well for them. The very long training period for physicians, however, creates particular problems for that profession.

26. As with its investments in the HIF, these funds for the loan guarantees and forgiveness programs will first come from the UCP's acceptance of future health care obligations. In the long run these programs may be phased out.

27. Note that the focus here is on fee, not overall cost, increases. The latter reflect the combined effects of changes in fees and volume of services. Increases in volume may not necessarily signal shortages; indeed they may indicate an oversupply of services. Competition among physicians will return fee changes to their more usual role as price signals. The focus here is also on *changes* rather than levels of fees. Some specialties and geographic areas have high or low fees because of level of skill or cost of living and other factors. These would not be directly factored into these calculations. If fees began to increase rapidly because of shortages of primary care physicians or physicians of any type in rural areas, those are the types of slots that would get the increased loan forgiveness, even if hourly fees for specialists in metropolitan areas were still well above average.

28. There are some diagnosis codes for tobacco use disorder and history of tobacco use, but they may need to be modified for these purposes.

29. Claims data do not currently include some simple measures such as height and weight (to calculate body mass index) or blood pressure (to assess hypertension). As CIM payments would require the submission

of such information rather than just the presence of the diagnosis, changes in their values could be tracked over time.

8. How SecureChoice Would Work for Patients and Physicians

1. Harvey's employer has undertaken some careful analyses in making this offer because, as is the case with many employers, the PPO "benefit" appears to be worth more than it costs. That is, the benefit is available only to employees who are willing to "take up" coverage by paying their share of the premium. Before the individual mandate, many people eligible for coverage did not take it. Even when employees do cover themselves, they often forgo the extra employer contribution for family coverage. An employer like Harvey's with a rich benefit package would suddenly find more employees asking for contributions associated with family coverage. Some employers will make this available only to those who had previously taken such coverage; others will slowly adjust their overall compensation package to make tax-preferred contributions independent of family structure.

2. This is partly speculation, and will require some testing with simulations and actual behavior. It will certainly be the case that people who choose low co-payments will use more minor acute care than those who choose large co-payments and deductibles. As long as in most instances this reflects differences in stoicism rather than an unmet need for care, it is not a problem. Physicians and payment intermediaries may develop policies to prevent high co-payment arrangements from deterring people from seeking necessary care, such as not offering plans that combine high deductibles and charges for telephone consultations. In general, selection is a problem for *insurers* only if it cannot be reflected in premiums; it is a problem for *patients* if high premiums reflect health needs rather than preferences. Neither will be significant under SecureChoice.

3. See Table 3.1.

4. The PIs compete for physicians' business by offering efficient and low-cost claims processing, informational tools, and new approaches to coverage. Ideas such as waiving co-payments on the first five phone calls or e-mails per year would be tested by some PIs and, if effective, rolled out

to all their clients. Other PIs may then adopt or modify their approaches to coverage and information delivery.

5. A small number of people either will resist choosing a medical home or are so transient that a geographically based medical home will not make sense. Most of these people would be eligible for completely, or nearly completely, subsidized coverage. Safety net clinics will have supplemental funding to serve as de facto medical homes for such people, and they will develop electronically linked medical records to provide reasonable continuity of care.

6. These calculations reflect the care and fees not only of the "medical home" but also of the providers usually used by the patients who choose that medical home, weighted by the utilization patterns of those patients.

7. We went through such an exercise with three pediatricians before the birth of our first daughter. Their clinical approaches differed markedly, yet their technical skills were reputed to be comparable. We have friends who swear by each and would clearly be unhappy with either of the others.

8. Although the practice pattern information associated with each practitioner is available to PIs, researchers, comparative Web sites, and other analysts, fee information is included only on the claims submitted and is stripped off from most datasets to preclude price-fixing by providers or PIs. Premium quotes for specific medical homes can be obtained from the PI for each on the basis of a "generic" patient of a given age and sex. This is what is usually shown in the "comparison shopping" sites. Even though the UCP directly covers major acute/interventional costs and chronic illnesses, the actual expected costs for a person will also depend on the interaction of his or her chronic illnesses, coverage, and patterns of using care. Harvey is inclined to use CDTs and other specialists who may charge fees higher than what the UCP calculates as being required by providers achieving superior-quality outcomes. He also wants coverage that pays a significant fraction of those extra costs, and a PI cannot estimate its premium without knowing something about his chronic illnesses. The SecureChoice legislation could have precluded PIs from using such information in their premium calculations, but that would

have adversely affected physicians like Dr. Killy who attract a disproportionate share of such patients. In response, Dr. Killy would have incentives to encourage patients like Harvey to switch to other providers. Instead the legislation allows PIs to incorporate information derived from
billing data in their premium calculations because the vast majority of
the costs of chronic illness are covered by the UCP and are not transferred back to the patient. It is only the differential costs associated with
patient preferences that show up in individual premiums.

9. This constraint is designed to reduce the opportunity for HMOs to attract low-risk enrollees or to encourage those patients who develop
costly medical problems to switch back into the UCP. The UCP moni-
tors such switching carefully and adjusts (in the background) the "premiums" for risk differences. When primary care practitioners work only
within a given HMO and enrollees stay in the HMO for extended periods of time, selection issues are minimized. The principal reason why
people in such situations switch into or out of the HMO is that they
move. Unlike in the present situation, under SecureChoice employment
changes will not affect their HMO options.

10. To illustrate this, on the basis of the data used in Chapter 3, the average
cost for all minor acute and preventive services for males eighteen to
twenty-nine years old in 2003 was about $40 a month (see Table 3.1).
Even for men aged eighteen to twenty-nine who were hospitalized for a
chronic problem in the prior year, this figure was only a little over $100 a
month. In contrast, the cost for all services, including major acute and
chronic illness management, was over $320 a month. The latter two fig-
ures come from the same data subset by the categories used in Figure 3.1.

11. The federal legislation requires the income-based subsidy to incorporate
all income for the year. Given Sam's intermittent employment, this is
difficult to calculate on a "real-time" basis. The Federal Health Equity
Agency (FHEA) facilitates the process by providing a line of credit to
cover his premiums, adding that cost to his income taxes due, after
accounting retroactively for the income-based subsidies. This is done
seamlessly by coordinating with the Internal Revenue Service. The
FHEA needs to charge only a very low interest rate because it can "pig-
gyback" on IRS enforcement.

12. The transfer of information and funds matches that outlined in Figure 5.2.

13. Although the chronic illness management payments are typically constant per month, over time the UCP and PIs work out increasingly sophisticated approaches. For example, conditions that require extensive workups to determine the diagnosis will have an initial up-front payment to the PI that essentially offsets the costs incurred in reaching the diagnosis. This would be important for Louisa's multiple sclerosis, which requires imaging and various other tests, but would not have been important for the initial assessment of her diabetes. When certain chronic illnesses commonly occur together, such as hypertension and chronic heart disease, a new combined category will have to be developed, because the treatment protocols and management costs are unlikely to be just the sum of what is needed to treat the two conditions separately.

14. As with a move, the identification of a new chronic condition triggers a mid-year opportunity for a person to change medical homes. Given the extra payments from the UCP to the PIs associated with the new condition, such a change will have little impact on the patient's premiums, except if the new condition leads him or her to choose a different co-payment schedule or a new clinician with a markedly different practice style.

15. This is not a pure pass-through because unusual cases in an individual physician's practice can cause too much random variation in premiums, even if the risk offset by the UCP is accounted for. PIs essentially include a degree of reinsurance in the policies they offer, which smooths out such variability. Physicians practicing in larger primary care groups may forgo much of that reinsurance because they can average costs internally.

16. The general model in which physicians need to decide either to be part of a CDT or to focus their work on ambulatory care is really designed to prevent physicians from deciding to admit their patients for expensive (and possibly unnecessary) procedures and then participate in the financial gain associated with that decision to hospitalize the patient. The Stark I and II laws are intended to address this problem, which was illustrated by the case of Redding Hospital in California, in which hun-

dreds of patients received apparently unnecessary cardiovascular procedures. Stephen Klaidman, *Coronary: A True Story of Medicine Gone Awry* (New York: Scribner, 2007). The "choose a setting" rule is less an issue if the physician, such as a radiologist, is simply being paid for his or her time and expertise and is not sharing in the productivity gains of the CDT.

9. Getting There

1. The UCP is designed to be as neutral and "hands off" as possible. For example, it delegates to other expert agencies specific decisions such as whether an expensive new treatment is eligible for routine coverage or should still be considered experimental.

2. The careful reader will note that the option of subsidies for low-income people preferring Platinum coverage was never fully discussed, largely because it seems politically impracticable.

3. The recent transfer of responsibility for the retiree health costs of the United Auto Workers from the employers to a Voluntary Employee Benefit Association—$35 billion for General Motors alone—highlights this opportunity. There is substantial concern whether the VEBA will be sufficiently well funded to meet its obligations, but the UAW apparently was willing to accept this "bird in the hand" because of fears that if GM were to go into bankruptcy, its obligations for retiree coverage could be in jeopardy. The problem with the VEBA is that it has no levers, other than benefit reduction, to contain costs in the long term. The UCP includes strong incentives to achieve such a goal and would be able to offer a better guarantee of coverage for retirees. Mark Bruno, "VEBAs Moving into Fast Lane," *Pensions and Investments,* October 15, 2007, www.pionline.com (accessed February 6, 2008).

4. Some large multispecialty group practices do have such information, but they may want to continue to be paid as single entities, and they would not necessarily represent the practice patterns of widely dispersed independent physicians.

5. The patterns of use reflected in these data will be sensitive to the co-payment and deductible provisions faced by the enrollees. Carriers will need to provide some information on these along with the claims. The

data necessary to make these estimates already exist. The main road-blocks are (1) an unwillingness of carriers to share the data, which they will likely do voluntarily in exchange for early access to the pooled data, and (2) the AMA licensing fees on the use of the codes representing procedures. This licensing agreement dates back to the Reagan administration and would be renegotiated as part of the Compact.

6. The CCHs are intended simply to serve as efficient transmitters of data from clinicians' offices to other entities. In some ways the CCHs are similar to data interchanges such as Availity that process claims electronically for multiple payers in Florida and elsewhere. See www.availity.com. In contrast, the automated clearing houses described in Chapters 4 and 5 facilitate transactions among PIs.

7. The analogy here is to the electronic equipment that stores and restaurants use to transmit credit card information regardless of the card company, making it relatively easy for the store to switch to another vendor. This effort will be focused primarily on small office practices. Large medical groups and hospitals already have such capabilities.

8. Health insurers wishing to become PIs would not be allowed to pass information from one side of their operation to the other, much as is currently the case for insurers that act as fiscal intermediaries for Medicare.

9. There may be selection problems if this option is offered to individuals, but large employers may decide to place all their enrollees in such networks, allowing those who see less expensive physicians to have somewhat lower monthly payments.

10. Most analysts believe that Medicaid payment rates are among the lowest, but what is less clear is whether this translates into substantially lower total costs on an episode-of-illness basis. If transitioning Medicaid is fiscally unattractive for states, additional funding via the UCP might be used to offset part of the extra costs.

Glossary

automated clearing house (ACH)   An entity, useful when a patient sees a provider who has a different PI from that of the patient's PCP or medical home, allowing PIs to communicate with one another and net out transactions. Its functions are modeled after similar functions for clearing checks. The provider's PI receives payment via the ACH and then credits his or her bank account.

avoidable compensable event (ACE)   An injury to the patient that should not have occurred if the execution of care was ideal. There is typically a schedule of compensation amounts, and the standard of evidence to show that an ACE has occurred is usually lower than that needed to show negligence under a medical malpractice claim.

care delivery team (CDT)   A voluntary collaboration between hospitals or interventional facilities and the clinicians working in them. CDTs accept EDRG payments and design ways to allocate those funds internally to improve efficiency and quality. CDTs accept at least part of the financial responsibility for the production risk associated with MA/I episodes. Revisions to existing laws prohibiting gainsharing will specifically allow the sharing of risk and reward among those who are part of the CDT.

chronic illness management (CIM)   The ongoing management of the care for a person with one or more chronic conditions. It includes both the coordination of care and the services rendered, some of which may be nonmedical, such as stress reduction programs, nutrition counseling, or massage. CIM may be lifelong, or may taper down and terminate with recovery, such as from depression. It is typically difficult to predict whether or when CIM episodes of care will end. The costs of acute exacerbations of the underlying chronic illness are not included in CIM payment, but there may be some incentives for those responsible for CIM to reduce the occurrence of such exacerbations. In many instances in which it is not necessary to distinguish between payments for MA/I and CIM care, these are jointly referred to as major acute and chronic illness care.

claims clearing house (CCH)   Serves as the electronic interface between a provider's office and the claims payment systems embedded in SecureChoice. A CCH will provide the hardware and software needed to submit claims, initially to Medicare and other insurers, and later to the PI chosen by the provider.

consumers   People making choices about their financial coverage or the style of physician practice they prefer. See also *patients.*

diagnosis-related group (DRG)   A system in Medicare that classifies hospital visits into one of approximately five hundred categories of events expected to have similar resource use, determined by ICD diagnoses, procedures, age, sex, and comorbidities. Hospitals are paid a fixed amount for each patient in a specific DRG irrespective of the resources actually used for that case.

educational loan reinsurance pool   Established by the UCP to guarantee medical educational loan repayment to lenders, thereby lowering the interest rate. Students choosing to specialize in high-demand areas may also have a portion of their loan forgiven with funds from the UCP. Those entering practice in shortage areas in which fees are rising rapidly will have a further portion of their loans forgiven. In essence, the UCP will provide selective incentives to trainees to enter those segments of the profession in which the UCP is facing the most rapid fee increases, thereby lowering its costs in the long term.

electronic health record (EHR)   A digital format for record keeping whereby an individual patient's record can be stored and retrieved by a computer. It can be made up of electronic medical records from many locations and/or sources.

episode of care   An episode of care links all the services associated with a given condition or problem, regardless of when or by whom the services are provided. Various software programs or "groupers" can collect these disparate claims together.

expanded diagnosis-related group (EDRG)   The mechanism used by SecureChoice to pay for MA/I episodes. Building on the DRG concept used by Medicare, EDRGs will also include payments for professional services used in the episode and for immediate preadmission and some postdischarge care. Relative to DRGs, EDRGs may include more risk adjustment for patient comorbidities that cannot be controlled by the care delivery team but less adjustment for complications that may be its responsibility. EDRGs will not include higher payments for complications that develop during the admission but will instead base payment on what treatment costs CDTs demonstrating superior outcomes, typically those with fewer than the average number of complications.

Federal Health Equity Agency (FHEA)   Coordinates and provides the income-based subsidies to the Funds Clearing House. In contrast to the FCH, which may be a private firm operating under contract to the UCP, the FHEA will be a government agency with codes of confidentiality comparable to those of the Internal Revenue Service, from which it seeks limited information about subsidy eligibility.

first-tier claim   An individual patient's medical error case that is submitted to a health court to determine whether an avoidable compensable event occurred and if so, the amount of compensation to be paid.

Funds Clearing House (FCH)   Established to allow co-payment and premium costs, as well as contributions and subsidies, to be handled at a family level. It also further protects patient confidentiality by isolating medical information, such as the dates and reasons for medical visits, from the entities that may be financing coverage. The FCH will receive employer and government contributions for coverage and co-payments on behalf of all those associated with a "family" account and pay the PIs as they present bills for premiums and co-payments. The FCH will probably be a private entity collectively owned by the PIs to facilitate their transactions. It will adhere, however, to all federal privacy and confidentiality rules.

gainsharing   Occurs when a party—typically a hospital—shares some of its gains with or otherwise rewards physicians not in its direct employ. Two important pieces of federal legislation, often referred to as Stark I and II after their author, Congressman Pete Stark, prohibit gainsharing. The underlying concern this legislation was designed to address is the potential for hospitals to reward physicians for (1) steering patients to their facility or (2) admitting patients for care that is unnecessary. Many states also have anti-kickback or anti-fee-splitting laws to preclude gainsharing between physicians.

Gold coverage   The standard coverage offered by the UCP. It is based on the services used by clinicians and care delivery teams that achieve superior-quality outcomes for their patients. It includes coverage for experimental treatments if the patient enrolls in a trial. See also *Platinum coverage*.

health care card (HCC)   Contains an individual's HIN and some other coded information. It will be used in place of a credit card for all health care goods and services, issuing immediate payment to the provider of such services. Co-payments and other amounts due, such as for non-covered benefits, are billed to the party responsible for the patient.

Health Care Compact   The Compact is a political agreement among the broad set of parties needed to reach a consensus on legislation establishing SecureChoice or something like it. It identifies not just the governmental structures required to operate the system but perhaps nongovernmental entities, such as an endowed foundation, that independently monitor how the system is performing and report on whether Congress and the executive branch are fulfilling the intent of the Compact. Over time, the Compact should acquire the same public acceptance and support as Social Security, being modifiable only after extensive public debate.

health court   Patients who have experienced an injury may bring their claim before a dedicated court that uses administrative law procedures to determine if the injury was due to an avoidable compensable event (ACE). If so, there would be a schedule for compensation. Health courts hear first-tier claims.

health identification number (HIN)   Unique identifier assigned to individuals for the purpose of linking all their medical and health information. The UCP will assign these numbers when people initially enroll in SecureChoice, either directly or through a participating employment-based health plan. People who have not yet enrolled despite the individual mandate to do so will be assigned an HIN when they seek care.

health innovation fund (HIF)   A for-profit company that bids for the rights to various innovations and takes them to market. HIFs subcontract with other firms for the actual trials and production, and with the IRP for reinsurance. In many ways similar to conventional drug companies, the HIFs set out without the large sales staffs and with the expectation of having market risk reinsurance. With initial investment from the UCP and public pension plans, HIFs also set out with a greater commitment to research and product transparency.

hospitalist   A relatively new medical specialty in the United States, although the model has been commonplace in Europe for decades. Typically working in teams, hospitalists provide twenty-four-hour on-site expertise to respond rapidly to changes in a patient's status. Because they specialize in caring for the sickest patients, they develop expertise in knowing which other specialists to call upon to achieve optimal care.

individual tax identification number (ITIN)   A tax processing number issued by the Internal Revenue Service. ITINs are issued to people who do not have Social Security numbers.

innovation reinsurance pool (IRP)   Provides reinsurance to drug and other manufacturers against the risk that a product they successfully bring to market may suddenly lose market share to a better alternative. The IRP does not ensure success; it only covers the risk that a future stream of earnings expected from a successful product may be cut short by a new (and clinically better) competitor. The IRP may be established by the UCP to help drug and other research-intensive firms become accustomed to the new incentives built into SecureChoice. It is intended to break even over the long run, and is likely to pass on this function eventually to private reinsurers as they develop the expertise.

major acute or interventional (MA/I)   Characterized by the use of high-cost, high-intensity care in a relatively short period of time. Under SecureChoice all hospitalizations will be in the MA/I category, as well as significant procedures and other services usually requiring multiple physicians and a specially equipped facility. Some MA/I episodes will be truly sudden and unpredictable, such as a heart attack or automobile trauma; others may be acute exacerbations of a chronic illness such as congestive heart failure; still others may involve patient decisions whether to go forward with care, be it in choosing to be admitted for pneumonia in the last stages of cancer or deciding to undergo a hip replacement to improve one's quality of life.

medical home   A clinician or care system with responsibility for tracking an individual's health over time, maintaining records, and serving as an initial point of contact for advice and referral. Typically this is the patient's PCP; for patients who have certain chronic illnesses, it may be a specialist.

minor acute   Those acute care episodes not requiring hospitalization or major interventional services. By definition, acute episodes are expected to be resolved in a reasonably short period of time. Determining whether an episode is in the minor acute category must occur after the fact; some patients may present with what seems to be an acute problem but is actually an early manifestation of a chronic illness or major acute episode. Not all minor acute episodes within a category are inexpensive: a single MRI exam can cost $1,000 or more but may be needed in only a small fraction of the cases within that type of episode.

occurrence risk   Reflects the uncertainty associated with whether an event, such as a potentially expensive episode of care, will occur.

patient- and provider-based premium   A premium reflecting the specific set of co-payments and other features chosen by the individual, combined with the practice patterns and fees of the providers used by the patients of that PCP, after accounting for those patients' CIM payments from the UCP. These premiums include a small markup by the PIs to cover their administrative costs and risk spreading. PCPs have incentives to monitor such costs and can switch to other PIs with lower margins. At times these are referred to as *provider-based premiums* when they do not account for the coverage options chosen by individual patients. The term *provider-based premium* does not specifically account for the influence of patient preferences on co-payments and deductibles.

patients   People already engaged in health care treatment who may find that their preferences have shifted because of a medical problem. Whereas *consumers* typically face somewhat abstract decisions and trade-offs, *patients* sometimes confront complex treatment choices in situations involving emotion and uncertainty. See also *consumers.*

payment intermediary (PI)   PIs serve to reorganize funds from several sources, including CIM payments from the UCP reflecting the chronic illness management that may be needed by a person, the coverage he or she may have purchased to pay for various types of minor acute and preventive care, and any income-based subsidies due the individual. The PI pools these funds to pay providers as needed on behalf of the patient. The PI provides a small amount of risk spreading to offset the random variability across patients in the amount of minor acute care they may need. Unlike current health plans, PIs do not attempt to organize providers or manage care.

PIs pay fee-for-service bills and smooth out the random variation across episodes of chronic and minor acute illness and preventive care. Each primary care physician will select a PI to handle all the claims of his or her patients. PIs will receive the monthly CIM payments from the pool and thus have no reason to avoid potentially high-risk enrollees. PIs do not function as do our current insurers but work more like Visa or MasterCard, earning a small fee for efficient payment.

Platinum coverage   Coverage of care not included in Gold coverage. Includes those procedures that are not proven medically effective. It may also cover provider fees in excess of the amounts paid by the UCP based on providers offering superior quality.

preventive episode   An episode of care intended to screen for or prevent illness, as well as the ongoing function of providing a place of first contact for acute problems or referrals. The latter may require a method of compensation even if rarely used by a particular person. Preventive episodes typically involve a health care provider or referral from such a provider (e.g., a smoking cessation program). Broad-based public health interventions (e.g., legislation prohibiting smoking in workplaces, restaurants, and bars) would not be included in this category but would be funded separately.

primary care practitioner (PCP)   The clinician (or clinic) serving as a point of first contact for many clinical problems; the provider of much of the primary care a patient may need, a referral source, and the medical home for the patient's records. PCPs by this definition include not just physicians such as family practitioners, internists, pediatricians, and gynecologists but also nurse practitioners and physician assistants if state scope-of-practice laws allow.

principal provider   Used in a generic fashion to identify the person or entity most responsible for a given episode of care. For an MA/I episode, this would be the care delivery team; if a PCP delegated chronic illness management to a subspecialist, the latter would be the principal provider for that CIM episode.

production risk   Reflects the uncertainty associated with the cost of taking care of a patient appropriately, typically with respect to a given episode of care.

reinsurance   Describes the situation in which an insurance company offsets part of its risk by purchasing coverage from other insurers. The primary insurer generally carries much of the risk; the reinsurance policy comes into play only if expenditures are very large. Thus an insurer may write fire insurance policies for individual homes but buy reinsurance against the possibility that a whole neighborhood may go up in flames, causing it to pay off on many policies at once. With SecureChoice, the UCP bears the occurrence risk and passes the production risk on to the CDT. The CDT, in turn, would usually cover most of its costs with the EDRG payments, but may buy reinsurance against the risk associated with the occasional case requiring an unusually long hospitalization. Reinsurance is a fairly specialized business, typically with a small number of customers and infrequent claims of large magnitudes. This allows detailed examination of each claim, facilitating exploration of the reasons why the case was unusually expensive.

risk model panels   Established by the UCP to select outcome measures for the major conditions that will be covered by EDRG and CIM payments. The panels will include clinicians and patients with knowledge of the conditions and care involved, researchers expert in outcome measurement and risk modeling, and health information and survey experts with experience in large-scale, routine data collection. The UCP will fund the staff work and analysis needed to develop the models.

second-tier claim   A claim that a provider has known about a series of adverse compensable events (usually demonstrated by paying compensation) and has not undertaken actions to avoid such events in the future. These would typically be tried as corporate negligence cases.

SecureChoice   The working name for the overall proposal. The proposal incorporates (1) assurance of coverage for key aspects of care, irrespective of one's employment situation, income, or health status; and (2) maximum choice and flexibility—accompanied by appropriate levels of financial responsibility—for patients and physicians.

selection   Favorable and adverse selection are critical problems that arise when people can choose whether or not to be covered or can choose among different plans. People generally know more about their own needs for care than do insurers, so the insurer assumes that those who voluntarily pay its premiums expect to get at least "their money's worth" and thus has to set its premium above what it would charge simply on the basis of observable risk factors.

superior care   The goal of SecureChoice. In practice this means that the UCP will select outcome measures, such as thirty-day survival after heart attack or the ability to walk two blocks without pain six months after hip replacement, and identify those CDTs achieving results in the top half of the outcome distribution. These are the superior care providers for that EDRG. The average resource use by those CDTs, adjusted for local wage differences, will determine the EDRG payment paid by the UCP to each CDT.

superior outcome   An outcome achieved by those clinicians or care delivery teams in the upper half of the distribution of providers. Outcome measures and patient risk factors used in assessing such outcomes are to be developed by the risk model panels.

universal coverage pool (UCP)   The entity through which everyone will be covered for major acute/interventional (MA/I) care and the costs associated with chronic illness management (CIM). Coverage through the UCP (or equivalent coverage) would be mandated by law and represents the "secure" component of SecureChoice.

Index